LIFE AND DESTINY

LÉON DENIS

Translated by
ELLA WHEELER WILCOX

FV EDITIONS

CONTENTS

INTRODUCTION BY THE TRANSLATOR ... 5
INTRODUCTION ... 8

THE PROBLEM OF LIFE

1. THE EVOLUTION OF THOUGHT ... 17
2. THE CRITERION OF THE SPIRITIST DOCTRINE ... 34
3. THE PROBLEM OF LIFE ... 57
4. PERSONALITY ... 62
5. THE SOUL AND DIFFERENT STATES OF SLEEP ... 65
6. TELEPATHIC PROJECTIONS ... 72
7. MANIFESTATIONS AFTER DEATH ... 78
8. VIBRATORY STATES OF THE SOULS' MEMORY ... 82
9. EVOLUTION AND FINALITY OF THE SOUL ... 86
10. DEATH ... 94
11. LIFE IN THE BEYOND ... 101
12. THE HIGHER LIFE ... 107

SUCCESSIVE LIVES AND THE LAW OF REINCARNATION

1. THE LAW OF REINCARNATION ... 113
2. RENOVATION OF THE MEMORY ... 126
3. REINCARNATION AND INFANT PRODIGIES ... 141
4. OBJECTIONS AND CRITICISMS ... 147
5. SUCCESSIVE LIVES - HISTORIC PROOFS ... 154
6. JUSTICE AND RESPONSIBILITY ... 162
7. THE LAW OF DESTINY ... 169

THE POWERS OF THE SOUL THE WILL

1. THE WILL ... 179
2. THE INNER SOUL ... 183
3. LIBERTY ... 193

4. THOUGHT	199
5. DISCIPLINE OF THOUGHT AND REFORM OF CHARACTER	204
6. LOVE	210
7. SORROW	216
8. REVELATION OF SORROW	227
PROFESSION OF FAITH	237

INTRODUCTION BY THE TRANSLATOR

Early in May, while in Dijon, France, the books of Léon Denis, the great spiritual philosopher, were brought to my attention by his friend and pupil, Miss Camille Chaise, a beautiful young refugee from Rheims. Profoundly impressed by the literary and religious importance of this volume, I asked Miss Chaise to inquire if I could obtain the rights of translation. This inquiry led to my coming to Tours, where Mr. Denis resides, and where I have pursued the delightful work. Feeling it to be a holy task, I resolved to begin it on a holy day, May 21st, which was the second anniversary of the birth of my husband into spirit life. Beginning with three pages daily, I gradually increased the number, and was able to complete the task on September 21st. The translation was made of peculiar interest to me, through messages received from my husband, while in Dijon, by the aid of a cultured lady in private life, Madame Soyer, who had no personal acquaintance with Mr. Denis or Miss Chaise. The messages urged me to make the translation, assuring me that I would not only benefit the world, but that I would be personally benefited, as the book contained great truths of life and death which would aid in my development. On numerous occasions while in Tours, messages received from the astral world referred to the translation with interest and approval. In giving this work of Léon Denis to the English-speaking world, I feel I am bestowing an inestimable favor on every intelligent mind capable of feeling love, sorrow, aspiration, or yearning for a larger understanding of life.

The work of translation of these beautiful thoughts has been an education to my mind, a solace to my heart, and an uplift to my soul. When I made this statement to the dear author, he replied: 'But you, long a student of spiritual research, and of theosophical lore, surely knew all these things before?' I replied, 'Yes, I knew them. But I feel as if you had entered a store-room of my mind, where were packed priceless paintings and rare statues, and as if you had taken them one by one, and hung them in a clear light on memory's walls, and placed the sculptured treasures on pedestals for the delight of my spiritual eyes; you have, in truth, set my intellectual house in order.'

It is rarely that a mind of such an analytically scientific bent, as that of Léon Denis, is at the same time so poetical. This, together with the writer's profoundly reverential nature, makes his work of threefold value. He appeals to those who pursue psychical research in a purely scientific manner; he appeals to those who value noble and moving literature; and he appeals to every soul that loves and believes in a God great enough to be the Supreme Creator of this magnificent universe.

This book is the crowning work of Mr. Denis's three score years and ten of life - the ripe fruit of more than half a century of continual study and research. It can be said of Mr. Denis (which cannot be said of all authors), that his personal life accords with his beautiful philosophy. From a troubled and painful youth, he has slowly climbed an ascending path of difficulties, overcome obstacles and surmounted sorrows, attained profound knowledge and a wide education, and put into daily practice the lofty principles he sets forth in this volume.

May it bring to every reader the uplift it has brought to the translator.

ELLA WHEELER WILCOX
September 1918.

A SCULPTOR

As the ambitious sculptor, tireless, lifts
Chisel and hammer to the block at hand,
Before my half-formed character I stand
And ply the shining tools of mental gifts.
I'll cut away a huge unsightly side
Of selfishness, and smooth to curves of grace
The angles of ill temper.
And no trace
Shall my sure hammer leave of silly pride.
Chip after chip must fall from vain desires,
And the sharp corners of my discontent
Be rounded into symmetry, and lent
Great harmony by faith that never tires.
Unfinished still, I must toil on and on,
Till the pale critic, Death, shall say, 'Tis done.'

— ELLA WHEELER WILCOX

INTRODUCTION

In the evening of life, the thinker is struck with a sorrowful impression of the futility of human existence. He perceives how the teachings dispensed by institutions of learning in general - churches, schools, universities - enable you to acquire many of those matters which are of vast importance in the conduct of terrestrial existence, and in the preparation for life Beyond. Those to whom is given the high mission of enlightening and guiding the human soul, seem to ignore its nature and its real destiny. In the midst of universities a complete incertitude reigns upon the solution of the most important problems ever presented to man in his passage through earth. This incertitude exists in every thing, which touches upon the problem of life, its aim, and its end.

We find the same impotence among the clergy. By their affirmations, denuded of all proofs, they have little success in communicating to the souls in their charge a faith which responds to sane criticism or the exigencies of reason. The inquiring soul, in fact, encounters in the universities and in the churches but obscurity and contradiction on everything which touches the problems of its nature and its future. It is to this condition of things that we must attribute in great part the evils of our times - the incoherence of ideas, the disorders of conscience, the moral and social anarchy.

The education dispensed to the generations is complicated, but it does not light the path of life for them, it does not gird them for the battle of existence. Classic education teaches the cultivation and the ornamentation of the intellect; it does not teach how to act, how to love, how to perform duty. Still less does it instruct how to form a conception of the destiny, which develops profound energies in us, and elevates our every aim toward a lofty goal.

Nevertheless, this conception of life is indispensable to every being and to all society, for it is the sustaining power and the supreme consolation in hours of trouble, the source of virile virtues and high inspirations. Carl du Prel tells the following fact:

> 'One of my friends, a professor in a university, had the sorrow of losing his daughter, which awoke his interest in the problem of immortality. He turned to his colleagues, professors of philosophy, hoping to find consolation. It was a bitter disappointment. He asked for bread and received a stone; he asked for affirmation, and received a "perhaps."' Francis Sarcy, an accomplished professor in a large university, wrote, 'I am upon this earth. I know absolutely nothing regarding the how or why of my existence. I know even less, how and where I will go when I leave earth.' A more frank avowal of ignorance on the all-important subject could not be uttered. After centuries of laborious study, the philosophy of the schools is without light, without warmth, without life.[1]

The minds of our children are tossed between diverse and contradictory systems: the positivism of August Comte, the naturalism of Hegel, the materialism of Stuart Mill, and many more - all uncertain, all without ideals, yet precise.

From these arises the precocious tendency toward destructive pessimism - malady of a decadent society, a terrible menace for the future; to which is added the skepticism of our young men, who believe in nothing but wealth and honor and material success.

Raoul Pictet, the eminent professor, speaks of this mental condition of the young, in the introduction of his first work on psychic science. He speaks of the disastrous effect produced by material theories, and concludes thus: 'These poor young men declare that all which occurs in the world is the fatal and necessary result of preceding conditions, and that human will can in no way intervene. They believe themselves the playthings of fate, tied hand and foot to a relentless destiny. These young men cease to make any effort to succeed at the first obstacle they encounter. They have no faith in themselves - they become their own living tombs wherein they bury their hopes, their efforts, their desires.' This applies, not only to a portion of our young men, but to many men of our time and generation in whom we recognize a moral lassitude and weakness.

Frederick Myers, author of Human Personality, has also said on this subject, 'Pessimism is the moral malady of the times; there is a lack of confidence in the true value of life.' The doctrines of Nietzsche, of Schopenhauer, of Haeckel, have largely contributed toward developing this state of things. Their influence has been far-reaching. To them we may attribute the skepticism and discouragement, in a great measure, which emanates from the contemporaneous mind: the utter lack of all that makes the ardor of life, its joyousness, its confidence in the future - those virile qualities of the race.

It is time to battle with vigor against these funeral doctrines, and to seek outside of the old official beliefs new methods of instruction, which respond to the imperious needs of the present hour. We must prepare souls for the necessities, for the combats of actual life, and life further on. We must above all teach human souls to understand and develop, in view of the final end, the latent forces which sleep within.

Until now, thought has been confined in narrow circles, religions, schools, and systems that exclude and combat all ideas at variance with their own. We must rise out of this rigid circle, and give our thoughts a larger freedom; every system contains a part of the truth, no one contains the *entire* truth. The universe and life have aspects too varied, too numerous for any one system of teaching to embrace wholly.

We must take the fragments of truth which each contains and fit them together until they form a united pattern; then add to them the aspects of truth which we discover from day to day, through the majestic harmony of our awakened thought. The decadence of our epoch comes largely from the imprisoned and restricted state of the human mind.[2] We must stir it out of its inertia and its creed-bound limits, and lift it toward high altitudes without losing sight of the solid base, which affords it and enlarged and renewed science. This science of the future we must work to establish. It will procure the indispensable criterion, the means of verification, and the control without which thought, left to its freedom, risks the danger of losing its way.

We have said that trouble and incertitude are everywhere found in our social conditions. Within and without, there is a state of inquietude. Under the brilliant surface of a refined civilization is hidden a deep malady. Irritation increases in social circles; the conflict of interests and the battle for life becomes every day more acute.

Humanity, weary of dogmas, and speculations without proof, is plunged in materialism or indifference. From whence, then, comes this doctrine? Toward what abyss are we being drawn? What new ideal will come to give man the confidence in the future and ardor for achievement? In the tragic hours of history, when the situation seemed desperate, succor was at hand. The human soul cannot perish: in the moment when our old faiths are hidden by a veil, a new conception of life and destiny, based upon science and facts, reappears. The Great Tradition is revived under new forms, larger and more beautiful. It reveals to all a future full of hope and promise. Salute, then, the new reign of the idea, victorious over matter, and work to prepare fair ways for its footsteps.

The task is great, and the education of mankind must be entirely reconstructed. This education, we have seen, neither the university nor the Church is prepared to give, since neither possesses the necessary synthesis to cast light upon the pathway of new generations. One doctrine alone can offer this synthesis - that of scientific spiritual research.

Already it shows a horizon to the world, and promises to illuminate the future. And this philosophy, this science, free, independent, liberated from all official restrictions, from all compromising politics, is adding every day new and precious discoveries to its storehouse of knowledge. The phenomena of magnetism, of radioactivity, of telepathy, are but applications of the one principle, the manifestation of the One Law, which, regulated at the same time, beings and universes.

A few more years of patient labor, of conscientious experimentation, of persistent research, and the New Education will have its scientific formulae, its essential base; this event will be the grandest fact since the coming of Christianity. Education, we all know, is the most powerful factor in progress. It contains the germ of the entire future; but to be complete, education should inspire the mind of man to study life in two alternating forms - the visible and the invisible: 'Life in its plenitude, in its evolution towards the summit of nature and of thought.'

The teachers of humanity have, then, an immediate duty to fill: it is to put scientific spiritual research at the base of education, and thus to remake the interior man and his moral health. The soul of man, sleeping under a funereal rhetoric, must be awakened, and its hidden powers developed into full consciousness until they recognize their glorious destiny. Modern science analyses the exterior world; its discoveries in the objective universe are profound, and this is to its honor and glory.

But it knows nothing of the universe invisible, and the world interior. It is a limitless empire, which remains to be conquered. To learn by what ties man is attached to the Whole; to descend into the mysteries of Being, where light and shadow are mixed as in Plato's cavern; to search the labyrinths and bring forth their secrets; to separate the ME normal from the ME divine, the conscious from the subconscious, there is no study more important.

Because the schools and the academies have not introduced this form of education into their programs, they have in reality done nothing definite for the education of humanity. But already there is surging a new and marvelous psychology, from which is being evolved a new conception of Being, and knowledge of One Law supreme, which explains all the problems of evolution and of the future. An era is finishing, a new era is dawning. We are like infants, crying in the night; the human spirit is in travail. Everywhere we see the apparent decomposition of old ideas and principles, in science, in art, in philosophy, and in religion.

But the attentive observer realizes that out of all this decay a new harvest will grow; science is scattering seeds rich, which promise. The coming century will be one of wonderful flowering. The forms and conceptions of the past do not suffice us. However respectable is the heritage, and in spite of the pious sentiment with which we consider the teachings of our parents, there is a growing consciousness that this teaching does not suffice to dissipate the agonizing mystery of the 'why' of life.

The state of the human mind today clamors for a science, an art, and a religion of light and of liberty to guide it toward the radiant horizon where it feels it is drawn by its own nature and by irresistible forces. We speak often of progress, but what progress? It is but a sonorous and empty word upon the lips of orators, more frequently materialists than otherwise, or has it a determined sense? Twenty civilizations have passed over the earth, lighting the path of humanity. Their flames shone in the nights of the centuries, and then became extinguished. And still man does not discern behind the limited horizons of his thoughts the Beyond without limit, which is the goal of his destiny. Powerless to dissipate the mystery, which surrounds him, he uses his forces in material labors, and neglects the splendors of the spiritual task, which would bring him true grandeur. The faith of progress must mean a faith in the future of all the races. Not until we possess that faith, and march with confidence toward that ideal, can true progress come.

Progress does not mean the creation of material things - of machines, and industrial growth. Nor does it consist in finding new methods in art, literature, and eloquence. The high objective of progress is to seize and attain the mother idea, which impregnates all human life, the pure source from which flows at once the truths, the principles, the sentiments, which inspire great works and noble actions. It is time we comprehended this fact; civilization cannot grow, society cannot better itself, save through the acquiring of thoughts that are more and more elevated, and the increase of light touching and renovating human hearts. The power to realize the fullness of being can alone lead the soul toward the mountain summits where every human endeavor will find its regeneration. Everything says to us - 'The universe is regulated by the law of evolution; it is there we find the word progress.' In ourselves and our principles of life, we are always subject to this law. But only by our own efforts do we learn that this same sovereign law carries the soul and its works across infinite time and space, toward a goal still more elevated. To make our work useful, to cooperate with evolution in general, and to reap its fruits, we must first lean to discern, to seize the reason, the cause, and the aim of this evolution, to know where it leads, in order to participate in the plenitude of the forces and faculties which sleep in us on this glorious path of ascension. Let us press on, then, toward the future, through the life always being renewed, and through paths of immensity, which open to us a regenerated spirituality.

Faiths of the past, sciences, philosophies, religions, illuminate yourselves with a new flame! Shake off your shrouds and the ashes, which cover you. Listen to the revealing voices of the tomb; they will bring you a renewal of thought, with secrets of the Beyond, which man has need to know, that he live better, better act, and better die.

---

1. A propos of the examinations in the universities, Mr. Ducas Doyen of the Faculty of Aix, wrote in the Journal of 3rd May 1912: 'There seems to be between the minds of the pupils and the things they study a sort of cloud - an opaqueness. It is particularly in philosophy that one feels this unfortunate impression.'
2. These lines were written before the war. We must recognize that, during the course of this gigantic strife, the young Frenchmen have shown a heroism above all eulogy; but the national education does not show in that, it is rather the result of sleeping qualities which have wakened in the heart of the race.

THE PROBLEM OF LIFE

1
THE EVOLUTION OF THOUGHT

We have said that one law regulates the evolution of thought, as it regulates the physical evolution of beings and worlds. The comprehension of the universe is developed with the progress of the human mind. This general conception of the universe and of life has been expressed in a thousand fashions, under a thousand diverse forms in the past. It is expressed in larger terms today, and will be amplified in the measure that humanity climbs the pathway of ascension.

Science enlarges without cessation its field of exploration. Every day, by the aid of powerful instruments of observation and analysis, science discovers new aspects of matter, of force, and of life. But that which those instruments record, the soul of man discovered long ago, for the flight of thought precedes always and surpasses the methods of positive science. The instruments know nothing, and are nothing, without the human will to direct them.

Science is uncertain and changeable; it continually reconstructs itself. Its methods, its theories, its calculations, arrived at with great trouble, crumble before a more attentive observation, or a more profound deduction, to give place to other theories which are no more definite.[1] The theory of the undividable atom, for instance, which for two thousand years was the base of chemistry and physical science, is now qualified and considered mere romance by our most eminent scientists. Many analogous mistakes have demonstrated the weakness of the scientific mind in the past. That mind will never attain to reality but by lifting itself above the image of material facts toward the realms of Cause and Law.

It is in this fashion that science has been able to determine the immutable principles of logic and mathematics. But it is not the same in the other orders of research. The scientist too often carries his prejudices, his personal tendencies, and his habits of routine into the domain of psychic research. This is particularly true of France, where there are indeed few scientists with the courage and the enlightenment sufficient to enable them to follow a pathway already traced by brilliant minds of other nations.

Despite these facts, the human spirit advances step by step toward an understanding of itself and the universe. Our ideas of force and matter are modified each day, and human personality reveals itself under unexpected aspects. In the face of so much phenomena established by experimentation, in face of accumulated testimonials from all quarters, no clear-seeing intelligent mind can deny the proof of the survival of the soul, or elude the moral consequences and responsibility, which follow that fact. That which we say of science, can be equally said of the philosophies and the religions, which succeeded one another down the centuries. They constitute so many steps or stations pursued by humanity still in its infancy - steps leading up toward spiritual planes, growing more vast and elevated at each turn.

The diverse beliefs of humanity are but the gradual development of the divine ideal reflected in the thoughts with more and more purity and brightness as the mind develops in refinement. The belief and the understanding of a period of time represent the measure of truth which men of that epoch can seize and comprehend, until the development of their faculties and their consciences enables them to perceive a higher form and a more intense radiation of the truth.

Seen from this point of view, even early fetishism explains itself, despite its bloody rites. It is the first babbling of the infantine soul, striving to spell the divine language, and to give in forms appropriates to its own mental state its vague, confused, rudimentary conception of a superior world. Paganism represents a more elevated conception, though exceedingly anthropomorphic. The pagan gods are all men, with the same passions and weaknesses; but even here the ideal of something higher is found. It brings a ray of eternal beauty to fertilize the world.

Still higher is the Christian idea of sacrifice and renunciation. Greek paganism was the religion of radiant nature! Christianity is that of suffering humanity, a religion of tombs and crypts and catacombs, born from the persecution and the sorrow it has suffered, and keeping the imprint of its origin.

Christianity should be regarded as the greatest effort attempted by the invisible world to communicate ostensibly with our humanity. According to Fred Myers, it is the first authentic message from the Beyond. The pagan religions were, to be sure, rich with occult phenomena of all kinds and in facts of divination. But the appearance of the materialized Christ after death constitutes the most powerful manifestation to which man has given testimony; it was the signal of an entry of spirits upon the world's stage. We are witnessing today a new advent of the invisible world into history. Isolated manifestations from the Beyond now indicate a tendency to become frequent and universal. A way is being established between the two worlds, which at first was a mere bridle path, then a narrow road, but which enlarges and widens and promises to become a large, sure route. Christianity has for its point of departure phenomena similar to that, which in our day constitute the proofs in the domain of psychical research: facts revealed through the influence and actions of a spiritual country of souls. Through these facts, and only through them, do we behold a pathway opening into infinity, and hope is born in anguished hearts, and humanity is reconciled with death.

The religions have opposed a barrier against violent passions and the barbarity of iron ages, and they have engraved clearly on the conscience of man the idea of morality.

The aesthetic part of religion has produced beautiful works in all domains of art, and aided largely in the revelation of art and beauty through the centuries. Greek art created marvels, Christian art attained sublimity in the Gothic cathedrals which lift themselves like bibles of stone under the heavens, with their proud sculptured towers, their imposing naves, which multiply the vibrations of the organ and the sacred chants, their lofty arches, from which floods of light ripple down on frescoes and statues, and then rest there as if exhausted.

The fault of religion is not an aesthetic fault; it is the fault of logic.

Religion is shut by the churches in walls of dogmas, and compelled to stand in rigid forms. Movement is the law of life, and the Church renders thought immobile, instead of inspiring it to flight.

It is the nature of man to exhaust all forms of an idea, and to carry it to extremes before allowing it to take its normal course of evolution. Every religious truth affirmed by an innovator is weakened and altered by its followers, who are almost always incapable of maintaining the height to which the master rose. The doctrine becomes, therefore, abused and distorted, and little by little creates counter-currents of skepticism and negation. Faith is succeeded by incredulity; materialism gets in its work, and only when materialism has shown its utter powerlessness in creating social order does the rebirth of idealism become possible. From the dawn of Christianity there have been divers currents of thought. Opposing ideas have crowded against one another in the bed of the newborn religion. Schisms and conflicts succeeded, in the midst of which the thought of Christ has been veiled with obscurity. True Christianity is the law of love and of liberty. The churches have it one of fear and dogmatism. From that has come the gradual weaning of 'thinkers' from the churches, and the weakening of religious feeling in many lands. And the inevitable result has been discord and discontent in the human family. Out of this discontent has come a crisis; in spite of all appearances of the death of faith, faith is not dead, but is being transformed and renewed. The doubt of today prepares the path for the conviction of tomorrow. An intelligent faith will govern the future and permeate all races. Humanity, still young and divided by the necessities of territory, climate, and distance, has nevertheless commenced to think for itself. Above the antagonism of politics and religions, groups of intellectual minds are formed; men pursued by the same problems, agonized by the same cares, inspired by the same invisible world, labor at a common work, and arrive at the same conclusions. Little by little the elements of psychical research are producing a universal faith all over the world. Numberless testimonials indicate the trend of human thought toward this glorious end. A higher spirituality is already here; religion is now the scientific effort of humanity to communicate with the spirit eternal and divine. Sir Oliver Lodge, the famous scientist of the University of Birmingham, and Maxwell, Attorney General in the Court of Appeals, Paris, both have declared the coming of a new religion of freedom and spirituality.

In the measure that thought ripens, missionaries of all orders awaken religious ideals in the breast of humanity. We are now witnessing one of these revivals, grander and more profound than any which have preceded. This new religious movement has not only men for interpreters, it has inspiring spirits, invisible helpers of space, who exercise their powers on all the surface on the globe and in all domains of thought at one time. Everywhere this new spirituality appears, and naturally the question arises, 'What is this new power? Is it science or religion?'

O human minds! Do you imagine that thought must sternly follow the ruts by the wheels of centuries?

Until now, all intellectual domains have been separated by walls and barriers - science on one side, religion on the other. Philosophy and metaphysics have been bristling with impenetrable thorns. In the domain of the soul, as in the domain of the universe, all is simple, vast, profound, but the system divined by man rendered it complicated, restricted, and divided. Religion has ripened in a somber cavern of dogmas and mysteries: science has been imprisoned in the lowest cellars of matter: that is neither true religion nor true science. We must lift ourselves above these arbitrary classifications to comprehend and reconcile the two with clear vision.

Do we not today, in even the elementary study of science, which relates to worlds in space, feel a sentiment of enthusiasm and admiration, which is almost religious? Read the great works of astronomers and mathematicians of genius; they will say to you that the universe is a prodigy of wisdom, harmony, beauty, and that already in the penetration of superior laws is realized the service of science, art, religion, and the vision of God through His works. Lifted to this height, study becomes contemplation, and thought is changed to prayer. The serious study of spiritism accentuates and develops this feeling and gives the mind a clearer and more precise understanding. On the experimental side it is only a science, but the aim of this research is to plunge into invisible regions and to lift oneself to the eternal sciences, from whence flow all life and force. This unites man with the Divine Power, and his study becomes a doctrine, a religious philosophy. It is the most powerful tie, which can bind humanity together, and it is, too, the voice of spirits delivered from the flesh calling to spirits still imprisoned in the body, and between them establishing a veritable communion.

We must not regard it, however, as a religion in the narrow acceptation of that word. The dogmas of established creeds and the new doctrine do not agree; it is open to all seekers; the spirit of free criticism and examination controls and presides at its investigations.

Dogmas, creeds, priests, and clergymen are nevertheless necessary to the world now, and will be for some time to come. Many young and timid souls in their journey through earth are unable to find their way or understand their own needs without direction.

The new spirituality, based on research and its proofs of life beyond the grave, addresses itself particularly to evolved souls who wish to find for themselves the solution of the grand problems, and to formulate their own creed. It offers to them a conception, an interpretation of truth and universal law, based on experience, upon reason, and upon the teachings of heavenly spirits. Add to that the revelations of duties and responsibilities, and you have a solid foundation for your instinct of justice. Then add to that the moral force, the satisfaction of the heart, the joy of finding again the loved being that you believed dead. To the proof of their survival is joined the certitude of joining them, and to live with them lives unencumbered, lives of ascending happiness and progress.

So in this research, the most obscure problems become radiant with light. The Beyond opens, the divine side of things is revealed; by the force of its teachings, sooner or later, the human soul mounts, and from its high altitude it sees that all the different theories, contradictory and hostile in appearance, are but various aspects of one truth. The majestic laws of the universe, for the enlightened souls are united in one single law of intelligent conscientious force, the source of thought and action; and by that law all the worlds and all beings are bound in one powerful verity, associated in one harmony, led toward one goal. The day will come when all the little system of narrow thought will be melted into one vast synthesis, embracing all the kingdoms of the mind. Sciences, philosophies, religions, today divided, will be joined together on this great light of life, the splendid radiance of the spirit, in this reign of knowledge. In this magnificent accord, science will furnish precision and method in the order of facts: philosophy, the vigor of logic and deduction: poetry, the radiation of its light and the magic of its color. Religion will add the qualities of sentiment and elevated aestheticism. So will be realized the beauty and force in the verity of thought. So will the human soul set toward the highest summits while maintaining the relation of equilibrium necessary to regulate the rhythmic march of intellect and conscience in their ascension toward the conquest of the good and true.

Physical research affirms and demonstrates the action of soul upon soul at all distances, without the aid of physical organs, and this order of fact is not made less positive by opposition and ridicule. The phenomena of telepathy and suggestion, of the transmission of thought observed and promoted everywhere today by millions, confirm these revelations. The experience of such eminent men as F. Colavida, and E. Marta, of Colonel de Rochas, and my own experiences, establish the fact that not only memory of the smallest details of life, even to childhood's hours, are remembered by the disembodied spirits, but those of anterior lives are engraved in the hidden recesses of the soul. An entire past, veiled in a waking state, reappears and lives again in a trance condition. Colonel de Rochas speaks of this in his book Successive Lives, and this subject will be specially dealt with farther on. Modern spiritual research cannot be considered as a purely metaphysical conception, as was the doctrine of the early spirituality. It now presents itself in quite another character and responds to the demands of an educated generation and to the school of rational criticism - a school rendered definite by the exaggerations of an agonizing and sickly mysticism.

To believe does not suffice for today - we want to know! No philosophical or moral conception has a chance of success if it does not lean on demonstration at once logical, mathematical, and positive, and if besides it is not crowned by the satisfying sanction of our ideas of justice. Leibnitz has said, 'If some one would write mathematically of philosophy and morality, nothing could prevent its being done with exactness. This' he adds, 'has been rarely attempted, and more rarely has succeeded.'

We might here remark, that in Allan Kardec's Book of Spirits, this has been done in a masterly manner. That book is the result of immense labor, classification, coordination, elimination, and gives only the messages from the spirit world, which the author was able to prove authentic beyond question. All the others were discarded.

This work of Allan Kardec is not ended; it continues since his death. Already we possess a powerful synthesis; the large lines were traced by Allan Kardec, and have been developed by the interpreters of his thought with the collaboration of the invisible world.

Each one brings a grain of sand to the common edifice, and the foundations are strengthened every day by scientific experimentation, while its towers reach higher and higher. For myself, I can say that I have been favored by teachings of spiritual guides, and that they have never failed me or misled me, during forty years. Their revelation have been of a particularly didactic character in the course of the last eight years. I have written fully of this in a former work, In the Invisible.

A rule scrupulously observed by Allan Kardec is that of presenting all his conclusions and ideas in a manner easily comprehended by any reader. That is why we purpose to adopt here the terms and method utilized by Allan Kardec, while adding to our own work the developments of fifty years of research and experimentation which have flowed by since the appearance of his works. Facts are nothing without reason, which analyses them and discovers the underlying law. Phenomena are transitory; the certitude that they give us is not enduring. History demonstrates this. During centuries, men believed (and many still believe) that the sun rises. To intellectual minds it was given to discover the movement of the earth, not grasped by the senses. What has become of the greater part of the old beliefs of science and chemistry? Our scientific men seem now only positive of the Law of Gravitation. In consequence, the methods I use in this work are observations of facts, their generalization, and search for the law governing them; and the rational deduction, which, beyond the fugitive and changing aspect of phenomena, perceives the permanent cause, which produces it.

In the study of spiritual phenomena there are two things to consider - a revelation from the spirit world, and a human discovery, that is to say, one part from invisible realms, essentially educative in itself, and the other a personal and human confirmation that pursues it with the laws of logic and reason.

Until now, we have had in this study only personal systems and individual revelations. Today there are thousands of voices the realm of the dead, which speak to earth. The invisible world enters into action, and eminent spirits, agents from beyond, are recognized by the beauty and power of their teachings. The great geniuses of space, impelled by divine impulse, have come to guide us to radiant summits. Is not this a grander dispensation than ever was ours in the past? The methods and the results are equally remarkable.

Personal revelation is always fallible. All the individual theories whether of Aristotle, of Thomas Aquinas, of Kant, of Descartes, or of Spinoza, are necessarily influenced by the opinions, tendencies, and prejudices of the revealer, and by the times and condition in which they are received. One might say the same of all religious doctrines. The revelations of impersonal spirits are free from the greater part of these influences; no man, no Church, no nation has the power to stifle them. They defy all inquisitions, and we have seen the most hostile minds brought to a new viewpoint by the power of their manifestations, and souls moved to the depths of their being by appeals and exhortations from the dear dead who urged them to become instruments of spiritual propaganda. Friends and relatives bring to doubting minds proofs unquestionable and irrefutable of their identity, and in this way spread the great truths of life without end over the earth. There seems to be a majestic accord in all the voices, which are simultaneously lifter to make a skeptical society listen to the good news of the survival of the soul, and to the explanation of the problems of life and sorrow.

This revelation has penetrated into the heart of family and society. The multiplication of the sources of this revelation, and its diffusion, constitutes a permanent basis for this science, which renders sterile all opposition and intrigues. Spiritual truth, if extinguished for a moment by falsification, is illumined again soon at a hundred other points. In this immense movement of spiritual revelation, souls are obeying orders from on high; they act under a plan traced in advance, and which unrolls and amplifies with majesty. An invisible council presides in the bosom of space; it is composed of great spirits of all races and all religions, and souls of the spiritual elite who have lived on earth according to the law of love and sacrifice. Their powerful influence unites earth with heaven by rays of light on which mount the prayers of the fervent and on which descends inspiration for mortals.

Certain students of spiritual revelations are puzzled by the contradictory nature of many communications. There are, for instance, spirits who affirm the law of successive lives, and others who deny it. This subject will be more thoroughly examined in later chapters of this volume.

Like all new doctrines, this modern spiritual revelation has met with criticism and objections: its followers have been called hasty in their assertions, and accused of building hurriedly on a foundation of phenomena, a frail and premature system of philosophy.

There are always the skeptics, and the indifferent, and the laggards to attack every new movement. No progress would be possible in the world if pioneers awaited the cooperation of laggards. It is amusing to hear such minds attempt to criticize men like Allan Kardec, who gave years of laborious research to his study before giving it to the world; or such brilliant scientists as Frederick Myers, the eminent professor of Cambridge, author of The Survival of Human Personality; or Sir Olive Lodge, the world-famous scientist and Member of the Academy, who stands bravely forth as the leader of this philosophy today.

In face of such appreciations, the recriminations of lesser minds fall through their own weakness.

To what can we attribute an aversion to a belief in communication with our dead? It must be because this belief and its teachings impose a moral responsibility of thought and action, which becomes very troublesome to many minds incapable of grasping, and indifferent to, an intellectual philosophy. In his Survival of Human Personality Professor Frederick Myers says, "For every conscientious seeker, psychical research leads logically to vast syntheses of philosophy and religion: the observations and experiences it brings open the door to a revelation."

It is evident that the day when such relations are established with the world of spirits by the force of events, the problem of life and destiny will also be established under new aspects. At no epoch of history has man been able to flee from the great problems of life, of death, of sorrow. Despite his incapability to solve them, they have without cessation haunted him, returning each time with more force as he attempted to escape them, gliding into all the events of his life, and knocking at the doors of his conscience. And when a new source of knowledge, of consolation, and moral force with vast horizons of thought open to the mind, how can he remain indifferent? And does it not indeed appeal to all of us? Is it not our future, our tomorrow, which is in question? Why this torment, this anguish, which has besieged the human heart across the centuries - this confused intuition of a better world, longed for and desired - this anxiety, that God and Justice should exist in a larger and more satisfying measure? Is there not in this desire - in this need - of the thought to probe the great mystery, one of the most beautiful privileges of human existence? Is it not therein lies the dignity and reason of being in this life? And each time that man has failed to recognize this privilege and has renounced turning his eyes Beyond, refused to direct his thought toward a higher life, and has circumscribed his horizon to earth, has he not seen the miseries of mortals aggravated, the burden grow heavier upon the shoulders of the unfortunate, despair and suicide multiply, and society descend toward anarchy and decadence?

It is claimed by our opponents that the spiritual philosophy is inconsistent, and that the communications come frequently from the mind of the mediums, or from those present, and who have formed their ideas upon this subject. But how can our critics explain the fact that in my own group, three mediums through whom I have made investigations gave descriptions of the worlds beyond, utterly at variance with the teachings of the church in which they were reared! All their ideas and views, when not in trance state, differed radically from their statements made when under control. The main statements made by mediums entirely unknown to one another, and scattered over the whole earth, are curiously consistent regarding the realms attained by the soul after death.

It is true, however, that there are as many orders of minds in the Beyond as there are here. There are infinite degrees of beings climbing the ladder that leads from earth to the higher heavens. The noble and the vulgar are to be encountered there as here. Yet sometimes the vulgar souls, in describing their moral situation and their impressions of the Beyond, furnish us with precious material for determining the conditions, which exist in that world. The prudent experimenter learns how to separate the gold from the dross in studying psychical phenomena. Truth does not always reach us nude, and the invisible helpers leave to our reason and perseverance the work of developing fully that which they give us in part. Meanwhile the utmost precaution should be taken, and continual control exercised. Fraud, conscious and unconscious, is to be encountered in these realms of research, and we must demand absolute proofs of identity, and never depart from righteous methods in our dealings with mediums and psychics.

When the authenticity of the communication is assured, we should again analyze them, with severe judgment applying the principle of scientific philosophy, and accept only those, which can be convincingly established as incontrovertible. Besides the possibility of fraud employed by mediums, there are occult dangers to be encountered in this study. All those who experiment in these realms know there are two orders of spiritualism. One, practiced at haphazard without method and without devotion of thought, attracting from space light and mocking spirits, which are numerous in the earth vicinity. The other, serious and reverent, practiced with caution and given respectful attention, which puts the student en rapport with advanced spirits who are desirous of comforting and enlightening those who call them with a fervent heart. That is known as the 'Communion of Saints' by the religious.

Again we are asked, 'How can the communications which come from superior spirits be distinguished from others? To this question there is but one answer. How can we distinguish between the good and bad books of authors long deceased? How distinguish a noble, elevating language from that which is banal and vulgar? We have only one law by which to measure the quality of thoughts, whether they come from our world or the other. We can judge mediumistic messages, above all, by their moral force and effect. If they purify and uplift the character and conscience, it is the surest criterion of their source; in our communications with the Invisibles, there were signs of recognition to distinguish the good from the bad spirits.

Sensitive psychics recognize quickly the approach of good spirits by the agreeable fragrance, which precedes the approach; while an odor difficult to endure surrounds evil visitors from the unseen realms.

There are spirits, which employ a certain musical note to distinguish their arrival. (That eminent author, Stainton M. Moses, mentions this in his book Annals of Psychic Science.). One of our mediums announced the coming of her control as a 'blue spirit'; brilliant radiations and harmonious vibrations accompanied this spirit. That which persuades and convinces us in our search for spiritual truths, more than all else, are the conversations established between friends and relatives who have preceded us into the world of space. When incontestable proofs of their identity assure us of their presence, when the old-time intimacy and confidence is newly established between us, the revelations obtained under these conditions take on a most suggestive character. Before them the last hesitations of skepticism vanish, to give place to ecstatic emotions of the heart. Can we resist, when the companions of our youth and our virility, who one by one have departed, leaving us solitary and desolate, return with a thousand proofs of their identity; incidents meaningless to strangers, but moving to us? When they advise, counsel, and console us, the coldest and most skeptical cannot resist their influence. We have proof of this in the conversations of Professor Hyslop, the American professor, with his father, brother, and uncle. Then add to these the pages written feverishly in half obscurity by mediums incapable of comprehending their beauty or value, but where splendor of style is allied to profundity of ideas. And again add impassioned discourses, such as we have heard in our study group, discourses pronounced by the organs of a simple and modest medium of honest character, who discussed the eternal enigma of the world and the laws which regulate the spiritual life. Those who had the privilege of attending these reunions know well what a penetrating influence they exerted upon all. In spite of the skeptical tendency of our generation, there are accents and forms of language and heights of eloquence, which cannot be resisted. The most prejudiced are obliged to recognize the incontestable mark of moral superiority. Before those spirits who descended for a moment into our obscure world to glorify it with their rays of genius, criticism hesitates and becomes silent. During eight years we received, here in Tours, messages of this order. They touched on all the great problems, all the important questions of moral philosophy, and comprise several volumes of manuscripts. It is the résumé of this work, too long and too involved to publish entirely, which I wish to present here.

Jerome de Prague, my friend, my guide of the present and the past, the magnanimous spirit who directed the first flights of my infantile intelligence in the far off ages, is the author. How many other eminent spirits have thus spread their teachings over the world, in the intimacy of various groups, almost always anonymously, revealing themselves only by the high value of their conceptions.

It has been given to me to lift some of the veils, which hide the true personalities. But I must guard their secrets, for the choice spirits are particular in this respect, and wish to remain unknown; the celebrated names which one often finds attached to empty and fleet communications are but a decoy. By all this details I wish to demonstrate one thing - this work is not exclusively mine, but rather the reflection of a higher thought which I seek to interpret. I have considered it a duty to endow my earthly brothers with these teachings, a worthy work of itself. Whatever one may think of the revelation of spirits, I am not ready to admit that because our universities teach immense systems of metaphysics, built by human thought, that we should regard as negligible, and reject the principles divulged by the noble intelligences of space. Though we love the human masters of reason and knowledge, it is not an excuse for disdaining the superhuman masters, who represent a higher and more serious knowledge. The spirit of man, limited by the flesh, deprived of the fullness of his perceptions and his resources, cannot attain by mortal powers alone a full acquaintance with the invisible world and its laws. The circle in which our life and thoughts struggle is restricted, our point of view limited, the insufficiency of the ideas we acquire render all generalization impossible, or improbable; we must have guides to penetrate the unknown domain and its laws. It is by the collaboration of the eminent thinkers of the two worlds - the two humanities - that the highest truths are attained, or at least perceived, and the noblest principles established. Better and surer than our earthly masters, those of Space know how to present to us the problem of life and the mystery of the soul, and how to aid us to realize the grandeur of our future. There is another question presented to us, and a new objection made by the critics. In presence of the infinite variety of communications received from the Invisible Realms, and the liberty given each mind to interpret them according to will, what, asks the questioner, becomes of the verity of doctrine, this powerful verity which has produced the force and the grandeur, and assured the devotion of sacerdotal religions? We have said that spiritism is not a dogma - it is not an orthodox sect. It is a living philosophy, open to every mind, and which progresses in evolving. It imposes nothing, it 'proposes', and what it offers leans upon facts of experience and moral proofs.

It excludes no other beliefs, but lifts itself above them all, and embraces them in vaster formulae, higher and more extended expressions of truth. Superior intelligences open the way; they reveal eternal principles, which each one of us adopts and assimilates in the measure of his comprehension, following the degree of development attained by his faculties in his succession of lives.

Generally the verity of doctrine is only obtained by the price of blind and passive submission to an ensemble of principles fixed in a rigid mould. It is the petrification of thought, the divorce of religion from science, which does not know how to exist without liberty and movement. This immobility, this fixed rigidity of dogma, deprives religion of all the benefits of evolution of thought; in considering itself as the only source of truth, it arrives at proscribing all which is outside of itself, and so ripens in a tomb, where it would carry all with it, all the intellectual life and genius of the human race. The greatest solicitude of the spiritual world is to prevent the funereal consequences of orthodoxy; its revelation is a free and sincere exposition of doctrines which are not unchanging, but which constitute new stations in the climb toward infinite and eternal truth. Every one has the right to analyze those principles, and they require no anchor but that of the conscience and reason, yet in adopting them one should conform his life and perform the duties, which are the result. Those who fail to do this cannot be considered serious. Allan Kardec always tells us to be on guard against a dogmatic and sectarian attitude. Constantly in his works he warns us against the unfortunate methods, which undermine other religions. Psychic research is a neutral territory where we meet one another and clasp hands with all. No more dogmas! No more mysteries! Open our hearts to all the whispers of the Spirit, draw from all the sources of the past and present; let us say that in every doctrine there are portions of truth, but that no one contains it all! For truth in its plenitude is vaster than the human spirit. It is only in the accord of sincere hearts and disinterested minds we can realize harmony of thought, and the conquest of the greatest sum of truth possible for man to assimilate on earth in this human history. A day will come when all will comprehend; there is no antithesis between science and religion, there is only misunderstanding. The antithesis is between science and orthodoxy. In bringing near to us the sacred doctrines of the Orient, touching the verity of the world and the evolution of life, the recent discoveries of science prove this fact. That is why we affirm that in pursuing their parallel march upon the grand route of the centuries, science and faith will meet one day forcibly, for their aim is identical, and they will finish by a reciprocal penetration. Science will analyze religion, will become the synthesis. In them the world of facts and the world of cause will unite. The true terms of intelligence, human and divine, will become one. The veil of the invisible will be torn away, the divine work will appear to all eyes in its majestic splendor.

The allusions that we have made to ancient doctrines might suggest another criticism, viz. that the teachings of spiritism are not entirely new. No, certainly they are not! In every age of humanity rays of light have flashed upon the pathway of thought, and the requisite truths have appeared to sages and seekers. Always men of genius, as well as psychics and clairvoyants, have received revelations from Beyond appropriate to the needs of human evolution. It is scarcely probable that the first men could have arrived of themselves, and through their own resources only, to an idea of law and a form of early civilization.

Consciously, or otherwise, the communication between earth and space has always existed. So we find easily in the doctrines of the past the greater part of the principle brought into full light by the teachings of spiritism. But these principles, understood by a few, have never penetrated the soul of the masses. Their revelations were spasmodic, in the form of isolated communications, and were usually regarded as miracles. But after twenty or thirty centuries of silent gestation, the critical mind of man has developed, and reason has grasped a concept of the highest laws. Spiritual phenomena, with all the instruction belonging to them, reappear to guide a hesitating society along the arduous way of progress.

It is always in the troubled hours of history that the grandest conceptions form in the breast of humanity. For there the old doctrines, with their voices enfeebled by age, and the philosophies, with their abstract language, no longer suffice to console the afflicted, to raise the courage of the crushed, and to lead souls to the summits. Nevertheless, they contain latent forces, and the light of their hearts can be reanimated. We do not partake of the views of those who, in this domain, seek to demolish rather than to restore; this would be wrong. Wisdom consists in gathering the portions of eternal life and the moral truths they contain, while casting away the superficial and useless, which the ages and the passion of men have added.

This work of discernment, of sorting, of renovation, who can accomplish? Men are badly prepared for it. In spite of the imperious wavering of the hour, in spite of the moral decadence of out time, no voice of authority is lifted, either in the sanctuary or the academy, to say the strong and grand words for which the world waits. The impulsion could only come from on high - it has come! All those who have studied the past with attention, know there is a plan in the drama of the centuries.

The divine thought manifests itself in different fashions, and the revelation gradually unfolds in a thousand manners, following the needs of society. When the hour of a new dispensation arrives, the Invisible World comes out of its silence; in all parts of the earth flow communications from the departed, bringing elements of a doctrine which give a foundation for the religions and the philosophies of two humanities.

The aim of psychical research is not to destroy, but to verify - to renew, to complete. It separates in the domain of faith that which is living and that, which is dead. It gathers and assembles, from the numerous systems by which until now, the conscience of humanity has been enclosed, the relative truths that they contain, and unites them with the order of truth proclaimed by itself. In brief, this new spiritism attaches to the human soul, still weak and uncertain, the powerful wings of wide space, and by this means elevates it to the height where it can embrace the vast harmony of laws and worlds, and at the same time obtain a clear vision of its destiny.

And that destiny it finds incomparably superior to anything, which has been murmured to it by the dogmas of the Middle Age and the theories of other times. It is an immense future of evolution, which opens for it, and leads it from sphere to sphere, from light to light, toward a goal always more beautiful, always more fully illumined with rays of justice and love.

---

1. Professor Richet says: 'Science has ever been a series of errors and approximations, constantly in a state of evolution, constantly overturning themselves, and changing more quickly than they form.'

2
THE CRITERION OF THE SPIRITIST DOCTRINE

(¹)

Modern Spiritualism is based on a complete set of facts. Those simply physical reveal to us the existence and mode of action of forces long time unknown. Others have an intelligent character and these are: direct or automatic writing, tiptology, and speeches delivered through trance communication or psychophony. We have already reviewed and analyzed these manifestations in another work.[2] We have seen that they are frequently accompanied by signs and proofs that establish the identity and the intervention of human souls that once lived upon the earth, and to whom death gave freedom.

It was through these phenomena that the Spirits[3] diffused their teachings throughout the world. As we will see, these teachings were confirmed by experience, on many points.

The new spiritualism, then, is directed both to the senses and the intelligence. It is experimental, when it studies the phenomena that serve as its basis; it is rational, when it verifies the teachings derived from them and constitutes a powerful instrument for the inquiry of the truth, as it can be employed simultaneously in all dominions of knowledge.

The Spirits' revelations, as we have said, are confirmed by experience. Since 1850[4] the Spirits taught us theoretically and demonstrated in practices the existence of imponderable forces that Science till then rejected "a priori." The Spirits refer to these forces as fluids. Later on Mr. W. Crooks, who amongst the intellectuals enjoyed great authority, was the first to verify the reality of these forces. Present day Science is gradually starting to recognize the importance and the variety of these forces, thanks to the celebrated discoveries of Roentgen, Hertz, Becquerel, Curie, G. Le Bon, and others.

The Spirits affirmed and demonstrated the possible action of one soul over another, from any distance and without the benefit of the physical organs. Notwithstanding, that order of facts has raised opposition and incredulity.

Nevertheless, the phenomena observed and widely performed today of telepathy, mental suggestion, and transmission of thoughts came by the thousands to confirm these revelations.

The Spirits taught us about the preexistence, the survival, and the successive lives of the soul. The experiences of F. Colavida, E. Marata, and the ones from Colonel de Rochas, mine, etc., establish that not only the memory of the smallest peculiarities of the current life, regressing far back to the most tender moments of childhood, but also remembrances of past lives are recorded in the inner recesses of our consciences. An entire past, which is protected in a vigilant state, resurfaces and comes to life during a trance state. This recollection can effectively be reconstituted in a certain number of sleeping patients, as we will establish later on, when we deal especially with that question.[5]

You see that modern Spiritualism cannot be considered purely as a metaphysical conception, as an example of the ancient spiritualistic doctrines. Rather, it presents a distinct character that suits the requirements of a generation educated in the schools of criticism and rationalism, and that was once rendered skeptical by the exaggerations of the morbid and agonizing mysticism.

Today it is not enough just to believe; one wants to understand. No philosophical or moral conception has a probability of triumph if it does not have for its basis a demonstration that is at the same time logical, mathematical, and positive, in addition to being crowned by a sanction that satisfies all our instincts of justice.

"If a mathematician wanted to write about philosophy and morals using mathematical formulas, he could without obstacle do it." Said Leibniz.

However, adds Leibniz: "It has rarely been tried, and much less with good results."

It should be observed that these conditions were perfectly accomplished by Allan Kardec in his magisterial exposition made in "The Spirits' Book."

That book is the result of an immense work of classification, coordination and elimination that had for its basis millions of communications and messages obtained from different origins, each one unknown to the others. These messages were obtained from all points of the world and assembled together by the eminent compiler, after establishing their authenticity. He was careful to set aside any isolated opinions, and suspect testimonies, keeping only the points where the statements were in agreement.

There is still much to be added before this work is complete. Despite the death of its brilliant initiator, this work has not suffered interruption. In fact, we already possess a powerful summary whose main lines were drawn by Kardec himself. Now, the heirs of his thoughts in conjunction with the invisible world are making an effort to further develop it. Each one brings his grain of sand for the common establishment of this edifice, whose fundamentals scientific experimentation renders more solid every day, and whose adornments will enable it to rise taller day by day.

For thirty uninterrupted years I myself received teachings from spiritual guides, who relentlessly provided their assistances and advices. Their revelations proceeded to take on a particularly didactic character during the sessions that lasted eight years, and of which I wrote about in a prior work[6].

In Allan Kardec's book, the teachings of the spirits are accompanied, on each question, with a consideration, commentary, and clarification. His style makes clear the beauty of its principles and the harmony of its whole. It is there that the qualities of the author become evident. First, he cleverly provides a clear and precise meaning of the expressions he often employed in his philosophical argumentation. Then, he proceeds to clarify the terms whose meanings could be interpreted in different ways. He knew that the confusion that arises in most philosophical systems is the result of a lack of clarity of expressions used by the authors.

Another rule of equal importance used throughout the entire

methodic exposition, and one that Allan Kardec meticulously observed is that which consists of circumscribing the ideas, and presenting them in a way that enables the readers to better understand them. Next, he developed those ideas in an orderly fashion and correlated them so as to promote their interconnection. Finally, he knew how to draw conclusions that already represent a reality and a certainty within the rational order, and in accordance with human conceptions.

For the above reasons and for the purpose of safety, we propose to adopt the terms, the views, and the methods observed by Allan Kardec for this book. We have added to our work all developments resulting from the investigation and experiences that took place during the fifty-year period since the appearance of his works.

In view of the above validation, we see that the Doctrine of the Spirits (of which Kardec was the interpreter and judicious compiler), similarly to the most appreciated philosophical systems, encompasses the essential qualities of clarity, logic and rigor. Unlike any other system, however, the Spiritist Doctrine offers its vital set of manifestations, through which it first affirmed itself in the world. Since its establishment the Spiritist Doctrine has continuously withstood all kinds of examinations. It addresses people of all social classes and conditions; it speaks not only to their senses and intellects, but especially to their best possessions - reason and conscience.

Do not these inner potencies, in their union, constitute a criterion of good and evil, truth and falsehood, more or less clear or concealed, evidently in accordance with the advancement of the soul? Further, don't we find that each of these is a reflection of the Eternal Reason from which they emanate?[7]

There are two aspects to the Spiritist Doctrine. One aspect shows a revelation from the spiritual world; the other shows a human discovery. With the first we have teachings that are universal, extra terrestrial and identical both in its essential parts and in its general sense. The latter shows that a personal and human confirmation continues to be made according to the rules of logic, experience and reason. The conviction emerging from these two aspects is reinforced and becomes progressively more rigorous in direct proportion to the increase in the number of communications received, thus multiplying and expanding the means for its verification.

Until now we were only acquainted with individual systems, that is, private revelations; but today, thousands of voices coming from the deceased make themselves heard. The invisible world is coming into action, and among its agents, we find eminent Spirits allowing themselves to be recognized only through the strength and the beauty of their teachings. The great geniuses of Space, moved by a divine impulse, come to guide our thoughts to radiant summits[8].

Isn't this a vast and grandiose manifestation of Providence, never equaled in the past? The difference of the means can only be compared to that of the results; let us compare.

The personal revelation is fallible. All human philosophical systems, all individual theories, whether they come from Aristoteles, Tomas of Aquino, Kant, Descartes, Spinoza or from our contemporaries are unavoidably influenced by the opinions, tendencies, prejudices, and sentiments of their revealers. They also suffer influences regarding the conditions of time and place in which they are produced. Incidentally, the same can be said of religious doctrines.

The Spirits' revelation, however, being impersonal and universal, escapes the majority of these influences, while supplying a greater number of probabilities, if not certainties. It cannot be suppressed or tarnished. No man, no nation, no church has privilege over it. It challenges all inquisitions and produces itself wherever one may least expect. The power of its manifestations has converted the most hostile oppositions, illuminating them with the new ideas. These men, when moved deep within their souls by the supplications and exhortations from their deceased relatives, spontaneously made themselves active instruments of its publicity.

Phenomena analogous to that, which happened to St. Paul on the road to Damascus do no lack in Spiritism, and have caused many to convert.

The Spirits have incited a great deal of mediums from all walks of life, from the bosom of all social classes, from among the most diverse factions, and even from the depths of sanctuaries. Clergymen have received instructions and propagated them either openly or under the veil of anonymity.[9]

Together, their deceased relatives and friends carried on the dual roles of teachers and revealers, adding formal and irrefutable proofs of identity to their teachings.

It was through such an approach that in fifty years Spiritism was able to stake its claim throughout the world and to convey its enlightenment. There is a majestic accord in all these voices that have simultaneously arisen to compel our incredulous societies to hear the Glad Tidings of the survival of the soul, and to solve the problems of death and pain. The revelations brought forth by means of mediumship have penetrated the hearts of families, reaching deep down into the atriums and social infernos. Did not the prisoners of Tarragona Prison address, as it is well known, the International Spiritist Congress of Barcelona in 1888, a moving adhesion in favor of a doctrine that, as they said, had converted them to goodness and reconciled them with their duties?[10]

The multiplicity of teaching sources and diffusion methods of the Spiritist Doctrine constitute a permanent contrast, which frustrates and renders sterile all oppositions and intrigues. Due to its own nature, the revelations of the Spirits escape all monopolization and falsification efforts. All attempts of domination or dissidence are powerless against it, for if they succeeded in extinguishing or corrupting it in one point, it would immediately re-emerge in a hundred other diverse points, thus rendering ineffective any harmful and treacherous ambitions.

Within this immense movement of revelation, the souls declare that they obey orders derived from Above. Their actions are regulated in accordance with a plan designed in advance, and which progresses with majestic amplitude. From the bosom of space an invisible council presides over its execution. It is composed of great Spirits from all races and religions. These enlightened and wholesome souls once lived in this world in accordance with the laws of love and sacrifice. These charitable potencies hover between heaven and earth, uniting the two through a trace of light through which prayers and inspirations continuously arise and descend.

Concerning the concordance of spiritual teachings, there is a fact - an exception - that most impressed certain detractors, and which they have held as a capital argument against Spiritism.

Why did the Spirits announce to most Latin countries the law of successive lives and the soul's reincarnation on earth, while they either denied or bypassed them all together in Anglo-Saxon countries? They question how one can explain such a flagrant contradiction?

Isn't this enough reason to destroy the unity of doctrine that characterizes the New Revelation?

Let us mention that there is no contradiction, but simply a dissemination approach developed because of prejudice inherited in the caste systems, races and religions that are deeply embedded in certain countries.

Since its beginning, the Spirits' teachings were more complete and extensive in the Latin centers. For reasons of opportunity, however, its start was restricted and gradual in other regions. It is verified that the number of spiritist communications affirming the principle of successive reincarnations have increased daily both in England and in America - many of them even offering precious arguments to the debates taking place among spiritualist of different schools.

In fact, the idea of reincarnation has spread beyond the Atlantic in such a way that one of the main American spiritualistic organizations[11], is today fully favorable to it. The "Light" of London that until recently pushed away this issue, is today discussing it with impartiality.

It seems that the shadows and contractions existent in the beginning were only apparent and offered almost no resistance to a serious exam[12].

∼

As it happens to all new doctrines, the Spiritist Revelation has incited many objections and criticisms.

Let us consider some of them. Firstly, we are accused of taking great satisfaction in philosophizing. We are also accused of having edified - on the basis of phenomena - an anticipated system, a premature doctrine, and having therefore jeopardized the positive character of modern Spiritualism.

A commendable writer, serving as interpreter for a certain number of psychics summarized his critique in these terms: "A serious objection against the spiritist hypothesis is the "philosophy" that certain hasty men have bestowed upon Spiritism. Spiritism which should only have been a science in its beginning, is already an immense philosophy for which the Universe has no secrets."

We remind the above author that the men he speaks of simply represented the roles of intermediaries, limiting themselves to coordinating and publishing the teachings received through mediumship.

On the other hand, we should notice that there will always be indifferent, agnostic and tardy spirits ready to think we advance too fast. There would not be any possible progress, if we had to wait for latecomers. It is truly amusing to see people - whose interest for this subject dates back only to yesterday - trying to offer guidelines to men of the likes of Allan Kardec who dared to publish his works only after years of laborious investigations and mature reflections, hence complying with formal orders and drinking from fountains of information that our excellent critics can hardly imagine.

All those who devotedly follow the development of psychic studies, can verify that the results acquired from such a work came to confirm and to further strengthen all the points of Kardec's work.

Charles Richet tells us that the eminent professor at Cambridge, Frederich Myers (who was for twenty years the soul of the "Society for Psychical Researches," of London, and who was subsequently promoted in 1900 to honorary president of the official International Congress of Psychology of Paris) makes the following declaration in the last pages of his magisterial work, La Personnalité Humaine, sa Survivance - a publication that produced a profound sensation in the intellectual world: "For all enlightened and conscious researcher these inquiries will provide place, logic, and obviously a vast philosophic and religious synthesis." Focusing on this information, he devotes the tenth chapter of that work to a "generalization or conclusion that establishes a more obvious connection between these new discoveries and the scheme of thoughts and beliefs already existent of the civilized man." [13]

The exposition of his work ends as follows:

"Bacon had predicted the progressive victory of observation and experience in all fields of human studies; in all except one: the control over "divine things." I am determined to show that this great exception is not justified. I insist there is a method to obtain the knowledge of divine things with the same certainty and safety with which we have reached the progress that we possess in the knowledge of terrestrial things. The authority of the church will, therefore, be substituted by that of observation and experience. The impulses of faith will be transformed into rational and firm convictions, giving rise to a superior ideal well above all that Humanity has known thus far."

Consequently, what some critics of little sagacity consider as a premature endeavor appears to F. Myers as "a necessary and unavoidable evolution." The philosophical synopsis that concludes his work received the highest support in scientific circles. Sir. Oliver Lodge, the English academic declares: "it constitutes one of the most extensive, comprehensible and well founded proposals concerning existence, that has been seen."[14]

Prof. Flournoy of Geneva gives it his highest praise in his "Archives of Psychologie de la Suisse Romande" (June 1903).

In France, other men of the scientific field, though unrelated with Spiritism, comes to similar conclusions.

Mr. Maxwell, a medical doctor and the substitute Attorney General at the Court of Appeals of Paris verbalized it as follows [15]:

"Spiritism arrives at its own time and corresponds to a general need... The expansion this doctrine is taking is one of the most curious phenomena of the current epoch. We watch what seems to me to be the birth of a true religion, without ritual ceremonies and without the clergy, but with assemblies and practices. Regarding myself, I find extreme interest in these meetings and have the impression of observing the birth of a religious movement predestined to a great future."

In view of these appreciations, our challengers' arguments and recriminations come to a halt. What, then, should we attribute their aversion to the Spiritist Doctrine? Could it be due to the fact that the spiritist teachings – with its laws of responsibilities, its linkage of cause and effect developed in the moral dominium, and its sanctioning through the examples they bring to us – cause a terrible embarrassment for a great number of people who pays little importance to philosophy?

Speaking on psychic facts, F. Myers says [16]: "these observations, experiences and inductions open the door to a revelation." It is evident that the day relationship with the Spirit world was established by the natural force of events, the problem of the being and its destiny - with all its consequences and with new aspects - was also immediately raised.

Say what they may, it was not possible to communicate with deceased relatives and friends and avoid concerning ourselves with their way of existence, or without taking an interest in their views, forcibly expanded and different from those they possessed while on Earth - at least for the souls already developed.

No time in History could mankind withdraw from the great problems of being, life, death, and pain. Despite man's inability to solve these problems, they have continuously worried him - returning with more determination each time he tried to push them away - infiltrating themselves in all events of his life, lodging deep into the recesses of his mind, knocking so to speak at his conscience's door. How could he be indifferent to a new source of teachings, consolation and moral force? How could he ignore the vast horizon that opened to his thoughts? Isn't it pertaining to both, our relatives and us? Isn't it our future destiny and our tomorrow's fate that is in question?

Why! The torment, the anguish resulting from the unknown that has afflicted the soul through the times; the confusing intuition of a better, forefelt and desired world. The anxious search for God and his justice can be - in a new and more expansive approach - appeased, clarified, and satisfied. Could we ignore the pathway to accomplish that? Isn't the desire and need of our minds to inquire into that great mystery one of the most beautiful privileges of the human being? Isn't that what constitutes the dignity, the beauty, and the reason for being in one's life?

Have we not seen that every time we have ignored this right, this privilege; every time we have momentarily renounced to turn our sights to the Beyond and to direct our thoughts towards a more elevated life; or else when we have sought to restrict that horizon, have we not seen, concurrently, the moral miseries aggravated, the weight of existence befalling heavier on the shoulders of the miserable, desperation and suicide increasing its area of devastation and societies retreating back towards decadence and anarchy?

There is still another kind of objection: the spiritist philosophy, they say, has no consistency; the communications upon which it is based originate most often from the mediums, from their own subconscious mind, or else from the audience's spirits. The medium in trance "reads from the consultees' spirits the doctrine accumulated therein, and that these eclectic doctrines are drawn from philosophies from all over the world, but mostly from Hinduism."

Did the author of these lines reflect thoroughly upon the difficulties that such a task could bring? Would he be able to explain the process by which one could, at first sight, read the accumulated doctrines in a person's mind? If this is possible, then do it! As it stands, we have basis to see in his allegations nothing more than words employed deceitfully and at the work of a passionate critic. Those who do not want to seem mistaken with their sentiments are often cheated by their words. The systematic disbelief on a point, at times, turns into naive credulity on another[17].

Before proceeding we remind you that the opinions of the majority of the mediums, at the beginning of the manifestations, were entirely opposite to those enunciated in their communications. Nearly all the mediums had received a religious education and were imbued with ideas of a paradise and an inferno. Their ideas concerning the future life, whenever they had them, differed significantly from those exposed by the Spirits. The ideas of heaven and hell are still most frequently the case today. In fact, that was the case of three mediums from our group, all practicing catholic women, who despite the philosophical teachings they received and transmitted, never fully renounced their cultural habits.[18]

As for the audience, listeners, or people considered as "consultees," let us recall that at the dawn of Spiritism in France - that is, in Allan Kardec's time - the men and women who possessed notions of oriental or druidic philosophy acknowledging the theory of transmigration or the successive lives of the soul, were a very small number. Information on the subject was not readily available; it was necessary to seek them in the bosom of the academies or in some secluded scientific centers.

We ask our challengers how could it be possible for such a vast number of mediums spread throughout the whole earth, working independently and being strangers to each other, by themselves alone constitute the basis of a doctrine with sufficient strength to resist all attacks and criticisms. A doctrine so exact, that its principles would be validated time and again by the daily receipt of confirming experiences, as described at the beginning of this chapter.

Regarding the sincerity of the mediumistic communications and their philosophical achievement, we are going to cite the words of an orator, whose opinions will not seem suspect, knowing the aversion most ecclesiastics have concerning Spiritism.

During a sermon given on April 7, 1899, in New York, Reverend J. Savage, a well-known preacher said:

"The supposed nonsense said to come from the other world makes up a legion. Along with it, however, there exists one of the most pure and complete moral literature - of incomparable spiritualistic teachings. I know of a book whose author is a graduate from Oxford and also a minister of the English Church. That book was written through automatic writing. At times, in order to deviate his thoughts from the work his hand executed, the author read Plato in Greek. In contrast to what is commonly admitted for that kind of work, that book was in absolute opposition to the author's religious beliefs. (This author and medium converted into Spiritism, before concluding the book.[19]) That work contains moral and spiritual teachings worthy of any of the Bibles that are in existence throughout the world."

The first periods of Christianity were composed of people who were looked down upon and deemed unworthy of any attention by those of the established society. One should read Saint Paul's story to recall it. Modern Spiritualism was launched on similar circumstances; only, in the shadow of its banner, we find many of today's honored names, followed by the best and most enlightened men. Observe then, that in general, it is a great and most sincere movement."[20]

In his speech, reverend Savage knew to give each thing its proper place. It is certain that not all mediumistic communications offer the same degree of interest. Many of them are simply composed of foolishness, repetitions and trivialities. Not all Spirits have the capability of transmitting useful and profound teachings. As it happens on earth, but even more meticulously in space, the scale of beings holds an infinite number of degrees. In that scale we find the noblest intelligences, as well as the most vulgar souls. At times, however, even the inferior Spirits, by describing their moral situations, their impressions at the moment of death and their situations in the Beyond - thus initiating us in the particulars of their new existences - furnish us with precious material to determine the conditions of survival of the diverse categories of Spirits.

Thus, from our relationship with the Invisibles, we can cultivate elements for our own education, though not all should be taken into consideration. The cautious and astute experimenters must know how to separate the glitter from the gold. The truth does not always reach us in its purest state. Interaction with those from the Above provides man with an ample field for the exercising of his faculties and reasoning abilities.

It is necessary to act with the utmost caution, be attentive and apply continuous examination to all [21]. In addition, we have to guard against conscious or unconscious frauds, while ascertaining that the written messages are not a mere case of animism. In order to accomplish this it is critical to verify if the communications are superior to the medium's capabilities, by analyzing the form and depth of the messages. It is necessary to request proofs of identity from the manifesting spirits, and not to relinquish the severest control - except in cases in which the teachings make an impression, because the superior nature and exceptional amplitude of the messages are well above the faculties of the transmitter.

Once the authenticity of the communications is established, it is necessary to compare them among themselves and submit the scientific and philosophical principles they express to a severe examination; only the points where a near unanimity of viewpoint is established are accepted.

In addition to frauds of a human origin, there are also the mystifications of an occult origin. All serious experimenters know there are two kinds of Spiritism. One that is practiced negligently, without method or thought elevation, which attracts to us the fools from space, the frivolous and mocking Spirits. These kinds of spirits are numerous in the terrestrial atmosphere. The other kind of Spiritism, which has a greater circumscription, is practiced with sobriety and a respectful sentiment. It places us in contact with the advanced Spirits, who are always eager to help and to enlighten those who call upon them with a heartfelt fervor. Religions have known and designated this kind of Spiritism as the communication of the saints.

It is often asked how is it possible to distinguish from the vast number of communications, whose authors are invisible, those that originate from superior entities and should be retained. There is only one answer to this question. How do we distinguish good and bad books from authors deceased a long time ago? How should a noble and elevated language be distinguished from one that is dull and vulgar? Do we not have a standard, a rule to appraise the thoughts - whether they come from our world or the other? Mediumistic messages are judged primarily by their moralistic effects. Countless times, these messages have improved many wicked traits and purified many consciences. That is the safest criterion of all philosophical teaching.

There are several ways to recognize and distinguish the good Spirits from the primitive souls, in our relationship with the Invisibles. The sensitive (medium) easily recognizes the nature of the fluids, which are subtle and agreeable with the good Spirits; these fluids are violent, glacial and difficult to withstand when dealing with the bad Spirits. One of our mediums always announced in advance the arrival of a "Blue Spirit," whose presence was revealed by harmonious vibrations and brilliant radiation.

Other Spirits are recognizable to certain mediums by their smell. In one case the smell is of a delicate and suave fragrance; [22] in another it is repugnant. A Spirit's elevation is evaluated by the purity of its fluids, the beauty of its form, and by its language.

With these kinds of investigations, the one thing that most intrigues, persuades and convinces us, are the conversations held with our relatives and friends that preceded us to the spiritual life. When incontestable proofs of identity give us the certainty of their presence; when the intimacy of the past, trust and friendship is again established among us, the revelations obtained under such conditions take on a most persuasive character.

Upon these proofs of identity, the last hesitations of skepticism forcibly dissipate, giving way to the impulses of the heart.

Is it possible, in reality, to resist the voices and the callings of those whom we shared our lives with? Can we ignore those who watched over our first steps with tender solicitude? Should we repel the voices and callings of friends from our infancies, adolescences and virility years? Can we disregard friends that one by one disappeared into death, leaving our path in life lonelier and more desolate upon their departure?

Through trance communications they come back with attitudes, voice inflections, reminiscence evocation, and with thousands upon thousands of identity proofs - silly in their particularities for strangers, but so poignant for those interested! They give us instructions regarding problems from the Beyond, admonish and console us. The most phlegmatic men, the most erudite experimenters, such as Dr. Hyslop, could not resist the influences from beyond the grave.[23]

The above facts show us that, unlike what some people think, we do not just find in Spiritism the so- called frivolous and abusive practices. On the contrary, we find in Spiritism a noble and generous cause, which is the affection for our deceased ones, and the interest we have for their memories. Isn't that one of the most respected aspects of human nature? Isn't that one of the sentiments, one of the forces that elevates man above matter and establishes the difference between him and the beast?

Besides the touching exhortations of our deceased relatives, we should also acknowledge the powerful outpouring of the genius from the Spirit World. Pages upon pages were written feverishly, under semi- darkness by mediums of our acquaintance, who were incapable of comprehending its value and beauty. These pages showed style of such a splendor whose beauty was only comparable to the wisdom of their ideas. In addition, remarkable speeches as we have many times heard in our study groups, were given through the organs of a medium of modest knowledge and character. Through such speeches superior Spirits have reasoned, speaking to us about the eternal enigma of the world and about the laws that govern the spiritual life.

Those who had the honor of participating in these meetings knew of the penetrating influence they exerted on all of us. Despite the skeptic tendencies and the mocking spirit of the men of our generation, they could not resist the bouts of eloquence that marked these communications, as they were characterized by accents and even peculiar forms of language. The most cautious men would be forced to recognize in them the characteristic of, and the incontestable sign of a greater moral superiority - the mark of the truth. In the presence of these Spirits, who for a short time descended upon our obscure and undeveloped world to brighten it with a sparkle of their wisdom, the most acute criticism grows dimmer, hesitates and becomes silent.

During eight years we received in the city of Tours these types of communications. They addressed all the great problems, all major moral and philosophical issues. These communications formed a manuscript of many volumes; the synopsis of that work, much too extensive and copious to be published in its integral form, I wanted to present herein. Jeronimo of Praga, my friend, my guide of the present and the past, the magnanimous Spirit who directed the first flights of my infantile intelligence in remote ages, is its author.

How many other eminent Spirits working in similar fashion and in the intimacy of some groups have spread their teachings throughout the world! Almost always anonymously, they reveal themselves only through the excellence of their concepts.

It was given to me the opportunity of lifting some of the veils that covered his true personality. I should however keep it a secret, as the finest of the spirits are distinguished precisely by their peculiarities of hiding behind borrowed names, desirous of remaining unidentified. The illustrious names that subscribe certain empty and shallow communications are no more than a hoax, in the majority of the cases.

With the above details I wanted to demonstrate that this work is not exclusively mine. Instead, it is a reflex of a more elevated thought that I seek to interpret. It is in agreement, in all its essential points, with the views expressed by Allan Kardec's instructors; points that they left obscure, however, begin to be discussed. I also considered the movement of thought and the human science - its discoveries - which I took care to indicate in this work. In certain cases, I added my personal impressions and comments, because in Spiritism, we can never say it enough times, there are no dogmas and each of its principles can, and should be discussed, judged, and submitted to the test of reason.

I considered it a duty to make these teachings available so that my brothers and sisters of Earth could benefit from them. A work is worth its substance. Whatever they may think or say of the Spirits' Revelation, I cannot admit that while the Universities teach metaphysical systems engineered by human thought, we allow ourselves to disregard and even reject the principles disclosed by the noble Intelligences of the space.

Having appreciation for the human masters-of-reason, and wisdom does not excuse our neglecting to bestow upon the above-human masters-of-reason, the representatives of a higher and more critical wisdom, our due appreciation. The human spirit compressed by the flesh, deprived of the plenitude of its resources and perceptions cannot by itself reach the knowledge of the invisible Universe and its laws. The circle in which our lives and thoughts transpire is limited, in the same way that our viewpoint is restricted. The insufficiency of information renders impossible all our generalization.

In order to penetrate the unknown and infinite dominium of the laws we need guides. It is with the collaboration of eminent thinkers of both worlds, of both humanities that we will reach the greatest truths - or at the least catch a glimpse of them. Then the noblest principles will be established. The masters of space, more efficiently than the masters of earth know best how to safely enlighten us concerning the problems of life and the mysteries of the soul, and to help us to acquire consciousness of our greatness and of our future.

~

Often when we are asked a question, a new objection is raised. Because of the infinite variety of communications and the freedom that each of us have to appreciate and verify them at will, many people ask what should be of the unity of the doctrine - that powerful unity that has been the strength, the greatness, and that has secured the duration of the sacerdotal religions.

We have said that Spiritism is not dogmatic; it is neither a cult nor orthodoxy. It is a living philosophy - a privilege of all free spirits, and that it progresses by evolution. It does not make any imposition; it proposes, and what it suggests is based on facts of experience and moral proofs. It does not exclude any other beliefs, but raises above them to embrace them in a vaster approach, in a more elevated and extensive expression of the truth.

The superior Intelligences open the pathways and reveal to us the eternal principles. Each of us adopts and assimilates these principles according to our own comprehension and in conformity with the level of development attained by our individual faculties – through the succession of our lives.

In general, the unity of the doctrine is obtained entirely at the cost of its blind and passive submission to a number of principles set on rigid rules - within inflexible molds. It is the crystallization of thought, the divorce of Religion and Science, through which it cannot pass without freedom and movement.

The self-imposed immobility and inflexibility of dogmas deprive Religion of all the benefits of social movement and thought evolution. Considering itself to be the only good and true belief, it goes to the extent of condemning all that is outside of it, consequently driving itself into a tomb whereto it wishes to pull along with itself the intellectual life and genius of the human races.

One thing that Spiritism takes most into account is to avoid the fatal consequences of orthodoxy. Its revelation is a free and sincere exposition of doctrines that has nothing of immutable; yet, it constitutes a new stage in the path leading to the Eternal and Infinite Truth. Everyone has the right to analyze its principles, which are sanctioned only by conscience and reason. But once these principles are adopted, each individual should strive to conform their lives to them, and accomplish the obligations they propose. Whoever avoids them cannot be considered as a true follower.

Allan Kardec always warned us against dogmatism and the spirit of cults; throughout his work he persistently urged us to do all we could to prevent Spiritism from crystallizing and to avoid the tragic methods that ruined the religious spirit of our country.

In our times of discord, political and religious battles in which Science and orthodoxies are at war, it is imperative to show to all men of goodwill – of all opinions, from all fields and beliefs, and to all truly free and far-reaching thinkers – that there is a neutral ground, that of experimental Spiritualism, where we can meet and hold each other's hands. No more dogmas! No more mysteries! Let us be open to understanding all facets of the spirit; let us drink from all the fountains of the past and the present. Let us acknowledge that all doctrines have a portion of truth; none, however, encompass it completely, because the truth in its plenitude is far more extensive than the human spirit.

It is only through the accord of people of good will; through the sincere hearts of the free and disinterested spirits that harmony of thought will be accomplished, in addition to the attainment of a greater sum of absorbable truth for the earthly man - in this current historic period.

A day will come when all mankind will comprehend that there is no antithesis between Science and true Religion. There are only misunderstandings. The discrepancy occurs between Science and orthodoxy, which is evident in Science's recent discoveries. These scientific discoveries prudently draw us closer to the sacred doctrines of the Orient and Gallia, in regards to the unity of the world and life evolution. That is why we affirm that although advancing in parallel marches through the long roads of the centuries, Science and faith will unavoidably meet one day. In fact, as their objectives are identical, they will inevitably intertwine with each other. Science will be the analysis and Religion, the synthesis.

The world of facts and causes will be united in them, the two aspects of the human intelligence will link and together they will tear down the veil of the Invisible. The divine work, in its majestic splendor, will appear to all eyes!

The allusions we made to ancient doctrines could bring another objection: "Are not the Spiritist teachings completely new, then?" they will ask. Absolutely not! Lighting has struck throughout all periods of Humanity; flashes of light have illuminated thought evolution and the necessary truths have appeared to the wise and the inquisitive. The men of genius, in addition to sensitive and clairvoyant mediums have always received from the Beyond the appropriate revelations to tend to the needs of human evolution [24].

It is unlikely that the first men could have arrived, spontaneously, and by their own mental resource, at the notion of laws and even to the first forms of civilization. Conscious or not, the communion between earth and space has always existed.

For this reason, we would find in doctrines of the past the majority of the principles brought to light again through the Spirits' teachings.

Finally, as these principles were reserved for the privileged minority, they had not yet penetrated the souls of the multitudes. In the past these revelations were produced, preferentially, in the form of isolated communications, and through manifestations that presented a sporadic character, which were often considered miraculous. However, after twenty or thirty centuries of lengthy work and silent progress have elapsed, the spirit of critique evolved and reason was raised up to the concept of superior laws. These phenomena along with their related teachings reappear, and once generalized they come to guide the hesitant societies through the arduous pathways of progress.

It is often in the midst of History's darkest hours that great synthetic conceptions are formed in the bosom of Humanity. It is also when the decrypted religions - with their voices weakened by age, and the philosophies with their abstract languages - are no longer sufficient to console the afflicted; to lift up the gloomy spirits; to pull the souls up to higher summits. Nevertheless, there is still a great deal of dormant force - containing glowing embers - that can be revived.

Hence, we do not agree with the views of some theorists who uphold its demolition, instead of its reconstruction; it would be a mistake. There are distinctions to be made from the inheritance of the past.

Such distinctions can even be extracted from esoteric religions - created for infantile spirits but that corresponds to the needs of certain categories of souls. Wisdom would consist of gathering the parcels of eternal life, the elements of moral direction they contain, while eliminating any worthless appendages added by the actions of time and passions.

Who could execute this work of discrimination, selection, and renewal? Man was poorly prepared for that task. Despite the imperious warnings of the current hour, despite the moral decay of our times, neither the sanctuaries nor the academic cathedras had promoted a voice authorized to say the strong and decisive words the world awaited.

Such impulses could only have come from Above. And so it did! All those who have carefully studied the past, know that there is a plan in the drama of the centuries. Divine thought manifests itself in different ways, and the revelation is adjusted in a thousand different ways, as per the requirements of the societies. It was for this reason that, having approached the time for a new concession, the Invisible World emerged from its silence. Communications from the dead emerged throughout the Earth bringing forth the elements of a doctrine that summarize and fuse together the philosophies and religions of both Humanities.

The purpose of Spiritism is not to destroy, but to unify and complete, thus renewing. It comes to separate from within the dominium of beliefs, that which has life from that which is dead. It collects the relative truths from the numerous systems that have until now encompassed the conscience of Humanity and adds them to the truths of the general order it proclaims.

In summary, Spiritism connects the human soul – which is still uncertain and fragile - with the powerful wings of infinite space, elevating it to heights wherefrom it can embrace the vast harmony of the laws and of the worlds, thus enabling it to obtain a clear sight of its destiny.

Such a destiny finds itself incomparably superior to all secrets kept by the doctrines of the Middle Age and the theories of other times. A future of immense evolution carried on from sphere to sphere and from clarity to clarity is open to the soul; its objective is an ending increasingly more beautiful and more illuminated by the rays of Justice and Love.

---

1. This chapter was left out when this book was first translated and published in English. The translator of this chapter is: Eliene Sherman; final editing: Louis Albert Day; revision against the French original (Nouvelle Edition - Conforme a l'edition de 1922 - Union Spirite Française et Francophone): Jussara Korngold.
2. See Dans l'Invisible - "Spiritisme et Médiumnité," 2nd part. Here we speak only of spiritist facts instead of animism or distant manifestations from the living.
3. We call the spirit a soul when clothed with its subtlebody.
4. See Allan Kardec –The Spirits'Book, The Mediums'Book.

    You can read in the Spiritist Magazine of 1860, pg 81, a message from the spirit of Dr. Vignal declaring that the body radiates obscure light. Isn't this the radioactivity verified by current Science, but until then ignored?

    In 1867 Allan Kardec wrote in his book Genesis, Chap. XIV (concerning fluids), the following: "Who knows the inner constitution of a tangible matter? Maybe it is in solid form only in relation to our senses. The proof of that is the ease with which it is crossed by spiritual fluids and by the Spirits themselves, as it offers no more obstruction than transparent bodies do to rays of light.

    Since tangible matter has the ethereal cosmic fluid as its primitive element, upon its disintegration, it should be able to return to its ethereal state - much like the diamond, the hardest of all bodies, can evaporate into impalpable gas. In reality the solidification of matter is no more than a transitory state of the universal cosmic fluid, which can return to its primitive state, when the condition of cohesion ceases to exist.
5. See Compte rendu du Congrès Spirite of 1900 pgs. 349 and 350 and Scientific and Moral Magazine of Spiritism, July and August of 1904. See also: A. de Rochas, The Successive Lives, Chacornac, ed. 1911.
6. See Dans l'Invisible, pg.299 on.
7. Facts do not have value without the reason that analyzes and deduces from them the law. Phenomena are ephemeral; the certainty they give us is only apparent and without duration. Only the Spirit possesses certainty, absolute truths are of a subjective order, and History shows it.

    Through the centuries it was believed, and many still believe, that the Sun is born every day. It was necessary to discover through intelligence the movements of the Earth, imperceptible to the senses, in order to understand the return of the same points to the same position in relation to the sun.

    What has been done with most theories of Physics and Chemistry? Clearly, there exists little more than the laws of attraction and gravity and, still, they may apply only to a section of the Universe.

    Consequently, the method at hand is as follows:

    1st) Observation of the facts;

    2nd) Its generalization and investigation of the law;

    3rd) The rational induction that goes beyond the fleeting and mutable phenomena and perceives the permanent cause that produces them.
8. See the communications published by Allan Kardec in The Spirits' Book and in Heaven and Hell.

    Spirit Teachings obtained by Stainton Moses.

We also indicate – Le Problème de l'Au-Delà (Conseils des Invisibles), Collection of messages published by General Amade. Leymarie, Paris, 1902; Sur le Chemin.., of Albert Pauchard and La Vie Continue de l'Ame, by A. Naschitz-Rousseau, a collection of messages of extreme interest (Editions Jean Meyer, Paris, 1922).

9. See Rafael, Le Doute, Father Marchal, The Consoling Spirit.
   Reverend Stainton Moses, Spirit Teachings.
   Father Didon wrote (August 4, 1876), in his Lettres to Mlle. Th. V. (Plon-Nourrit, edit., Paris, 1902), pg. 34: "I believe in the influence the dead and the saints mysteriously exert upon us. I live in profound communion with the invisibles, and feel the delights of the benefits received from such secret companionship.
   Mr. Alfred Benézech, an eminent preacher of the reformed church of France recently wrote to us (February of 1905) regarding the phenomena observed by him:
   "I feel that Spiritism can really become a positive religion, not one similar to those already revealed, but in the quality of a religion in accordance with reasoning and Science. What a strange thing! In our epoch of materialism, in which the churches - appearing to be about to disorganize and dissolve, the religious thought returns to us through the intellectuals, accompanied by the marvelous of ancient times. This marvelous - which I make a distinction from miracle, since it is no more than a natural, superior and rare fact - will not continue to be at the service of an exclusive church, honored with favors from the divinity. Rather, it will be a patrimony of Humanity, but without distinction of cults. How much greatness and morality is there not in this?"
10. See Compte rendu du Congrès Spirite de Barcelone, 1888. Library of Psychic Sciences, Paris, 42, rue Saint-Jacques.
11. The Banner of Light, which distributes 30,000 copies.
12. See ahead, chapters XIV, XV and XVI, the testimonies obtained in America and England supporting reincarnation.
13. F.Myers–La Personnalité Humaine, sa Survivance, ses Manifestations Supranormales, Felix Alcan, edition of 1905, pgs. 401 to 403.
14. Myers' synopsis can be abridged as follows: Gradual and Infinite Evolution, with multiple stages, of the human soul in wisdom and love. The human soul extracts its strength and grace from a spiritual universe. That universe is animated and governed by the Divine Spirit, is accessible to the soul and is in communication with it.
15. J.Maxwell – Les Phénomènes Psychiques, Alcan, ed., 1903, pgs.8 & 11.
16. F. Myers – La Personnalité Humaine, etc., pg. 417.
17. It is known that the suggestion and transmission of thought can only exert action in patients that have been prepared for a long time for that purpose and only when it is done by people who exert some ascendancy over them. Up to now, these experiences do not go beyond words or a series of words and were never able to constitute a set of doctrines. A thought-reader medium, inspired in the opinions of the spectators, if that were possible, would take from them, not precise notions on any philosophical concept, but the most confused and contradictory data.
18. Russell-Wallace, the English academic, in his beautiful work The Miracles and Modern Spiritism, verbalizes it as follows:
    "Having the mediums, in general, been educated in any of the usual orthodox beliefs, how can one explain that the notions of paradise are never confirmed by them? The extensive brochures of spiritualistic literature do not show any trace of a Spirit describing angels with wings, golden harps, or God's throne, where most modest orthodox Christians believe they would be placed, if they were to go to heaven.
    There is nothing more marvelous in the history of the human spirit than the following fact: Whether it is deep within the most remote American forest, or in the less important cities of England, ignorant men and women – most of which

were educated in the usual sectarian beliefs of heaven and hell – ever since they were taken over by the strange powers of mediumship, they gave on the subject teachings that were more philosophical than religious. Furthermore, those teachings differed considerably from all that was so deeply engraved within their spirit.

19. It refers to Stainton Moses – Spirit Teachings.
20. Reproduced by Revue du Spiritualisme Moderne, October 25, de 1901.

    Note that in cases like that of Stainton Moses, besides automatic writing, messages can also be obtained through direct writing, without any intervention of the human hand.

21. See conditions on experimentation – Allan Kardec, The Mediums' Book;" G. Delanne, Recherches sur la Médiumnité; Léon Denis, Dans l'Invisible, chapter IX.
22. See Dr. Maxwell, general advocate, Les Phénomènes Psychiques, pg 164.
23. See Dans l'Invisible, chap. XIX, Professor Hyslop's (of Colombia University) conversations with his deceased father, brothers and uncles.
24. See Dans l'Invisible, chapter XXVI – "La Médiuminité Glorieuse (The Glorious Mediumship)."

3

THE PROBLEM OF LIFE

The first problem which presents itself to the thought is of the thought itself, or of the thinking being. For each of us that is the leading subject who dominates all others, and its solution leads us to the very source of life and of the universe. What is the nature of our personality? Does it contain an element susceptible to survive death? To that question are attached all the fears, all the hopes of humanity.

The problem of life and the problem of the soul are one; it is the soul, which furnishes man with his principle of life and movement. Farther on in this work will be given facts of observation and experience to demonstrate this statement. The human soul is a will power, free and sovereign. It dominates all the attributes, all the functions, all the material elements of the being, as the divine soul dominates and unites all the parts of the universe to harmonize them. The soul is immortal because nothing is, and nothing can be, annihilated. No individuality can cease to be. The dissolution of forms proves only one thing - that the soul is separated from the organization by which it communicates with the earthly center. But it has not ceased to pursue its evolution under new conditions, and in a form more perfect, without losing it identity. Each time it abandons its terrestrial body, it returns to space united to its spiritual body, from which it is inseparable, in the form it has prepared by its thoughts and works.

This subtle body, this etheric double, exists always in us. Although invisible, it nevertheless serves as a mould for our material body. That does not play in the destiny of life the most important role. The physical body varies. Formed for the necessities of earthly stations, it is temporary and perishable; it disengages itself and dissolves at death. The etheric body lives; pre-existent to its births, it survives the decompositions of the tomb, and accompanies the soul in its incarnations. It is the model, the original type, the veritable human form upon which incorporates for a time the molecules of flesh, and which remains in the midst of all materializations and changing currents.

Even during life, the subtle form can detach itself from the carnal body under certain conditions, and act, appear, and manifest at a distance, as we will see later on, in a manner, which proves its independent existence.

Proofs of the existence of the soul are of two kinds, moral and experimental. Let us first look at the moral proofs: according to the materialistic school, the soul is but the result of cerebral functions - 'The cells of the brain', Haeckel says, 'are veritable organs of the soul; they grow, decay and vanish with it. The material germ contains the entire being, physical and moral.' To which in substance we reply - Matter cannot generate qualities it does not possess; atoms, whether they are triangular, circular or crooked, do not represent reason, genius, pure love, or sublime charity. The brain is said to create the function, but it is comprehensible that a function can know and possess consciousness and sensibility? How can we explain consciousness and sensibility, otherwise than by the spirit? Does it come from matter? It frequently combats it. Does it come from the instinct of conservation? It revolts against it, and commands us to sacrifice. The material organism is not the principle of life and its faculties; it is, on the contrary, a limitation. The brain is but an instrument, with the aid of which the mind registers its sensations. One can compare it to a keyboard on which each key represents a special order of sensations. When the instrument is in perfect tune, each key, under the action of the will, responds with its proper sound, and harmony reigns in the ideas and the actions. But if these same keys are out of tune, or if several are destroyed, the sound will be false, the harmony incomplete.

There will result a discord in spite of the effort of the intelligent artist, who cannot obtain from this defective instrument a consecutive harmony.

So are explained the mental maladies of neurotics and idiots, the temporary loss of memory and speech, madness, etc. In all these cases the mind still exists, but its manifestations are spoiled, or annihilated by a lack of correlation in its organs. Without doubt, the development of the brain usually denotes high faculties. For a soul delicate and powerful a more perfect instrument is required, which lends itself to all the manifestations of a thought rich and elevated.

The dimensions and circumlocutions of the brain are often in direct rapport with the degree of evolution of the mind. (Yet the rule is not absolute. The brain of Gambetta, for instance weighed less than that of the average man.) We should not infer from this that memory is but play of brain cells. These cells are modified and renewed constantly, says science, in the same degree in which the entire body renews itself after periods of years. How, then, can we recall the happenings of life ten, twenty, thirty years back? How do old people remember with surprising facility the smallest details of childhood? How can the memory, the personality, the ME persist and maintain itself in this continual destruction and reconstruction of physical organs? Nothing reaches the soul, say the materialists, save through the means of the senses; and the suspension of those is the destruction of the other. Let us remark, nevertheless, that in the condition of anesthesia, the momentary suppression of sensibility, the mind is not destroyed, but is, on the contrary, often extremely active. Buisson has said: 'If there exists one thing which can demonstrate the independence of the ME, it is assuredly the proof that we furnish in the patients under ether, whose intellectual faculties resist the agency of anesthetics.' Valpeau, treating the same subject, said: 'What a rich mine for the psychologists are the facts which separate spirit from matter, the soul from the body.' We shall see, also, in what fashion the soul can live, perceive, and act in ordinary sleep and in somnambulism. The soul, as Haeckel has said, represents only the sum of compound elements. There should always be in man a perfect correlation between the physical and mental. The rapport should be direct and constant, and the equilibrium perfect, between the faculties and the moral qualities on one side, and the material constitution on the other. The best portion of the qualities from the physical point of view should be possessed by the most intelligent and worthy. We know that this is not so, for often the rarest souls have inhabited poor bodies. Health and strength do not of necessity accompany brilliant and subtle minds. The phrase 'A healthy mind in a healthy body' is not an absolute rule. The flesh yields to sorrow. The soul, on the contrary, resists, and often exalts itself in suffering, and triumphs over exterior agents. We have the examples of Antigone, of Jesus, of Socrates, of Jeanne d'Arc, of the Christian martyrs, and many others who embellish history and ennoble the human race. They are there to remind us that the voices of duty and sacrifice can be heard high above the instincts of matter. The will of the hero knows how to dominate the body in the decisive hour.

If man were wholly contained in the physical germ, one would find in him only the qualities and the faults of his ancestors in the same degree, which they possessed. On the contrary, one sees everywhere children who differ from their parents, surpassing them, or being inferior. Even twin brothers with a striking physical resemblance, present, mentally and morally, entirely opposite characters. The theories of atavism and heredity are powerless to explain the cases of celebrated infant prodigies like the musicians Mozart and Paganini, the mathematicians Mondeaux and Inaudi, the painter Van de Kerkhove, and many other remarkable children whose genius cannot be traced back to their ancestors. The material substance transmitted by parents manifest itself by a physical resemblance in the children. But often this resemblance persists only a brief period of time; as soon as the character is formed, as soon as the child becomes the man, we see the features change, and at the same time the hereditary tendencies give place to other elements which constitute a different personality: a ME distinct in its tastes, its qualities, its passions from all that can be encountered in its ancestors. It is not, then, the material organism which makes the personality, but the interior man. In the measure that this develops and is established by its actions, we see the heredity of parents little by little fade, and often vanish utterly.

The idea of right - of what is good - engraved deeply at the bottom of our consciences, is another proof of our spiritual origin; if man was the mere issue of dust, or a result of mechanical forces of the world, we could not know good and evil, or feel remorse, or moral sorrow. Some one has said, 'These ideas come from our ancestors - from education -

from social influences.' But from whom did our first ancestors receive them? And why do they grow in us, if they find no natural soil and nourishment within us? If you have suffered at the sight of wrong, if you have wept for yourself and others in hours of sorrow, of revealing anguish, you have been able to perceive the profound secrets of the soul and its mysterious tethers to the Beyond; and you have comprehend the bitter chasm and the elevated aim of existence - of all existences. This aim is the education of beings by sorrow; it is the ascension of things finite to the life infinite. No! The thought and the conscience were never derived from a chemical and mechanical universe. They dominate it, on the contrary, direct it, and subdue it. In truth, is it not thought which measures the worlds and discovers the harmonies of the cosmos? We belong only partly to the material world; that is why we so resent its evils; if we belonged wholly to it, we would feel ourselves much more in our natural element, and be spared a large portion of our sufferings.

The truth about human nature, of life and destiny, of good and evil, of liberty and responsibility, will never be discovered on the point of a scalpel. Material science cannot judge the things of the spirit; the spirit alone can judge and comprehend the spirit in the measure of its own degree of evolution. It is by the consciousness of superior souls, by their thoughts, their works, their examples, by their sacrifices, that great light is cast on humanity to guide it toward a noble ideal. Man is at once spirit and matter - soul and body. But spirit and matter are but words, expressing in an imperfect manner the two forms of eternal life, which sleep in the matter of the brute, awaken in the matter organic, and grow and rise in the spirit. Is there not, as certain philosophers admit, but one only essence in things at once form and thought the form of the mind? That is possible: human knowledge is restricted, and the flashlight of genius is only one rapid ray in the infinite domain of ideas and laws. That which always characterizes the absolute difference of soul from matter is its unity with consciousness. Matter disperses and vanishes under analysis. Physical atoms divide and subdivide indefinitely. There is no unity in matter - such is the latest declaration of our greatest scientists. The spirit alone, in the universe, represents the one element simple, indivisible, indestructible, imperishable, immortal.

4
PERSONALITY

The conscience, the ME, is the center of the being, the foundation of the personality. To be a person is to have a conscience, a ME, which reflects, examines remembers. But can we analyze and describe the ME, its mysterious windings, its latent forces, its fertile germs, and its secret activities? The philosophies of the past have attempted it in vain. They have only skimmed the surface of conscious being; its internal and profound parts remained obscure and inaccessible up to the hour when hypnotism and spiritual phenomena projected therein some rays of light; and since then we have been enabled to see that in us is reflected the whole universe in its double immensity of space and time. We say space, for the soul, in its full, free manifestations, knows not distance. We say time, because all the past sleeps in the soul, and the future dwells there in an embryo state. The old schools admitted the verity and the continuity of the ME; the permanence and identity of the human personality and its survival. Their studies were based upon the sense which we today call introspection.

The new experimental psychology considers the personality as an aggregation, a composite, a 'colony'. The ME is regarded as a transient arrangement of cells without stability, which decompose eventually. These ideas are based on intellectual observations of alterations of personality, and the relation of maladies of memory to lesions of the brain, etc.

How shall we conciliate these dissimilar theories and observe both? Scientifically, in a most simple fashion. By observation itself - vigorous, attentive. Frederick Myers has given the subject the most magnificent effort that has been attempted by the human mind, in his book The Survival of Human Personality. He says in this work (which is recommended to all readers of this volume), 'After fourteen years of careful research, at the end of a long series of reflections based upon numberless proofs, I have come to the conclusion that the consciousness and the faculties of earth life assert themselves newly, in all their strength, after death.'

There are certain cases when there appears in us a being wholly different from our normal selves, possessing not only knowledge and aptitude more extensive than those of the ordinary personality, but besides, an endowment of more varied and more powerful perceptions. Often the observers of the phenomena of second personality believe they are in the presence of another individual.

It is necessary for the student to make the distinction between these cases and the controls of spiritual entities. The proofs furnished by careful students of these different manifestations permit no confusion. The cases of G. Pelham, of Robert Hyslop, and Fourcade, furnished in the book In the Invisible, are among these proofs. Dr. Binet, in his Alterations of the Personality, as does Myers, Dr. James, Dr. Merton Prince, Dr. Bouru and Dr. Bruat, all men of scientific renown. All the examples given by them demonstrate one thing. Above all the level of the normal consciousness, outside of the ordinary personality, there exists in us planes of consciousness - zones or layers, placed in such a manner that under certain conditions one can prove the alterations between these planes.

We see emerging to the surface, and manifesting themselves for a given time, attributes and faculties, which penetrate to a deeper consciousness: then they disappear, to plunge again into shadow and inaction. The ordinary superficial ME seems but a fragment of the ME total.

In the one is registered a world of facts, information, of memories reaching to a long past of the soul. During the normal life all these reservoirs remain hidden, as if buried under a material envelope. They appear in the somnambulistic state. The call of the will, the suggestion, mobilizes them; they come into action and produce the strange phenomena that the physiologist observes, but has no power to explain. All the cases of double personality, all the phenomena of clairvoyance, telepathy, premonition, enter the scene of the new senses and unknown faculties. All the ensemble of innumerable facts, constantly increasing, should be attributed to the intervention of the hidden personality. The somnambulistic state, which permits these manifestations, should not be regarded as morbid, but rather a superior state, following the experience of Myers' Evolution. It is true that organic degeneracy and weakness sometimes serves to facilitate the somnambulistic state. In a general way, it might be stated that all that reduces the physical vigor assists in allowing the spirit to free itself. The clear vision often found in the dying gives testimony to this fact.

But those who are regarded lightly by the materialistic psychologies as 'degenerates' are often the 'progenitors' instead. The highly nervous being is sometimes in a process of evolution toward a more intense state of planetary life. Morbidness sometimes is transformed into moral force. Myers speaks of the inspiration of genius 'as the emergence into the domain of consciousness of ideas formed quite independently of the will in the profound regions of the being.' Consequently, it is a most grievous theory of materialists who say that the 'official school' has arrived at the conclusion that genius is a species of nervous disorder. There is in us a reservoir of the subterranean waters, which sparkle and leap to the surface at times in a rapid bubbling current. The prophets, the martyrs of all religions, the inspired, the enthusiastic of all schools, have known these secret and powerful impulsions. They have procured for us the grandest works, which have revealed to man the existence of a superior world.

5

THE SOUL AND DIFFERENT STATES OF SLEEP

The study of sleep furnishes us with ideas of importance regarding nature and personality. We do not generally give enough serious thought to the mystery of sleep. An attentive examination of the phenomena, the study of the soul and its etheric form during the part of existence, which we consecrate to repose, leads us to a more extended comprehension of the conditions of life Beyond. Sleep promises, not only restorative properties, which science has never sufficiently emphasized, but also a power of co-ordination and of centralization upon the material organism. It can, as we will see, provoke a considerable extension of psychic perceptions, and a greater intensity of reasoning and of memory. What is sleep? It is simply the release of the soul from the body. Some one has said, 'Sleep is brother to death.' These words express a profound truth: sequestered in the flesh during our waking hours, the soul recovers in sleep, temporarily, its comparative freedom, and at the same time, the use of its hidden powers. Death will be its liberation complete - definite.

In the measure that outside perceptions are veiled when the eye is shut and the ear closed, other more powerful faculties awake in the depths of being. We see and hear by the aid of internal senses. Image, forms, and far-away scenes unroll and succeed on another. Conversations take place with the living and the dead. These experiences, often confused and incoherent in natural sleep, become precise and orderly in the sleep produced by trance or somnambulism. Often the soul goes far away in sleep, and its observations and impressions are translated into dreams. In this state an etheric cord unites it to the material organism, and by this subtle thread the impressions of the soul are transmitted to the brain. It is by the same process that in the other forms of sleep the soul controls, commands, and directs the earthly envelope. The walking of somnambulists in the night through perilous places with entire security is an evident demonstration.

It is the same force, which is employed in healing the body by suggestion. The soul is liberated and given the power to employ its forces in repairing the physical body. In the scientific reports of cases of double personality, it has been shown that the second personality, more complete and normal than the first, came and substituted itself for healing purposes. Suggestion is but an act of the will, which differs only from ordinary thought by its concentration and its intensity. In general, our thoughts are multiple and floating, are born and pass, or clash and confound themselves. In suggestion, the thought fixes itself upon one only point. It gains in power what loses in extent. By its action it becomes more penetrating, more incisive, and awakens in the subject on whom it is centered faculties revered in the normal state. Suggestion becomes then a lever, which mobilizes the vital forces, and directs them toward the point where they should operate. Rightly employed, the power of suggestion constitutes an important factor in education, and destroys pernicious habits and bad tendencies. It produces concentration of thought-increased energy and vitality. By fixing the attention on things essentially useful, and enlarging the field of memory, it manifests anew the internal senses and directs them to right ends. Let us return to ordinary sleep. When the soul is not fully released, the sensations and preoccupations of the day and memories of the past mix with the impressions of the night. In apparent disorder, the perceptions registered by the brain unroll in the incoherence of most dreams. But in the measure that the soul frees and elevates itself, the psychical senses become dominant, and the dreams acquire lucidity and a remarkable clearness. They unfold, and vast perspectives open on the spiritual world-veritable domains of the soul, penetrate hidden things, and even the thoughts and sentiments of other spirits. There is in us a double life, by which we appertain at one time to two worlds-two planes of existence. One is en rapport with time and space, as we conceive them in our planet, by our physical body and material life. The other, by our deeper faculties of the soul, unites us to worlds infinite. In the course of our terrestrial existence, it is in sleep that these faculties can find exercise, and the powers of the soul enter into vibration; then they resume contact with the universal world, which is their country from which the flesh has separated them. They invigorate themselves at the breast of eternal energies, to begin on awakening the penible and obscure task of daily life.

During sleep the soul can, following the necessity of the moment, apply itself in repairing the vital losses caused by the day's labor, and in regenerating the sleeping organism; infusing the forces of the cosmic world. Then, when this restorative action is accomplished, it takes the course of the superior life, and exercises its faculties of vision at a distance and penetrates hidden things.

In this independent activity it lives, in anticipation, the free life of the spirit. For this life (the natural continuation of the planetary existence which accompanies death) it must prepare itself, not only by terrestrial works, but also by its occupations in sleep. Thanks to reflections from that luster on high, which lights our dream paths and illumines the occult side of destiny, we can foresee the conditions of life Beyond. If it were possible to embrace in one glance of the eye the whole of our existence, we would recognize that the waking state is far from constituting the essential and most important phase. The souls who watch over us profit by our sleep to exercise their powers and develop our sense of intuition. They accomplish a work of initiation for the hungry humans, eager to elevate themselves - a work of which the dreams of the night carry indicating traces. The dreams of flying, or of moving rapidly above the earth, show that the etheric body is making an effort at freedom in the superior life. When we dream of mounting great heights without fatigue, of crossing space without difficulty, or floating over water freely, is it not a proof that our etheric bodies are free? For such sensations and images, completely reversing the laws of nature, could not come to the mind if they were not the result of a transformation in our method of existence. In reality they are not dreams, but real actions accomplished in another domain of sensation, and of which the memory is left in the brain.

These memories and impressions demonstrate that we possess two bodies; and the soul, the seat of the conscience, is attached to its subtle envelope, while the material body is plunged in sleep. There is always one difficulty: the farther the soul separates from the body and penetrates in the etheric regions, the weaker is the tie which unites them, and more vague is the memory of the dream. The soul soars far into immensity of space, and the brain cannot register its sensations. The result is, that we cannot analyze our most beautiful dreams. Often the last sensations of our night travels remain on awakening. If, at this moment, we take the precaution to fix them firmly in memory, they remain engraved there. One night I had the sensation of feeling vibrations in space - the last with a sweet, penetrating melody - and the souvenir of the closing words of a chant which terminated thus:

'There are Heavens innumerable.'

Sometimes one feels, on awakening, vague impressions of powerful experiences without precise memories. This sort of intuition, the result of perception registered in the deep consciousness, but not in the brain consciousness, persists with us for a certain time, and influences our actions at other times. These impressions are clearly translated in the dreams. Myers says of this subject: 'The permanent result of a dream is often such that it shows us clearly that the dream is not the effect of confused experiences in waking life, but possesses an inexplicable power, like that of suggestion or hypnotism, coming from the profound depths of our existence, which waking life is incapable of attaining.' Two groups of this sort are easily recognized - notably the dream which has been the point of departure of an obsessing idea, or acts of madness. We can explain this phenomenon in two ways: as a communication from the superior consciousness, or as the intervention of a lofty intelligence, which judges, disapproves, and condemns the conduct of the dreamer, and leaves with him a salutary sense of fear. The obsession might have been caused by evil spirits, which were exorcised by means of the dream. We should demand aid from the mysterious properties of sleep, and ask that our memory may be extended. Normal memory is restricted and precarious. It embraces only the narrow circle of the present, and the ensemble of daily events. The profound memory embraces all the history of life since its origin, its successive stations, its modes of existence, planetary and celestial. All the past souvenirs and sensations, forgotten in the waking state, are engraved in us; this past is awakened only during sleep - ordinary, or provoked by suggestion. It is a rule known to all experimenters, that the more profound is the sleep when produced hypnotically, the greater is the extension of memory. Myers deals fully with this subject in his book.

He says: 'Ordinary sleep is considered as occupying an intermediary position between waking life and profound hypnotic slumber. It appears probable, that the memory, which pertains to ordinary sleep, is attached on one side to actual daily life, and on the other, to that which exists in the hypnotic state. The fragments of memory in our nightly sleep are interlaced by the two chains.' We will see this in treating the question of reincarnation. Myers has been pushed much farther than he foresaw, and the consequences are immense. Not only can we, by hypnotic suggestion, reconstruct the smallest souvenirs of actual life, which have disappeared from the normal memory, but also we can restore the broken chain of past lives. At the same time that a vast and rich memory is awakened, we see appear in sleep faculties superior to all those which we enjoy awake.

Problems vainly studied, and abandoned as insoluble, are decided in dreams, or in the somnambulistic state; aesthetic works of an elevated order, poems, hymns, symphonies, have been conceived and executed. Is this done by the superior ME, or by the collaboration of spirits who come to inspire our work? It is probably that the two factors assist in phenomena of this order. Agassiz, Voltaire, La Fontaine, Bach, Fordini, all composed important works under these conditions.

We must not pass without mention another form of dreams, which until now has escaped explanation by science. I refer to premonitory dreams - an ensemble of images and visions bearing on future events of which the exactitude is later verified. They seem to indicate that the soul has power to penetrate the future, or that the future has been revealed to it by superior intelligences.

There was the dream of the Duchess of Hamilton, who saw, fifteen days in advance, the death of Count L----- with the details of an intimate order, which surrounded the event. A similar fact was published in The Progressive Thinker, of 1st November 1913. A magistrate of Hauser, Mr. Reed, was killed in an automobile. His ten-year-old son had twice in succession, in a dream, seen this catastrophe in all its details. Despite his supplications, and those of the wife and mother, Mr. Reed refused to abandon his project, and found death under the identical circumstances perceived by the child in his dreams.

In the Journal des Débats, May 1904, there is a curious story guaranteed as true. A man disappeared from his home, and a little dog, devoted to his Mistress, disappeared with the husband. One night she dreamed the little dog came to her, barking furiously, and after a few moments, scratched at the door to go out. She followed the animal through various streets and finally saw him disappear in a restaurant. The street, the house, the locality - were all clear in her memory when she awoke. She spoke to three friends of the matter, and decided to make a search for the place. She found it, and there was her husband, and with him the little dog. Innumerable other authentic cases of this kind could be given.

The perceptions of the soul in sleep are of two orders. First the vision of things at a distance- clairvoyance, lucidity; then comes an ensemble of phenomena known under the name of telepathy, of the reception and transmission of thoughts and sensations and impulses. In this category are cases of apparitions, known under the names of phantoms of the living. Official psychology has recorded great numbers of these cases. They form a continuous chain of facts.

The great astronomer, M. Flammarion, in his book, The Unknown and Psychic Problems, mentions a series of vision directed to a distance in sleep, resulting in verifying inquests. In the Annals of Psychic Science, September 1915, page 551, a detailed account of a proven psychic dream is given, which revealed the death of a man who had disappeared ten years previously, and the finding of his skeleton in the place indicated. In the same periodical, Professor Newbold, of the University of Pennsylvania, relates many examples, which prove the activity of the soul in sleep, and the knowledge it gains of worlds invisible. In all these cases the body reposes, its organs sleep, but the psychic being continues to be awake-to act. It sees, hears, and communicates, without the aid of words, with other beings like itself; that is to say, other souls. In a certain manner this phenomenon is found in each one of us. In sleep, when our ordinary means of communication with the exterior world are suspended, new outlets open for us, and through them our vision reaches out on intense rays of light. We see revealed another form of life - the life psychic - which proves to us that there exists for the human being a mode of perception different from that of the normal senses.

Besides the visions of natural sleep, there is that of provoked clairvoyance. Doctor Maxwell plunged a psychic, Mme. Aguelana, in magnetic slumber. Dr. Maxwell suggested to her to go to one of his friends, Mr. B - and see what he was doing. 'The medium,' says Dr. Maxwell, 'to my great surprise, said she saw Mr. B. - only partly dressed, walking bare-footed on stones. It was then 10:30 P.M. I could see no sense in the medium's statement, yet, when I saw my friend the next day, I told him the tale, and he was greatly astonished. He said, the previous evening, he had not felt well, and a friend had urged him to try to Kneipp cure, and walk bare-footed of doors. So, partly dressed, he walked up and down some stone steps outside his home.' Verified cases of clairvoyance are innumerable; and only those have made no careful investigations in this realm can deny their reality as facts.

6
TELEPATHIC PROJECTIONS

We arrive now at an order of manifestations that are produced at a distance, without the assistance of physical organs, and during the waking state. These are known under the general vague term of telepathy. As we have already stated, these occurrences are not an indication of a morbid or diseased personality, as some observers have believed, but, on the contrary, they are the coming to light of superior powers in the human breast. We should regard them as the dawning of future qualities with which man will be endowed. The examination of these facts leads to the proof that the exterior ME, and the ME surviving death, are identical, and represent two aspects of one and the same existence.

Telepathy, or projection of the thought to a distance, and even of manifesting thought in pictures, causes us to mount one more step on the ladder of psychic life. Here we are in the presence of a powerful act of the will. The soul itself imparts its vibrations - a proof that it is not a composite aggregation of forces, but on the contrary, the center of life and of will in us - a dynamic center that commands the organism and directs the functions. Telepathic communications do not admit of limitations. The power and independence of the soul reveals itself in a sovereign fashion, for here the body takes no part. It is more of an obstacle than an aid. So it produces phenomena after death, with even greater intensity, as we will see by the following. Myers says: 'Autoprojection is the one definite act which man is capable of accomplishing equally as well before death as after.' Telepathic communication at a distance has been established by experiences which have become classic. M. Pierre Janet, Professor of Sorbone, and Doctor Gibert of Havre, called mentally to Léonie, a telepathic subject, to come to them - a distance of two miles - and she came.

These experiences have been constantly multiplied. The Daily Express of London, 17th July 1903, relates exchanges of thought that took place in the office of the Review of Reviews, Strand, London. Six people witnessed these experiments - among them Doctor Wallace, 39 Harley Street, and W. Stead. The messages were sent by Mr. Richardson of London, and received by Mrs. Franck of Nottingham, at a distance of 110 miles.

The Banner of Light, of 12th August 1905, relates that an American, Mrs. Burton Johnson of Des Moins, sitting in her room at the Victoria Hotel, received four times telepathic messages from Palo Alto, California, a distance of 3000 miles. These facts were rigorously investigated, and verified beyond question.

Visions of people who are living are frequent occurrences. My own mother, during the last days of her life, saw me often near her in Tours, though I was far away, traveling in the East. This phase of phenomena is explained by the projection of the will of the one manifesting toward the recipient. In the following cases we will see the psychic personality, the soul, disengaging itself entirely from the body and appearing as a phantom. Testimony of this kind is abundant. The Society of Psychical Research in London has records of nearly a thousand authentic cases of apparitions of living persons. These cases are attested to by people of high moral and mental integrity. They form several volumes, and bear the names of men of science belonging to academies and scientific societies. Among other names are those of Gladstone and Balfour.

This order of phenomena is generally attributed to a subjective character. But this opinion does not submit to careful examination. Certain apparitions have been seen successively by several people in different stories of a house. Others have impressed animals - dogs and horses. In certain cases the phantoms opened doors, deplaced objects, and left their traces in the dust of the furniture. Voices have been heard, giving information on unknown facts, afterwards verified. An ensemble of such occurrences has been published by Doctor Dariex and Professor Charles Richet, in the Annals of Psychic Science, and by Flammarion in his book, The Unknown. Three prominent journals of London reported, on 17th May 1905, a case of an apparition in Parliament. The phantom of deputy Sir Carne Rasch, who was at that moment ill at his home, was seen by three other deputies. Sir Gilbert Parker says of the occurrence: "I was to participate in the debate that day in Parliament, but they forgot to call my name. As I resumed my place, my eyes fell on Sir Carne Rasch sitting in his usual place. As I knew him to be ill, I made a friendly gesture, and said, "I hope you are better." He made no response; that surprised me. He was very pale; he was sitting tranquilly learning on one hand, his expression impassible and hard.

'I pondered a moment on what I ought to do, and when I again turned toward Sir Carne, he had disappeared. I went to look him up, thinking he was in the vestibule; but he was not there, and no one had seen him. It was undoubtedly the etheric double of Sir Carne, which had been projected by his great desire to be there and cast his vote for the Government.' Sir Arthur Hayter adds his testimony to that of Sir Gilbert Parker. He says he not only saw Sir Carne Rasch, but drew the attention of Sir Campbell-Bannerman to his presence in the Chamber.

The exteriorization of the double can be produced by magnetic force.

These experiences have occurred, and before the proofs doubt is impossible. Consult history, and we will find the past full of facts of this nature. The phenomena of appearance of the living in religious annals are frequent. The past is no less rich in testimony of the spirits of the dead, and this abundance of affirmations and their persistence across the centuries, indicates that in the midst of superstitions and errors there must be a portion of reality. In effect, the manifestation and the communication at a distance between incarnated spirits, leads to the possible communication of the incarnate and the discarnate. To quote Myers again, 'We can affect each other at a distance,' and if our spirits incarnated in our bodies act thus, independently of the physical organism, we have there a presumption in favor of the existence of other spirits, independent of the body, and able to affect us in the same manner. 'The inhabitants of space' have furnished many proofs of this law of universal communion in the restrained and difficult measure that they are able to establish. The Society for Psychical Research experimented with two mediums, one in England and one in America. Professor Hyslop of Columbia College took all necessary precautions to prevent fraud. Four Latin words, unknown to either medium, were transmitted from spirit to spirit, across seas. This experiment was related in full in the Daily Tribune of Chicago, 31st October 1904, and in the Proceedings of the Psychical Research Society.

When we study under their divers aspects the phenomena of telepathy, we are led to recognize in it a process of communication of incalculable import. At first we saw therein a simple, almost mechanical transmission of thoughts and images between two brains; but the phenomena began to assume the most varied and impressive forms. After thoughts came the projections at a distance of phantoms of the living - those of the dying, and often, without any interruption in the continuity of the chain of facts, the apparitions of the dead.

In the greater number of these cases, the clairvoyant who saw and described these apparitions ha no acquaintance with the personages appearing. We have on record a series of continual manifestations of this nature, which demonstrate the indestructibility of the soul.

Telepathy knows no bound; it mounts over all obstacles, and binds the living on earth to the living in space - the world visible to the worlds invisible - man to God. It unites them closely, intimately. The means of transmission that it reveals to us constitute the foundation of social relations between spirits and their usual mode of exchanging ideas and sensations. The phenomenon called telepathy on earth is nothing but the process of communication between all spirits in the life superior, and prayer is one of its most powerful forms, one of its highest and purest applications. Telepathy is the manifestation of a law universal and eternal.

All beings, all bodies, exchange vibrations; the stars influence one another across shining immensities. In the same manner, souls, which are systems of thought and centers of force, impress one another, and can communicate at any distance. Sir William Crooks, in an address to the British Association on vibration, declared it was the natural law that regulated all psychic communications. Telepathy seems even to extend to animals; there are facts existing that indicate such communication between men and animals. The attraction spreads from star to star and from soul to soul. All are drawn toward one common center, eternal and divine. A double rapport is established. These aspirations mount toward Him in the forms of appeals and prayers, and descend in the forms of grace and inspiration. The great poets, writers, artists - the wise and the good, have known these impulsions, these sudden inspirations, theses rays of genius which illuminate the brain like flashes from a superior world, and reflect its grandeur and inebriating beauty. Visions of the soul in an ecstatic flight, they open the inaccessible world with its radiations and its glories.

All this demonstrates to us that the soul is capable of being impressed by other means than through its physical organs; of gathering information beyond the reach of earthly things, and proceeding from a spiritual cause. Thanks to these rays of light, the soul perceives in the universal vibration the past and the future; it beholds the genesis of forms - forms of art and thought, of beauty and holiness, from which flow for even new forms, which they emanate. Considering these things from the immediate point of view, let us see their consequences in the earthly center. Already, by the fact of telepathy, the human evolution is accentuated.

Man, conquering new psychic powers, will one day be permitted to manifest his thoughts at any distance, without a material intermediary. This progress constitutes one of the most magnificent stages of humanity toward a free and more intense life. It should be prelude to the grandest moral revolution ever produced on our globe.

By its effect, evil would be vanquished, or greatly diminished. When man has no more secrets, when others can read the thoughts in his mind, he will not dare think evil, or consequently do evil. So ever the human soul mounts, climbing the ladder of infinite development.

The time will come when more and more intelligence will predominate, and disengaging itself from the bodily chrysalis, reach out and affirm its empire over matter, creating by its efforts new and more extended means of perception and manifestation. The sense, in their turn refined, will see their circle of action enlarge; the human will become a mysterious temple filled with harmonies and with perfumes, an admirable instrument for the service of a spirit. At the same time, with the human personality, and soul, and organism, the earthly organism will be transformed. In order that society evolves, the individual must evolve himself first. It is man who makes humanity, and humanity by its constant action transforms its dwelling. There is an absolute equilibrium between the moral and the physical; the thought and the will are the excellent utensils by the aid of which we can transform everything in ourselves and around us. Having but high and pure thoughts, aspirations toward all that is great, noble, and beautiful, little by little we will feel our being regenerated, and with it, gradually, society, the globe, humanity. In our ascension we will come to better understand and practice this universal communion that binds all beings. Unconscious in the lower states of existence, this communion will become more and more conscious in the measure that the life is elevated and travels over the innumerable degrees of evolution to arrive one day at that state of spirituality where every soul, shining with the glory of acquired powers, in an ecstasy of love sees and feels itself united to all in work infinite and eternal.

7
MANIFESTATIONS AFTER DEATH

In the preceding examination we have followed the spirit of man through the different phases of extrication. Ordinary sleep, somnambulism, transmission of thought, telepathy under all forms: we have seen its sensitiveness and its means of perception increase, in the measure that its ties to the body relaxed. We are going to see it now in the state of absolute liberty - that is to say, after death, manifesting itself at the same time physically and intellectually to its earthly friends. No chasm separates them in the different psychic states. Whether these phenomena take place during or after the material life, the cause is identical in its laws and in its effects.

Let us eliminate the idea of the supernatural, which has long been looked upon with suspicion by science. The old adage, 'Nature makes no breaks,' verifies itself once more. Death is not a break; it is a separation and not a dissolution of the elements that compose the earth man. It is that passing from the world visible to the world invisible, whose limits are purely arbitrary, and due simply to the imperfection of ourselves. The life of each one of us in the Beyond is the natural and logical prolongation of actual life, the development of the invisible parts of our being. There are links in the psychic domain as in the physical. We have seen in the two orders of apparitions, whether living or deceased, that it is always the etheric form - this vehicle of the soul, the reproduction or the picture of the physical body - which becomes perceptible to the medium. Science, according to Curie, Lebau, and Becquerel, familiarizes itself day after day with the subtle and invisible states of matter, with its fluids, in a word, utilized by the spirits in their manifestations, and well understood by them.

Thanks to recent discoveries, science has entered into contact with a world of elements, of forces, and of powers unsuspected, and the possibilities of forms of existence long unknown at last appear to him. The scientists who have studied spiritual phenomena - Sir W. Crookes, R. Wallace, R. Dale Owen, Sir Olive Lodge, Paul Gibier, Myers, Aksakof - have testified to numerous apparitions of the dead. The spirit of Katie King was materialized during three years in the home of Sr. William Crookes, member of the Royal Academy of London, and was photographed on 2nd March 1894 in the presence of a group of experimenters, as he relates in his book Researches. Myers speaks of 231 cases of apparitions of the deceased. Among them was one announcing an imminent death. A commercial traveler had a vision one morning of a sister dead nine years. When he related this to his family it met with incredulity and skepticism; but in describing the vision he mentioned a scratch on her face. This detail caused the mother to faint. After coming to consciousness, the mother related how she had inadvertently made this scratch on her daughter's face as she lay in her coffin, and had covered it with powder, so that no person in the world knew of the occurrence. The fact that it had been seen bye the son impressed upon the mother the veracity of the vision, which she believed was a forerunner of her own death. In fact, she died some weeks later.

In a report made before the 'International Congress of Psychology' in Paris, 1900, Dr. Paul Gibier, Director of the Pasteur Institute, spoke of the materialization of phantoms obtained by him in his laboratory in presence of regular assistants in his biological work and of several ladies of his family. These were given the special mission of watching the medium, Mme. Salmon; of disrobing her before the séance, in order to verify her garments, always black, while the phantoms appeared in white. The medium was also locked in a metallic cage, and Dr. Gibier kept the key; yet under these conditions, in a half-light, numerous forms of various heights appeared, from little children to those of tall stature. The formation was gradual, and took place before the eyes of all the assistants. Interrogated, they spoke, declaring themselves personalities who had lived on earth, whose mission it now was to demonstrate the existence of another life.

In Paris, 23rd September 1900, Doctor Bayal, Ex-Governor of Dahomey, and Senator of Bouches-du-Rhône, described the apparitions he had witnessed at Arles. The phantom of Arcella, a young Roman girl whose tomb is at Arles, was materialized in the presence of many people, among whom were the poet Mistral, and a general of the division, a noted doctor, and others. Professor Milesi, of the University of Rome, testified in the Revue of Psychic Studies, 11th September 1904, to the materialization of his sister three years after her death. 'She appeared with the exquisite smile which was habitual to her,' he said. In an article in the Figaro, 9th October 1905, Mr. Charles Richet, of the Academy of Medicine of Paris, Member of the Institute, wrote; 'The occult world exists; at risk of being regarded by my contemporaries as insane, I believe in phantoms.' In my own group of students that I long directed in Tours, the mediums described apparitions of the dead whom they had never seen or known so perfectly that they were readily recognized by those present. In the works of Aksakof, he relates the reproduction by a spirit of the penmanship of the banker Livermore, which was identical with that in the possession of his wife. Often spirits incorporate in the body of the sleeping medium, and speak and write, furnishing proofs of their identity. The medium abandons momentarily her body to their use. Voice, language, and gestures are those of the spirit, not of the medium at those times. A curious case is testified to by Abbé Grimond, director of the Asylum for Deaf-Mutes at Vaucluse. By the means of the organs of Mme. Gallas, medium, while in trance, he received from the spirit of Focade, eight years deceased, a message by the silent motion of the lips. This was after a special method of speech for the mute which this spirit had invented and communicated to Abbé Grimond, and that this venerable ecclesiastic alone knew. Twelve witnesses who were present have given their signatures to the truth of this remarkable séance. Doctor Maxwell, Avocat-Géneral, speaks in his book of a case of incorporation as follows; 'A curious personality is that of a doctor who has been dead a hundred years; his medical language is archaic. He gives the ancient names to medicinal plants. His diagnosis is generally exact, but the description of internal symptoms which he perceives are astonishing to a physician of the twentieth century! I have studied my confrère from beyond the tomb for ten years, and he has not failed to present a striking continuity of logic.'

If we take into consideration the difficulties which surround the communications by the aid of an organism, and particularly a brain which he has not himself fashioned and accustomed himself to by experience, if we consider that by reason of the difference in planes of existence one cannot demand of discarnate man all the proofs we demand of a material man, we must them recognize that the phenomenon of incorporation is one of those which co-operates the most powerfully to demonstrate the spirituality of life and its survival.

It is not a question in these cases of a simple influence at a distance, it is an impulsion which the subject cannot resist, and which often takes possession of the entire organism. These phenomena are analogous to that of the second personality. There the profound ME substitutes itself for the normal ME, and directs the physical body, with the purpose of regeneration. But here it is a strange spirit which plays a role and substitutes itself in place of the personality of the sleeping medium. The word 'possession' which we have just used has often been employed in an evil sense. One attributes to it facts which are designed as diabolical. But as Myers has said, "The evil is not a creature recognized in science. In these phenomena we find ourselves in presence of spirits who have been men like ourselves, animated by the same motives which inspire us.'

Thanks to these experiences, to these observations, to these testimonials a million times repeated, we must see the existence of the soul rising out of the domain of hypothesis, or of simple metaphysical conception, to become a living reality, a fact vigorously established.

All the terror, all the superstitions suggested by the idea of death to man vanish. Our conception of the universal life and of divine work enlarges, and at the same time our confidence in the future is fortified. We see under the alternate forms of existence, carnal and etheric, that the progress of life and the development of the personality continues, and one law supreme presides over the evolution of souls through time and space.

8
VIBRATORY STATES OF THE SOULS' MEMORY

Life is an immense vibration which fills the universe and of which the center is God. Each soul is a detached spark from which this divine center becomes in its turn a center of vibrations which vary and augment with amplitude and intensity, following the degree of the elevation of life. This fact can be verified by experiment. (Doctors Baraduc and Joire have constructed a registering apparatus which measures the radiant force escaping from each human person, and varying according to the psychic state of the subject). Each soul has then its particular and different vibration; its proper movement, its rhythm, is the exact representation of its dynamic power, of its intellectual value, of its moral elevation. All the beauty, all the grandeur of the living universe is summed up in this law of harmonic vibrations. The souls that vibrate in unison recognize each other, and call across space with sympathy, friendship, and love. The artists, the sensitives, the delicately harmonized beings know this law and feel its effects. The superior soul vibrates in unison with all the harmonies.

The psychic entity penetrates with its vibrations all its etheric organism - that subtle form and image, that exact reproduction of its radiant and harmonious personality. But incarnation comes, and these vibrations are under veils of flesh. The interior center cannot project outward more than a feeble intermittent radiation; nevertheless in sleep, in somnambulism, in trance, as soon as a passage is opened to the soul through the envelope of matter which chains and oppresses, the vibratory current is established, and the center restored to activity. The spirit finds in these interior states power and liberty. All that sleeps in it awakens; its numerous lives reconstruct themselves, not only with treasures of thoughts and memories, but also with all the sensations, joys, and sorrows unregistered in the fluidic organism. In trance, the soul, vibrating with memories of the past, affirms its anterior existences and renews the mysterious chain of its transmigrations.

The smallest details of our life are registered in us and leave their ineffaceable traces; thoughts, desires, passions, acts good or bad, all are there fixed, all are there engraved. During the normal course of life, then memories accumulate in successive layers, and the most recent efface in appearance the most ancient. We seem to have forgotten a million details of our departed existence; but in the experiences of hypnotism, it is only necessary to evoke the past and to turn the subject by will to an anterior epoch of his life in his youth or childhood to bring back those memories in crowds. The subject reviews his past with the associations of ideas which pertained to that epoch; (ideas often wholly unlike those he actually professes); and with the tastes, habits, and language of that time, he automatically reconstructs a series of phenomena contemporaneous to that period. This leads us to recognize that there is a close correlation between the psychic individuality and the organic state. Each mental state is associated with a state physiological. The evocation of one in the memory of a hypnotized subject leads to the reaparition of the other.

This law is known in psychology under the name of 'psycho-physical parallelism.' A notable instance of this law is the case of Rose, a hypnotic subject of M. Pierre Janet, Professor of Psychology in Sorbonne. He relates in his work on this subject, that when he willed her to go back two years in her life while in trance state, there were reproduced in her all the symptoms of pregnancy, which was her condition at that time. This phenomenon would be incomprehensible without the explanation that the etheric double retains all the impressions of the past. It is that which furnishes the soul the sum-total of its states of consciousness; even after the destruction of the brain memory. Spirits demonstrate this by their communications, for they have conserved in space the most minute details of terrestrial life.

This automatic registration seems to be effected in groups or zones within us - zones corresponding to periods of our existence. If the will causes the awakening to memory of an event pertaining to any past period, all the facts belonging to this same period unroll in a methodical series. M. G. Delanne compares these vibratory states to the layers in the section of a tree, which permit us to calculate its age; this renders comprehensible the variations of personality already mentioned. Superficial observers explain these phenomena by the disassociation of consciousness. Studied closely they represent, on the contrary, a unique consciousness corresponding to many phases of one existence. These aspects are repeated as soon as the sleep is profound enough and the etheric double is released.

This release is facilitated by magnetic action. The more profound the hypnotic state, the more fully can the soul detach itself and recover full powers of vibration. The active life of the spirit is resumed, while the physical life is suspended. To lead the hypnotic subject to a determined epoch in his past, longitudinal passes, practiced downward, should be made until profound sleep results. One can obtain facsimile penmanship from such subjects, varying with the different epochs of their lives.

We have ourselves assigned to a subject one precise date in his far past, and caused him to recall it, with details afterwards verified. Such experiences cast a bright light on the mystery of life. All the varied aspects of memory, the existence of souvenirs of normal life, and their revival in trance condition, are explained by the different vibratory movements which unite the soul and its psychic body to the material brain.

With every change of state the vibrations, varying in intensity, become more rapid in the measure that the soul is released from the body. Sensations felt in a normal state register with a minimum of force and durability, but memory conscious, memory implacable, conserves the imprint of all its faults, and becomes its own judge, and sometimes its own executioner. But at the same time, the ME, broken into fragments and distinct layers during the earth life, reconstructs itself into a magnificent unity. All the experience acquired in the course of centuries, all the spiritual riches and fruits of evolution, often hidden or buried and lessened by this experience, reappear in their brilliancy and freshness to serve as a foundation of new acquisition. Nothing is lost! The deep layers of being, if they recount the faults and falls, proclaim also the slow, difficult efforts made in the course of the ages to beauty the personality, in the unfolding of the acquired faculties, qualities, and virtues.

9
EVOLUTION AND FINALITY OF THE SOUL

The soul, we have said, comes from God; it is the principle of intelligence and life in us. Mysterious essence, it escapes analysis, like all things which come from the Absolute. Created by love, created for love, so tiny it can be restrained in a fragile form, so great that with the flight of a thought, it embraces the Infinite, the soul is a portion the divine essence projected into the material world. From the hour of its descent into matter, what has been the way it followed to remount to the point of its actual course? It has been obliged to pass through obscure paths, reclothe forms, animate organisms it rejected at the end of each existence as one does with a mantle which has become useless.

All its bodies of flesh perished; the winds of destiny scattered the dust. It pursued its ascending march through the innumerable stations of its journeys, and goes toward a goal grand and desirable, a goal divine, which is perfection. The soul contains in its natural state all the germs of its future developments. It is destined to know all, to acquire all, to possess all! And how can it achieve this in one existence? Life is short and perfection is long! Can the soul in one life develop its understanding - enlighten its reason - fortify its conscience - assimilate all the elements of wisdom, holiness, and genius? No! To achieve its ends it must, in time and space, have a field without limits to travel; it is by transformations without number, after millions of centuries, that the coarse mineral changes to the pure diamond, shining with a million fires. It is so with the human soul. The aim of evolution, the reason of life and being, is not earthly happiness, as many erroneously think, but the perfecting of each one of us. And this perfection we must realize by work, by effort, and by alternating joy and sorrow until we attain the celestial state.

If there is on earth less joy than sorrow, it is because sorrow is the instrument par excellence of education and progress. A stimulant for the being which without it would be retarded in paths of sensuality. Pain, physical and moral, forms our experience; wisdom is the price of it. Little by little the soul is elevated, and in the measure that it mounts, there accumulates in it an always-growing sum of knowledge and virtue. The soul feels itself united more and more to its own world, and communicates more intimately with its planetary center.

Eventually by powerful ties it unites itself with the company of space, and then with the Eternal Being. So the life of conscious being is a life of solidarity and liberty. Free in the limit assigned to it by the eternal laws, it becomes the architect of its own destiny. Its advancement is its work. No fatality oppresses it, knowing that only the consequences of its own acts fall upon it. It can grow and develop but in the collective life, with the assistance of, and to the profit of all. The more it mounts, the more it fells and suffers with all and for all.

In its need of its own upliftment it attracts to it all the human beings who people the world where it has lived, to help them attain the spiritual state. It seeks to do for them what the older brothers, the great spirits, have done for it in guiding its progress. The law of justice desires all souls to be emancipated in their turn and freed from that lower life. Each soul which arrives at full consciousness should work to prepare for its brothers a social condition which eliminates all save the inevitable evils. These necessary evils, operating as a law of general education, will never be completely suppressed in our world; they represent one of the conditions of terrestrial life. Matter is a useful obstacle; it provokes the effort of developing the will - it contributes to the ascension of beings by imposing on them the necessity to work. How learn joy without pain? Without the shadow, how appreciate the light? How, without privation, enjoy acquisition? Behold why difficulties in all forms are found in us and around us. It is a grand spectacle, this strife of the spirit against matter, this strife for the conquest of the globe, this strife against the elements, the floods, life and death. Everywhere matter opposes itself to the manifestation of thought. In the domain of art, it is the indiscernible, the infinitely tiny particle which hides itself from observation. In the social order, there are obstacles without number, epidemics, catastrophes, and conflagrations; and facing the powers which menace him on all sides, man stands a fragile being, with no resource but his will.

By the aid of this unique resource, through all time the fierce strife is pursued without truce, without mercy; when one day, by human will, the formidable power is vanquished. Man has willed, and matter is subdued. At his gesture, the enemy elements, water and fire, are united and toil for him. It is the law of effort - the law supreme by which spirit asserts itself and triumphs and grows. It is the magnificent epoch of history, this exterior strife which fills the world. The interior strife is not less moving. With each rebirth, the spirit must fashion a new envelope which will serve its dwelling and express the conceptions of its genius. Often the instrument resists, and the thought falls back on itself, powerless to lift the burden which smothers it. But accumulated efforts of thought and desire through centuries will develop the soul's high faculties.

There is in each of us a silent aspiration, an intimate mysterious energy which carries us toward the summits and pushes us toward the beautiful and the good. It is the law of progress, of eternal evolution, which guides humanity across the ages and spurs each one of us on. For humanity in all ages is composed of the same souls. They come from century to century, to follow in new bodies their work of self-perfection, until they are ripened for better worlds. The history of one soul does not greatly differ from that of all humanity; the ladder only differs, the ladder of relative proportions. Spirit moulds matter; it communicates its life and beauty. So evolution is par excellence the aesthetic law. The forms we have acquired are the point of departure for more beautiful forms. Yesterday prepares tomorrow. The past gives birth to the future. The human work reflects the word divine which will blossom in more beautiful and perfect form.

The law of progress does not apply only to man; in every domain of nature, evolution has been recognized by the thinkers of all time. From the green cell, the vague embryo floating upon the waters, through innumerable changes, the chain of the species has unfolded its lengths down to us. (The mono-cellular beings are found today by millions in each human organism. It is not through one cell alone that the chain of species has come, but rather by multitudes of these cells grouped to form more perfect beings, and round upon round converging toward unity.)

Upon this chain every link represents a form of existence which leads to a superior form, to an organism better adapted to the growing needs and manifestations of life. But on the ladder of evolution thought, conscience, and liberty appear only after many degrees; in the plant intelligence sleeps; in the animal it dreams; in man alone it wakens recognizes itself, and becomes conscious. From this hour progress fatal in some ways in the inferior forms of nature can only be realized but with the accord of human will with eternal laws.

It is by this accord and this union of the human and divine will that are build the works which prepare for the reign of God - that is to say, the reign of justice, wisdom, and goodness which every reasoning and conscientious being feels intuitively must come.

So the study of the laws of evolution, instead of weakening the spirituality of man, gives it instead new sanction; it shows us how our bodies can obtain an inferior form by the law of moral faculties of a different origin, and this origin we find in the invisible universe, the sublime world of the spirit. The theory of evolution ought to be completed by that of percussion; that is to say, by the action of invisible powers who direct this slow and prodigious ascensional march of life on our globe. The occult world intervenes at certain epochs in the physical development of humanity, as it intervenes in the moral and intellectual domain by psychic revelations.

When a race, having attained its apogee, is followed by a new race, it is rational to believe that a family of superior souls is incarnated among the vanishing race to help it mount to a higher estate and to fashion a new type. It is the eternal hymen of heaven and earth, the intimate penetration of matter and spirit, the increasing overflow of the psychic life into forms in the course of evolution.

The appearance of man on the ladder of beings explains itself as follows; man is the synthesis of all living forms which have preceded him - the last link in the long chain of inferior lines, which unroll through time. But this is only the exterior aspect of the problem of origins; the interior aspect is more ample and imposing. Every birth is explained by the descent into flesh of a soul from space, and the first appearance of man on our planet must be attributed to the intervention of invisible powers which generated life. The psychic essence came to communicate the breath of new life to animal forms. It created for the manifestation of intelligence an organ unknown till then - speech. Powerful element of all social life, the word appeared, and at the same time, by its etheric envelope, the incarnated soul retained the possibility of entering into contact with the center from which it came.

The evolution of worlds and souls is regulated by the divine will which penetrates and directs all nature. But physical evolution is only a preparation for psychic evolution, and the ascension of soul is pursued by the chain binding the material worlds to the Beyond.

That which dominates the lower regions of life is the incessant combat, the perpetual warfare without check waged by every being to conquer and obtain a place for himself, almost always to the detriment of others. This furious strife decimates and destroys the inferior beings in its whirlpool. Our globe is an arena of incessant battles; nature renews without pause its army of combatants. In its prodigious fecundity it creates new beings when again death presses into their ranks. This strife, frightful at first sight, is yet necessary to the development of the principles of life. It will last until the higher day when a ray of higher intelligence comes to illuminate the sleeping consciousness. By this struggle the will is developed. From pain is born understanding; material evolution and the destruction of organisms is but a transitory phase. It represents the primary epoch of life. The imperishable realities are in the spirit; they only survive the conflict. All these ephemeral envelopes are but the vestments given the permanent etheric form for temporary use. It clothes itself in these costumes to play the numerous acts of the drama of evolution upon the grand stage of the universe. Emerging degree by degree from the abyss of life to become spirit, to gain its future, hour after hour to release itself a little more day by day from the grasp of the passions, to free itself from suggestions of egotism and idleness and discouragement, and to aid all the human race toward a more elevated estate - behold the role assigned to each soul, and, in order to fill this role, it has all the succession of innumerable existences which are evolved upon the magnificent ladder of the worlds.

All which comes from matter is unstable - all vanishes, all disintegrates. The mountains sink little by little under the action of the elements; the great cities fall in ruins; the stars fade out and die; the soul alone soars imperishable through eternal duration. We are limited and restrained by terrestrial bonds, but when though detaches itself from changing forms and embraces the extent of time, it sees the past and the future unite and live in the present. The chant of glory, the hymn of infinite life, fills all space. It rises from the bosom of ruins and tombs, and upon the debris of civilizations grow new flowers, and union is made between the invisible and visible, between the humanity of earth and that which peoples space. Their voices call and respond, and these murmurs, still vague and confused for many, become for us the message, the vibrant word which confirms the communion of universal love.

Such is the complex character of the human being - spirit, force, and matter, in which are contained all the powers of the universe. All that is in us is in the universe; all that is in the universe is in us. By his etheric and his material bodies, man finds himself united to all the worlds invisible and divine. We are made of light and shadow. What is in us is in every other being. Each soul is a projection from the eternal center. It is that which consecrates and assures the fraternity of man. We have in us the instincts of the beast, and we have, too, the chrysalis of the angel - of the radiant and pure being that we can become by moral aspirations of the heart and the constant sacrifice of self. We touch depths of abysses with our fee, and with our brows the high altitudes of Heaven, the glorious empire of the spirit. When we listen to what is passing in the depths of our being, we hear the rumbling of hidden and tumultuous waters, the ebb and flow of the stormy sea of personality, with its waves of anger, egotism, and pride.

These are the voices of matter, the appeals of the lower regions, which still influence out actions. But this influence we can dominate by will; upon these voices we can impose silence; and when the murmur of the passions is quieted, then the powerful voice of the Infinite Spirit is heard, the canticle of Life Eternal, whose harmony fills immensity. The more the mind is elevated and purified, the more accessible it becomes to the vibrations and the voices from on high. The divine mind which animates the universe acts upon all minds. It seeks to penetrate, clarify, and fertilize them. Too gross still, the greater number remains closed and dark. They cannot feel the influence nor hear the appeal. Often the divine mind surrounds them, envelops them, seeks to reach the depths of their natures and to answer them spiritually. But the human soul is free, and may resist this effort; others feel its influence only in solemn moments of their lives, during great trials, or in desolate hours when they need help from on high. To live the higher life, where these influences reach us, we must have known sorrow, practiced abnegation, renounced material joys, and lighted in ourselves this flame, this interior illumination which is never extinguished, and of which the bright gleams in this world are but the reflections from Beyond.

Multiple and sorrowful planetary existences prepare us for this life. It is thus the mystery of the 'psyche' is unveiled to the human soul, shut for a time in flesh, and mounting toward its origin through millions of deaths and births. The task is rude, the steps steep to climb, the frightful spiral seems to wind without apparent end; but our forces are unlimited, for we can renew them by the will and by universal communion. And we are not alone upon this great journey! Not only do we sooner or later rejoin our companions and our friends of past lives, those who shared our joys and troubles, but other great celestial spirits come to our side in difficult places. Those who have gone ahead of us on the sacred way, not losing sight of our needs, reach out their helping hands to aid us over the tormenting spots in our route. Slowly, sadly we ripen for higher and higher tasks. We participate more completely in the execution of a plan whose majesty moves to admiration those who read between the imposing lines. In the measure that ascension is accentuated, greater revelations are made to us - new forms of activity given to us, new psychic senses are born in us, and new sublimities appear to us. The etheric universe opens more widely to our flights and becomes a source of inexhaustible joy.

Then comes the hour when after its peregrinations through those worlds, the soul in the regions of higher life contemplates its ensemble of existences, its long cortège of sufferings subdued. At last it comprehends! Those sufferings were the price of happiness; those trials gave birth to its joys, and then its role changes. The protégé becomes the protector. It envelops with its influence those who are still striving with earth difficulties; it whispers to them and counsels them by its own experience, and sustains them through the rude paths they are treading. Does the soul ever arrive at the end of its voyage? As it advances along the prepared way it sees ever opening before it new fields of study and discovery. Like the currents of a stream, the waves of a supreme knowledge descend toward it in a tide of increasing power. It penetrates the holy harmony of things, and understands that no discordance, no contradiction exists in the universe, that everywhere reigns order, wisdom, and foresight, and its confidence, its enthusiasm augments. With a greater love for the Supreme Power, it enjoys with intensity the felicity of well being.

From that moment the soul is intimately associated with the divine work; it is ripe to fulfill the missions devolving on higher souls in this hierarchy of spirits, who under various titles govern and animate the cosmos. For these souls are the agents of God in the eternal work of creation. They are the marvelous books upon which God has written His most beautiful mysteries. They are like streams which bring to the earth from space forces and radiations from the Infinite Soul. God knows all these souls which He has formed with His thought and His love. He knows what great part each one will take for the realization of His wishes. At first, He lets them slowly pursue the sinuous path, mount the somber defiles of terrestrial lives, accumulate little by little in themselves the treasures of virtue and patience, and lean what is to be acquired in the school of suffering. When one day, softened under the rains of adversity, ripened by the rays of the divine sun, they come out of the shadow of time, of obscurity, of lives innumerable, and their faculties blossom in glorious sheaves, and their works reveal the reflection of divine genius.

10
DEATH

DEATH is but a change of state; the destruction of a fragile form which no longer furnishes life with the necessary conditions for its evolution. On the other side of the tomb, another phase of existence opens. The spirit in form etheric, imponderable, prepares for new incarnations. It finds in its mental state the fruits of the finished existence. Everywhere is life; all nature shows to us the perpetual renewing of everything. Nowhere is death, as we understand the word - nowhere is annihilation. The principle of life never dies. The universe overflows with life physical and psychic. Everywhere is the immense fortification of beings, the elaboration of souls preparing for their magnificent ascension through slow and obscure paths of matter.

The life of man is like the sun of summer in Polar Regions; it descends slowly. It drops, it weakens, and seems to disappear for an instant on the horizon. In appearance that is the end, but quickly it rises to follow again its immense orbit in the skies.

Death is only a moment's eclipse in the revolution of our existence. But this instant suffices to reveal to us the grave and profound meaning of life. Death also has its nobility, its grandeur. We should not fear it, but rather seek to embellish it, and to prepare for it by research and the conquest of moral beauty - the beauty of the spirit, which moulds the body, and ornaments it with an august reflection at the hour of the supreme separation. The fashion in which we know how to die is in itself an indication of what will be our life in space. Something like a pure, cold light surrounds some deathbeds. Faces heretofore insignificant seem aureoled with rays from Beyond. An imposing silence surrounds those who have left earth. The living witnesses of death feel great and austere impressions disengage themselves from the banality of their habitual thoughts. Hate and all evil passions cannot exist before the spectacle of death. Before the body of an enemy animosity is vanquished, and all desire for vengeance dies. Before a casket, forgiveness seems easy and duty imperative.

All death is a rebirth; it is the manifestation of a life which binds us to the Invisible. After a time of trouble we find ourselves on the other side of the tomb, in the fullness of our faculties and consciousness, near to the beloved beings who shared our earthly existence.

The tomb held only vain dust; we must elevate our thoughts if we would find the trance of souls who were dear to us. Do not appeal to the stones of cemeteries for the secrets of life. Know that the bones and dust which lie there are nothing; the souls which animated them are gone. They will come again in more refined and subtle forms. From the bosom of the Invisible, where your prayers reach and move them, they follow you with their loving eyes; they smile, and they respond to your thoughts. Spiritual revelation will teach you how to communicate with them, and to unite yourself with them in the same love and in an ineffable hope. They are often at your side - these beloved beings you seek in the cemetery. They come and watch over you - they who were the companions of your joys and sorrows. Around you float a throng of beings who disappeared in death, a throng which calls to you, and tries to show the path for you to pursue.

O death! O serene majesty! Thou whom we regard with terror, thou art for the thinker but an instant of repose - the transition between two acts of destiny, one ending - one beginning. When my poor soul - wandering for centuries through many worlds after strife, vicissitudes, and disappointments inconceivable, after extinguished illusions and delayed hope - at last goes to repose again in thy breast, with joy it will salute the dawn of etheric life. With intoxication it will lift itself from earth's dust, and though fathomless spaces seek those cherished ones who await it yonder.

To the greater part of men, death remains the profound mystery, the somber problem they dare not look in the face. For us, it is the blessed hour for releasing the imprisoned soul and giving it free passage to the eternal country. That country is the radiant immensity studded with suns and spheres. Compared with them, how poor and mean appears our little earth! The Infinite envelops us on all sides; there is no end to space or time for the soul freed from body limitations.

As each existence has its period, and then vanishes to give place to another life, so each sphere in the universe must die to give place to other more perfect worlds. A day will come when all human life will be extinguished on the cold earth. The planet will roll on in melancholy silence; imposing ruins will stand where once stood Rome - Paris - Constatinople - cadavers of great capitols, the last vestiges of an extinguished race, gigantic books of stone with no eye of flesh to read them. But humanity will only have disappeared from earth in order to pursue upon spheres better endowed other paths of ascension. The waves of progress will have pushed all the terrestrial souls toward planets better suited for life. It is probable that prodigious civilizations will flourish then on Saturn and Jupiter, and humanity reborn will there flower in a glory incomparable.

A new field of action will be given humanity to love and work toward perfection. In the midst of their work, sad souvenirs of earth will perhaps come to haunt their spirits; but these souvenirs, with memories of troubles overcome and sorrows endured, will be only a stimulant to greater heights. The voice of wisdom will say to them: 'What matters the shadow of the past! Nothing perishes; all life reforms itself, and mounts from sphere to sphere - from sun to sun, up to God. Spirit is imperishable! Remember this - there is no death.' The teachings of the churches and their ceremonials have contributed not a little to the representation of death under lugubrious forms, and to awakening a sentiment of terror in the minds of mortals.

Materialistic doctrines have not reacted against this impression. At the hour of twilight, when night descends upon the earth, a certain sadness touches us. We drive it away, saying, 'After darkness the light returns; the night is but the herald of dawn.' When the summer is followed by sad winter, we console ourselves with the thought of future springs. Why, then, this fear of death - this poignant anxiety regarding the act which is not the end of life?

The spiritualist knows death ends nothing. It is for him the entrance into a mode of life full of rich impressions and sensations. Not only are we still in possession of spiritual joys, but they are augmented by new resources and more varied powers of enjoyment. Death does not even deprive us of the things of the earth; we continue to see those we loved and left behind us. From the bosom of space we follow the progress of this planet; we see the changes which take place, and we assist in new discoveries, in the development of nations politically, socially, and religiously: and until the hour of our return to flesh we participate, etherically, to the measure of our power and our advancement, in the labors of those who toil for humanity.

Instead of avoiding the idea of death, we should look it in the face, and know what it is. Let us disengage it from the shadows and chimeras with which it has been enveloped, and ask of it in what manner we should prepare ourselves for this necessary and natural incident in the course of life. Necessary, we said. In truth, what would happen if death were suppressed? This globe would become too small to contain the throngs of humanity. Age and decrepitude would lend their aid to make life insupportable. A day would come, when, having exhausted all the means of study - of travel and of useful cooperation, existence would assume for us a character of overwhelming monotony.

Our progress demands that one day or another we should be relieved from this earthly envelope which, after having rendered its service, becomes unsuitable for other plans of destiny. How can those who believe in the existence of a Supreme Power think of death as an evil?

The universe cannot fail. Its aim is beauty, its means, justice and love. Let us fortify ourselves with the thought of unlimited futures; confidence in the survival of life will stimulate our efforts and render them fertile. No work done with patience and a high motive can fail of success on some tomorrow. Every time death knocks at our door in its splendid austerity it is an invitation to us to live better, to act better, and to increase the worth of our lives by ceaseless efforts.

Often the imagination of man peoples the Beyond with frightful creations. Certain churches teach that the conditions of our future life are determined irrevocably at death, and this affirmation troubles the existence of many believers. The revelation of spirits puts an end to all these apprehensions, bringing from beyond the tomb precise information. It dissipates the cruel incertitude, the haunting fear of the unknown. Death, it tells us, changes nothing in our spiritual nature or our character - that which constitutes the veritable ME. It simply sets us free in the measure of our advancement. On that side as on this, we have the possibility of choosing good or evil, and the faculty to advance, progress, and reform. Everywhere reign the same laws, the same harmonies, the same divine powers. Nothing is irrevocable; the love which calls us to this world attracts us later to the other; and in all places friends and protectors attend us. While here we weep over the departure of those who are lost to us in seeming nothingness, above us beings glorified welcome their arrival in the light in the same manner that we welcome the arrival of an infant whose soul comes to blossom newly on earth. Our dead are the living in Heaven. Many people fear the physical phases of death, but the spirits tell us that the moment of death is almost always painless. Death is but falling asleep. The knowledge which we have been able to acquire of the conditions of the future life exercises a great influence on our last moments. It gives us more assurance, and enables the soul to quickly disengage itself.

To prepare oneself usefully for the life Beyond, it is not only necessary to be convinced of its reality, but to comprehend its laws, and by their aid to see the advantages and the consequences of efforts toward moral ideals. Our psychical studies and relations established during life with the invisible worlds, and our aspirations toward a more elevated mode of existence help to develop latent faculties; and when the definite hour comes, the final detachment from the body will be easily accomplished. The spirit will quickly recognize its position; all that it sees will be familiar, and it will adapt itself without effort or pain to its new environment.

Often at the approach of the last hour the dying enter into possession of their psychic powers and perceive the beings and the things of the invisible world. There is an immense library of authentic facts open to all who desire proofs of such occurrences. In the annals of Scientific Psychology of March 1906, the last hours of the Rev. Dwight L. Moody, the Evangelist, are described by his son (page 485). The dying man said, 'The earth is disappearing, the heavens open before me; do not call me back. If this is death, it is beautiful. Dwight! Irene! I see the children!' A few moments later he lost consciousness. In the same periodical, page 50, Alfred Smedley gives the story of the last moments of his wife, who cried out joyfully, 'Why, here are my sister, my mother, and my father and my brother! And they are bringing Betsey Heap. Oh, they have come to take me away.' Betsey Heap was a faithful servant of the family, greatly devoted to them. A few moments afterward, Mrs. Smedley died. These are but two of numberless cases of a similar nature. Mr. Stainton Moses, pastor of an English church, and a celebrated psychic, wrote of his study of the transition of a soul in the pages of Light. For twelve days and nights he was at the bedside of a dying friend, and was able to see the changes in the color of the aura, and, to use his own words, 'At the supreme moment, I saw the forms of spirit guardians appear and approach the dying man, and with no effort separate the soul from the body.'

The best means of securing a sweet and peaceful death is to live worthily, simply, soberly, and to vitalize existence with high thoughts and noble actions. There are good and bad conditions beyond the tomb, as here. What our condition will be there depends wholly upon the manner in which we have developed our tendencies, opportunities, and desires. It is in the present that we must prepare, act, and reform, and not at the moment when our earth end approaches. It is puerile to believe our future education depends upon certain formalities well performed at the hour of departure. It is our entire life here which responds to the Beyond. One is closely united to the other; they form a continuity of cause and effect which death does not interrupt. It is well to dissipate the chimeras by which certain brains are haunted, of regions reserved for souls after death, where hideous creatures torment them.

He who watched over our birth, and placed us in this world in loving arms outstretched to receive us, will reserve affection for us also at the hour of our arrival in the Beyond. Rid yourself of visions infernal and of vain terrors. The future, like the present, is activity. Work! It is the conquest of new regions. Have confidence in the goodness of God, in His love for His creatures, and go forward with a firm heart toward the goal He has fixed for each life. Your conscience will be your judge and your executioner beyond the tomb. Release from the fetters of earth, it acquires an acumen difficult for us to comprehend; too often drowsy during life, it awakens at death and lifts its voice. It evokes the memories of the past, and stripped of all illusions, they appear in full light, and every least fault becomes a cause of regret. Of this Myers has said, 'There is no need of purification by fire! The knowledge of himself is complete punishment and the complete reward of man.'

Harmony is everywhere; in the solemn march of worlds, as in that of human destinies, each one is classed according to his aptitude in the universal order. To great souls are given high tasks and creations of genius - to the weaker, mediocre works and mission inferior. With every effort of our lives we go toward the role which is ours by right. Make yourselves, then, great and powerful souls, rich with virtue and science, capable of noble works, and create for yourselves a high place in the eternal order. By culture, by the conquest of energy, dignity, and goodness, rise to the summit of the great spirits who labor for the cause of the humanities, and later you shall taste with them the joys reserved for the truly meritorious. Then death, in place of being a trial, will become in your eyes a benefit, and you can repeat the celebrated words of Socrates, 'If this is death, let me die again and again.'

11
LIFE IN THE BEYOND

We have said that the human being pertains to two worlds. By his physical body, he is tied to the visible world; by his etheric body, to the invisible. Sleep is the temporary separation of the two bodies; Death, the separation definite. In both cases the soul detaches itself from the physical body, and with it life concentrates itself in the etheric body. Life beyond the tomb is but the liberation and the persistence of the invisible part of our beings.

This mystery was understood in ancient eras; but for a long period of time, men have possessed only hypothetical and vague notions regarding the future life. Religions and philosophies transmit to us only uncertain ideas on these problems; ides absolutely unprovable, and in most points in disaccord with modern ideas of evolution. Science, meanwhile, has not until recently studied and known man, save on his earthly surface, his body. But that is to the entire being only what the bark is to the tree. The etheric man, of whom our physical brain has little consciousness, has been wholly ignored until of late; and that is why science has been powerless to solve the problem of survival after death, since it is the etheric man only who survives. Science has comprehended nothing of the manifestations which are produced in sleep and in trance, when the freed soul soars into the higher life. But it is solely by observation of these facts that we can acquire in this life a positive knowledge of the nature of the ME, and its conditions of life beyond the tomb. Thus experimentation alone can solve the question. It is necessary to study in the actual man now what will give us light on the man to be. Modern philosophy, traditional religion, and physical science have succeeded only by their insufficiency in driving human thought toward materialism, and materialism leads to anarchy.

It is only since the arrival of psychical research and experimentation that the problem of 'survival' has entered the domain of vigorous scientific observation. The invisible world has been studied by the aid of processes and methods conforming to those which contemporaneous science adopts in other domains of research. And already we can prove this. In place of diving into a void to establish a solution of continuity between the two modes of life, terrestrial and celestial, visible and invisible, as do the different religious doctrines, these spiritual studies have shown us in the life Beyond the natural prolongation and the continuity of what we possess here. Persistence of consciousness, with all its attributes of memory, intelligence, and effective faculties, has been established by the innumerable proofs of personal identity gathered in the course of experiences and researches directed by psychic societies all over the world. The spirits of the dead have manifested themselves by the thousand, not only with all their traits of character and accumulation of memories which constituted their moral personalities, but they have revealed their physical features through the forms of the etheric body which exists after death.

That etheric body is the mould of the physical; that is why the human faces and forms can be shown in materializations. Information of the conditions of life Beyond has been given by spirits themselves, through the aid of communications at their disposal. There are entire volumes of their communications received under test conditions, which serve as a foundation for a precise conception of the laws governing the future life.

Aside from these facts, the experiences of the dual personality of living beings furnishes with important knowledge of the existence of the soul in realms of the invisible. Birth is a death to the soul. It is imprisoned with its etheric body in the tomb of flesh. What we call death is simply the return of the soul to liberty, enriched by the acquisitions it has been able to make during the course of its earth life. We have seen that the different states of sleep are just so many moments of return to life in space. The more profound is the sleep the more the soul is emancipated, and the higher its flight. The deepest sleep borders on the first state of life invisible. In reality, the words sleep and death are inappropriate; when we sleep on earth, we awake in the spiritual life. The same phenomenon is produced by death; it differs only in duration.

Carl du Prel cites the two following significant examples: - A somnambulist spoke with regret of not recalling her experiences when awake. 'But,' she said, 'I will see them all after death.' She considered he state of trance identical with death. Prevorst, the medium, asked two spirits she saw why they had come to her. 'But it is you who have come to us,' they said. Numerous facts of a similar nature demonstrate that our world is not separated from the spiritual; they are within each other, closely interlaced. Men and spirits mingle; invisible witnesses share our joys and troubles. The situation of the soul after death is the direct consequence of the tendencies, be they toward things material or intellectual. If sensual tendencies dominate, the soul is forced to mobilize on inferior planes, planes dense and gross.

If the mind has been occupied with pure and beautiful thoughts, it will elevate the soul to spheres en rapport with the nature of these thoughts. Swedenborg said, 'Heaven is where man has placed his heart.' However, the classification is not immediate, nor the transition sudden. The human eye cannot quickly pass from obscurity to a brilliant light, and it is the same with the soul at death; we enter a transitory state, a prelude to the life spiritual. It is more or less troubled, according to the density or lightness of the etheric body. Delivered from the material burden which oppressed it, the soul finds itself enveloped by thoughts and images, sensations and emotions generated during the course of earthly lives. It must make itself familiar with its new situation and become conscious of its state before it can be carried toward the cosmic center for which it is prepared, according to its degree of light or density. At first, for the greater number, all is a subject of astonishment in the Beyond. Its laws of weight are less rigid, walls are no longer obstacles, and the soul can traverse and lift itself in the air. Yet there are certain fetters which it cannot define holding it. All this fills it with fear and hesitation at first, but the helping friends from above watch over and guide its first flights. The advanced spirits free themselves and pass rapidly out of all earthly influences and attain consciousness of themselves. The veil of materiality is torn by the force of their thoughts, and immense perspectives open before them. They understand their situation almost immediately, and adapt themselves to it. The spiritual body, the organism of the soul, floats for some time in the atmosphere. Then, according to its power and subtlety, it responds to higher attractions, and is drawn to groups of spirits of the same order as itself - spirits who surround it with solicitude and who initiate it into the new order of existence. Inferior spirits retain for a long period their impressions of material life. They try to live on the physical plane and pursue their usual occupations.

To materialists, the phenomenon of death is incomprehensible. Through faulty conceptions they confound the etheric body with the physical. Illusions of earth life remain with them. By their tastes and imagination they are riveted to earth. Then slowly, by the aid of good spirits, their consciousness is awakened to the comprehension of this new state of life. But their density and planetary attractions, and the currents in space, render high flights impossible at first. Those who have relied upon orthodox promises of immediate beatitudes, often meet with great surprise, and find a long apprenticeship necessary before they are initiated into the real laws of space. Instead of angels, they encounter the spirits of men who have preceded them by death, and their disappointment is great in encountering facts and conditions of existence wholly at variance with the education they have received. But if their lives have been good, their noble acts will have more influence on their destiny than mistaken ideas of faith, and they will be happy. Those who have refused to admit the possibility of a future life are plunged in a dream until their error dissipates itself.

After death, impressions are as varied as the value of souls. Those who, during earth life, have known and served the truth, gather immediately the benefits of their actions. The following communications were received from the spirit of Charles Fritz, editor of Life Beyond the Tomb, at Charleroi. All those who knew this man recognized his language. He described his experience at the hour of death thus: 'I felt the bonds of earth little by little loosen, and my soul disengage itself. I saw bands of spirits about me, and with them I rose from earth. Spiritual light, full of force, seemed born in me, for this light comes not from others, but from ourselves. The more you work for truth, love, and charity, the greater will be this light. My first steps were trembling, but I prayed to God for His assistance and forgiveness. I saw my past life written in the ether, and knew I had not been infallible; but I had worked and suffered for the spreading of spiritual light while on earth, and this light I found again here. I must still work to develop myself further and to see my past incarnations. I already see a part of this past, but not all. I possess enough light to go ahead, and already I am given the work of assisting unhappy and confused spirits.'

The law of grouping spirits in space is the law of affinities. The direction of their thoughts leads them naturally to their proper center, for thought are the essence of the world spiritual, and the etheric body the form, the vestment. Those who love and comprehend one another, assemble. Herbert Spencer, in a moment of intuition, said, 'Life is but an adaptation of exterior conditions.'

The spirits of those whose inclinations were all material remain bound to earth, and mingle with the men who partake of their tastes and appetites. Those whose ideals were high, are quickly borne toward superior beings, and unite themselves with societies in space, participating in their works and enjoying the harmonies of the infinite.

Thought creates, will constructs. The source of all joys and sorrows is in the mind. That is why we will find in the Beyond the creatures of our dreams and the realization of our hopes. But the memory of the unfinished task, together with the heart's affections, lead most spirits back to visit earth again. Each soul finds the place where its desires lead, and united to the beings it loves, lies with them in a world of dreams. In the ecstasy of their thoughts and the ardor of their faith, the adepts of every religion create images which they believe to be Paradise. But little by little they discover that theses images are only creations of their thoughts, like vast panoramas painted on canvas, or immense frescoes. They learn to detach themselves from these pictures, and to attain to the high realities.

In our present form, and with our narrow limit of faculties, we cannot comprehend the ravishing joys of the superior spirits. Beauty is everywhere, with varying aspects, following the degree of evolution and refinement of being. The advanced spirit possesses sources of sensations and perceptions infinitely more extended and intense than those of earthly man. In the clairvoyants, knowledge of the future co-exists in the indefinable synthesis which constitutes 'the central mystery of life', as Myers calls it. Speaking of those faculties, he says:

'The spirit, without being limited by time or space, has a partial knowledge of both. It can set forth and find a living person and follow him at will. It is capable of seeing in the present things which appear to us as situated in the past, and others which are situated in the future. The spirit is conscious of the thoughts and emotions of his friends who surround him.'

If such is the power of the entranced spirit still in earth life, we can understand how much more complete must be the life and power of the spirit when it is fully detached from the body by death. We can comprehend how the memories of its past must become an intense source of joy and sorrow. Alone, in presence of its past, the soul sees all its acts and their consequences reappear, and it becomes its own judge.

12
THE HIGHER LIFE

Every spirit desirous of progress and working for universal good receives from higher spirits a particular mission appropriate to its own degree of advancement.

Some have for their task the meeting of souls coming from earth, and of guiding and aiding them to rise out of the dense conditions surrounding them. Others are given the work of consoling and instructing the suffering backward souls. Spirits of chemists, physicians, naturalists, astronomers, pursue their researches, study the worlds, their surfaces, and their hidden depths, in a manner and with purposes which it is scarcely possible for the human imagination to conceive; others apply themselves to the arts, and beauty in all forms. Less advanced spirits assist them in their varied tasks as auxiliaries. A great number of spirits consecrate themselves to the inhabitants of earth and other planets, stimulating them in their researches, reviving their failing courage, and guiding the hesitating ones in the way of duty. Those who possess the secrets of curatives occupy themselves especially with the case of the sick. In Myer's Human Personality, he relates the case of the wife of a great doctor of European renown, who was completely cured by the spirit of a great physician, after being given up by her husband. Many similar cases are on record.

Most beautiful of all the missions is that of the spirits of light. They descend from celestial spaces to bring to humanity the treasures of their science, wisdom, and love. Their task is a constant sacrifice, for contact with the material world is painful to them; but they face the suffering in order to assist their protégés in their trials, and to pour into their hearts great and generous intuitions. It is only just to attribute to them those illuminating rays which radiate the thoughts, and that moral force which radiate the thoughts, and that moral force which sustains us in the difficulties of life. If we knew what these noble spirits suffered in coming to us, we should more fully respond to their solicitations, and we would more energetically detach ourselves from all that is evil, and unite ourselves to them in divine communion.

In hours of torment, it is toward those spirits, toward my guides beloved, that my thoughts and appeals soar; it is they who have always come with moral support and supreme consolation. I have painfully climbed the paths of life. My childhood was hard. Early in life I learned manual labor, and a heavy burden was placed on my shoulders by family duties. Later, in my career of propagandist, my feet were wounded by the stones of the way I trod, and I was bitten by the serpents of hate and envy. Now the twilight has come! Shadows mount and encircle me; I feel my strength decline, and my physical organs weaken. But never has the aid of my invisible friends failed me! Never have I invoked their help in vain. From my earliest childhood their influence has enveloped me. Often I have felt their soft touches on my brow, like the brushing of angel wings. It is to their inspiration that I owe my best pages and my most joys and sorrows, and when the tempest howled, I knew they were near me. Without them, without their assistance, long ago I would have stopped in my journey and given up my work. But their hands reached out to sustain me, directing me in the difficult path. Often in the gathering of evening or the silence of night their voices speak to me, and soothe and comfort me. They sound in my solitude like vague melodies; again they are like soft breezes which pass, bearing murmured counsels and admonitions upon my weaknesses of character, with wise instructions for their remedy.

Then I forget my human miseries in thinking of the day I shall see these invisible friends, and rejoin them in the light, if God judges me worthy, with all those I have loved, who from the bosom of the Beyond have helped me walk life's terrestrial paths. It is to you, O spirit instructors, protecting entities, that my grateful thoughts mount with their tribute of admiration and love.

The soul comes from God, and returns to Him after making the immense circle of its destiny. However low it may descend, sooner or later, by divine attraction, it returns to the Infinite. What does it seek? Always a more perfect knowledge of the universe, a more complete assimilation of its attributes - beauty, truth, love - and at the same time a gradual liberation from material servitude and a growing collaboration with eternal works.

Each spirit in space has its vocation, and pursues it with facilities unknown on earth. Each one finds its place in this superb field of action in this vast, universal laboratory. Everywhere subjects for study and travel, with means of education and participation in divine work, offer themselves to the industrious soul. Heaven is not the cold void of the place of inactive contemplation believed in by some. It is a living universe, animated, luminous, filled with intelligent beings on the way to continual evolution. The higher these spiritual beings ascend, the more accentuated are their tasks, the more important become their missions. In time they take rank among the messenger souls who go and carry to the limits of time and space the will and force of the Infinite One; for the most inferior spirit, as for the most eminent, the domain of life is without limit. Whatever the height to which we attain, there is ever a superior plane to reach.

For every soul, however low in the scale, a great future is prepared. Each generous thought, every living impulse, every effort toward a better life, is a vibration and an appeal from the higher world which will eventually receive all souls. Each burst of enthusiasm, each act of abnegation, helps us up the ladder of our destiny. In the measure that a soul detaches itself from inferior spheres, it perceives the high manifestations of intelligence, justice and goodness: and its life becomes more beautiful and divine. The confused murmurs, the discordant noises of the human centers, grow fainter, and finally are silent. At the same time, the harmonious echoes of celestial societies become perceptible. It is the clear call of happy regions where reign eternal light, serenity, and peace, and from whence come all things fresh and pure from the hands of God. The profound difference which exists between terrestrial life and life in space resides in the sentiment of deliverance and of absolute liberty enjoyed by purified spirits. The material cords are broken, and the pure souls takes its flight to the high regions. In a life exempt from physical necessities, it feels its faculties grow, and acquires a penetration into the veiled splendors of the infinite realms.

The language of the spiritual world is the language of pictures and symbols rapid as thought. That is why our invisible guides use symbols by preference in warning dreams of approaching danger. Ether, supple and luminous, takes with extreme facility the forms which they will to produce.

Spirits communicate with one another by processes which make the greatest human eloquence seem but dull babbling. The intelligent pupils perceive and realize without effort the most marvelous conceptions of art and genius. But these conceptions cannot be literally transmitted to man. Even in the most perfect mediumistic manifestations, the spirits have to submit to the physical laws of our world, and are but vague reflections or weak echoes of celestial spheres - broken notes of the eternal symphony which they would have reach even to us. All is grand in the spiritual life; the etheric body becomes more and more transparent and diaphanous, and leaves a free passage for the radiations of the soul.

With a greater aptitude to enjoy and understand the infinite splendors, and a more extended memory of the past, an increasing familiarization with things in superior planes, so the soul in its progression attains the supreme altitudes. Arrived at these heights, the spirit has conquered all passion, all evil tendencies; it is free for ever from the material yoke and the law of re-birth. It is the definite entrance into divine kingdoms from which it will no more descend in the circle of generations, save voluntarily, and to accomplish sacred missions.

Upon these summits existence is a perpetual fête of the intellect and the heart. It is the communion of love between those who have pursued the same cycle of reincarnations and trials. Add to it the constant vision of eternal beauty, a profound penetration of the holy mysteries and the universal laws, and you will have a feeble idea of the joys reserved for those who, by their efforts and their merits, have arrived at the higher heavens.

SUCCESSIVE LIVES AND THE LAW OF REINCARNATION

1
THE LAW OF REINCARNATION

After a time of sojourning in peace, the soul is reborn into human conditions, and carries with it the heritage, good or bad, of its past. It is born an infant, and reappears on the earthly scene to play a new act of the drama of life; to acquit old debts and to conquer new powers which will facilitate its ascension and accentuate its forward march.

The law of rebirth explains and completes the principle of immortality. The evolution of being indicates a plan and aim; this aim, which is perfection, could not be realised in a single life, no matter how long and fruitful it might be. We must see in the plurality of lives the necessary conditions of education and progress. It is by its own efforts, sufferings, and strife that it redeems itself degree by degree, first on the earth, and then on innumerable dwelling-places in the starry heavens. Reincarnation, affirmed by the voices from Beyond, is the only rational form under which we can admit the reparation of faults and the gradual evolution of being. Without it, there is no conception possible of a great Being governing the universe; nor can we feel a satisfying moral sanction of existing conditions.

If we declare that man lives actually for the first and last time here, that one existence only is experienced by us, we must then recognise the incoherence and the partiality shown in the distribution of good and evil conditions - of talents and faculties - of native qualities and original vices. Why to some lives constant good fortune and happiness, to others misery and inevitable misfortune? To one beauty, health, strength, to another weakness, deformity, and sickness? Why intellect, genius, and imbecility? Why so many admirable qualities, side by side with vice? Why the diverse races - some so near to animality, others favoured with powers which assure their supremacy? Why the blind, the idiots, the deformed who fill our hospitals? Heredity does not explain all that, nor can they all be considered as the result of natural causes. It is the same with those endowed with favors. Often the worthy seem crushed under trials while the wicked prosper. Why are these children born to suffer from the cradle, and why do some finish the earth life in youth, and others live a century? From whence come the infant prodigies, musicians, poets, painters, showing extraordinary talents for the arts and sciences, while others labour all their lives and remain mediocre? And how explain the inborn sentiments of dignity, or of evil, strangely exhibiting themselves in contrast with their environment?

If individual life commences on earth, if nothing anterior existed for us, we must seek vainly to explain these frightful anomalies, these painful contrasts, and to conciliate them with the idea of a wise, just, all-seeing Power. All the religions and the philosophies have run against this problem; no one has solved it. From their point of view, destiny rests incomprehensible and the plan of the universe is obscured, evolution is arrested, and suffering is inexplicable. Man, forced to believe in a blind force and fatality, and in the absence of all justice, is pushed toward pessimism and atheism. On the contrary, all is explained by the doctrine of successive lives; the law of justice reveals itself in the smallest details of life. The inequalities which shock us result from the different situations occupied by souls in their infinite degrees of evolution. The destiny of a being is but the development through the ages of a long series of cause and effect engendered by his acts. Nothing is lost; the effects good and bad accumulate and germinate in us up to favorable moments of their opening, sometimes after a long lapse of time, and many existences; but they never disappear until reparation has been made by the soul. Each one brings its seed of the past from beyond the tomb to the new-born soul. That seed, according to its nature for our happiness or misery, will spread its fruits upon the new life as well as upon those to come, if the one life does not suffice to exhaust the evil of past existences. At the same time, our daily acts, sources of new effects, come to add their causes to the old, to alleviate or aggravate them. They form a chain of good or evil altogether which composes the woof of our destiny.

Moral sanction, so insufficient when we study life from the point of view of one existence, finds itself absolute and perfect in the succession of lives. There is a complete correlation between our acts and our destiny; we find in the events of our lives the rebound of our former acts. Our activities under all forms are creative of good or bad elements, from far and near, which fall on us in tempests or joyous rays. Man constructs his own future. Until now, in his ignorance and incertitude, he has constructed it while blindly groping his way, submitting to his fate without the power to explain it. Soon with better light, penetrated by superior laws, he will comprehend the beauty of life which resides in courageous effort, and he will give to his work a nobler and higher impulsion.

The infinite variety of tastes, faculties, and characters is easily explained. All souls are not of the same age; all have not climbed the same paths in evolution. Some have already approached the apogee of earthly progress, after an immense career. Others have barely begun their cycle of evolution. These are the young souls, emanating recently from the eternal center - the center inexhaustible, from which gushes without cessation jets of intelligence, to descend upon the world of matter and animate its rudimentary form with life. Newly come to earth in human frames, these souls take rank among the savage races who occupy retarded continents - the disinherited regions of the globe. When they at length penetrate our civilizations, they are easily recognized by their awkwardness and inability, and often by their sanguinary tastes and their ferocity. But these souls will in their turn climb the ladder of infinite gradations through the means of numberless incarnations.

Another problem is the liberty of action of the spirit. There are those who are permitted to dally along the paths of ascension, to lose sight of the goal, and consequently lose precious hours in the pursuit of wealth or pleasure. Others are permitted to hasten along arduous paths and to attain rapidly the summits of thought, if they prefer the riches of the spirit to material seductions. Of this number are the sages, the geniuses, and the saints of all times and all lands; the noble martyrs of great causes, and those who consecrate their lives to accumulating, in the silence of cloisters, libraries and laboratories, the treasures of science and human wisdom. All the currents of the past mingle in each life. They contribute their elements toward making a soul great or mean, brilliant or obscure, powerful or weak. Among the majority of our contemporaries those currents unite to make indifferent souls, balancing constantly between good and bad, between truth and error, passion and duty.

So in the chain of earth lives is pursued and competed the grand work of education, the slow development of individuality and moral personality. This is why the soul should incarnate successively in divers places, and in all varieties of social conditions, experiencing the tests of poverty and riches in learning to obey, and then to command. It must know the obscure ways, the ways of labour and of privations, in order to renounce material vanities, and to detach itself from frivolity through discipline of the spirit. It must have lives of study and missions of duty and charity which will enrich the heart and illumine the mind. There must come lives of sacrifice for family, country, and humanity. Necessary, too, are the cruel tests of the furnace, wherein pride and egotism dissolve, and the desolate halting places where we pay ransom for the past and make reparation for faults, until the law of justice is accomplished.

The spirit is refined and purified by this suffering. It comes back to expiate its sins in the place where it was culpable. It happens sometimes that these trials make a Calvary of our existence, but a Calvary on whose summit we approach the heavens.

There is then, no fatality. It is man who by his own will forges his chains; it is he who weaves, thread by thread, the fabric of his destiny. The law of justice is but the law of harmony; it determines the consequences of acts which in our freedom we commit. It does not punish or recompense, but simply presides over the order and equilibrium of the moral as well as of the physical world.

Destiny has no other rule but that of good accomplished. Everywhere reigns the great and powerful law, which compels each being in the Universe to occupy the situation proportionate to his merits. Our happiness, in spite of often-deceitful appearances, is always in direct rapport with our capacity. This law finds its complete application in the reincarnation of the soul; it is that which fixes the conditions of each rebirth, and traces the large lines of our destinies. That is why the wicked often seem happy while the just suffer; the our of reparation has sounded for one, it is near for the other. To associate our acts with the divine plan, to act in concert with nature, in the sense of harmony and good for all, is to prepare for our own felicity. To act on the contrary sense, to ferment discord, and to work for oneself to the detriment of others, is to prepare sorrow for ourselves in the future. It is to place ourselves under the empire of influences which will long chain us to worlds inferior. Learn, then, the effects of the law of responsibility. The consequences of our acts fall on us across time as a stone thrown into the air falls to earth; and only by conforming our actions to this law can we bring order, justice, and solidarity into the world, and ameliorate the condition of humanity.

Certain schools of spiritualism combat the principle of successive lives, and teach that the evolution of the soul only continues after death. Others, while admitting reincarnation, believe it takes place only on higher spheres: the return to earth does not appear necessary to them.

To those of these opinions we would say that reincarnation on earth has an aim - the perfecting of the human being. But being given the infinite variety of conditions in the earth existence, whatever its duration or its results, it is impossible to admit that all men could attain the same degree of perfection in one life. The obligation to return permits them to acquire the qualities requisite to penetrate the more advanced worlds. The present is only explained by the past; it required a series of rebirths on earth to reach the point to which man has actually arrived, and it cannot be admitted that this point of evolution is a definite one, for on our sphere all inhabitants are not in a state to be admitted into a more perfect society immediately after death; the imperfection of their natures, on the contrary, indicates the need of new work and new trials to perfect their education and permit them to climb one higher degree on the ladder of life. Everywhere nature proceeds with wisdom, method, and leisure. Civilization was not born until long after periods of barbarism; evolution, physical and mental, is regulated by the same moral laws. We could never be satisfied with one existence, and why seek on other spheres the elements of a new progress when we find them right about us? Has not our planet offered a vast field of development for the spirit from savagery to refined civilization?

Contrasts and opposites are found under all their forms. The good and the bad, wisdom and ignorance are so many examples of education and so many causes of emulation. It is no more extraordinary to be reborn than to be born! The soul returns to the flesh to there submit to the laws of necessity. The needs and the strivings of material life are stimulants which oblige the soul to work, to augment its energy, and ripen its character. Such results could not be obtained in space by young spirits with untrained wills. For their advancement there must be the whip of necessity and numerous incarnations in which the soul learns concentration, self-reliance, and the strength indispensable to its immense journey in space.

The aim of reincarnation is then in a way the revelation of the soul to itself, or rather its comprehension of the value of developing its forces by knowledge, conscience, and will. The inferior new soul can only become conscious of itself but by the condition of being separated from other souls in a material body. It so constitutes a distinct being whose individuality affirms itself, and its progression is accentuated in the measure that it triumphs over difficulties and obstacles which earth life multiplies in its path.

Planetary existences put us en rapport with an order of things which constitutes the initial plan, the base of our infinite evolution. But this order of things and the series of lives attached to it, numerous as they might be, represents but one fraction of sidereal existence, an instant in the illimitable duration of our destinies.

The passage of souls from earth to the other worlds is effected under the empire of certain laws. The peopled globes vary in their nature and density. The etheric envelopes of souls could not adapt themselves to the new centers save under special conditions of purity. It is impossible for inferior spirits in their erratic life to penetrate high worlds and describe their beauty to mediums. The same difficulty occurs, still greater even, when it comes to reincarnation in other worlds. The high spheres are inaccessible to the majority of earth spirits, still gross, and not sufficiently evolved to permit them to be dwellers in those far worlds. They would find themselves like the blind in the light, or the deaf at a concert. The attraction which chains their etheric bodies to this planet no less unites their thoughts to inferior things. We must first learn to break the bonds which rivet us to earth before we take our flight to more advanced worlds. To tear earth souls from their center before their special term in this center expired, to send them to superior spheres before they realise the necessity of progress, would lack logic and reason. Nature does not so proceed; her work unfolds majestically and harmoniously in all its phases. Beings directed by its laws in their ascension, do not quit their field of action until they have acquired the virtues and the powers necessary to give access to higher domains of universal life.

The law of the return of the soul to flesh is the law of attraction and affinity. When the spirit reincarnates it is attracted to a centre conforming to its tendencies, character, and degree of evolution. Souls incarnate by groups; they constitute spiritual families whose members are united by tender and powerful ties contracted during existences pursued in common. At times these spirits are separated from one another temporarily, and choose new localities to acquire new faculties. This explains the analogies and the differences which characterize members of one family, children and parents. It has been said that reincarnation ruins the idea of family, and confuses the situation occupied by parent and child, husband and wife, etc. It is quite the contrary. In the hypothesis of one life, spirits disperse after a brief existence, and frequently become strangers. According to orthodox creeds, souls after death are placed in two diverse situations conforming to their merits, and the 'select' are separated for ever from the 'reprobates.' As a result the ties of family are broken at death never to be united. While by rebirths, spirits unite anew, and pursue in common their peregrinations through the worlds, and their union becomes in this way more complete. Our spontaneous tenderness for certain people here is easily explained; we have already known them, and are but reconstructing old affections. How many lovers, how many husbands and wives are united by innumerable existences pursued together! Their love is indestructible - for love is the force of all forces, the supreme tie which nothing can break. The conditions of reincarnation are such that reciprocal situations are rarely changed. The advanced spirit in the liberty it has gained chooses the place where it will be reborn, while the inferior spirit is pushed by a mysterious force which it obeys instinctively. But all are protected, counseled, and sustained in the passage through space and earthly existence, more painful and difficult than death.

The union of the soul to the body is effected through the means of the etheric form, of which we have spoken; by its subtle nature it serves as a tie between spirit and matter. The soul is attached to the germ by this plastic mediator which binds it more and more through the phases of progressive gestation and forms the physical body. Fibre by fibre, molecule by molecule, from conception to birth, the fusion operates slowly. Under the increasing flow of material elements and the force furnished by ancestors, the vibratory movements of the etheric body of the infant are reduced, while the soul faculties, the memory, and consciousness of other lives is annihilated. All the impressions of its celestial life and its long past are plunged in depths of unconsciousness. They will emerge again only at the hour of trance or of death, when the spirit regains the plenitude of its vibratory movements and elucidates the sleeping world of its memories. The role of the etheric double is large: it explains from birth to death all vital phenomena. Possessing in itself the ineffaceable traces of all states of being since its origin, it communicates the impression and the essential traits to the material germ. The key to embryonic phenomena is there during the period of gestation; the etheric body impregnates itself with the vital fluid, and materializes sufficiently to become the regulator of the energy and the support of the elements furnished by the progenitors.

It is the invisible armature which sustains the human frame; thanks to it, individuality and memory are conserved in spite of the vicissitudes of the changing and mobile part of being. And it assures, too, the memory of the present existence, a chain of souvenirs from the cradle to the tomb, furnishing us with intimate certitude of identity.

The incorporation of the soul is not spontaneous, but is gradually developed, and becomes complete but at birth. At this moment matter completely enfolds the spirit, which will vivify it in return by acquired faculties. Long will be the period of its development, during which the soul will apply itself to fashion a new envelope, and to make it an instrument capable of manifesting interior powers. But in this work the soul will be assisted by a spirit ordained as its guide, which watches over it and inspires and directs it during its long earthly pilgrimage.

Each night during sleep, and often in the day during childhood, the soul disengages itself from the body and returns to space to gain new force, and returns to its sleeping body to take up its painful existence. Before resuming contact with matter and commencing a new career, the spirit, we have said, must chose the place where it will be reborn on earth. But this choice is limited, circumscribed, and determined by multiple causes. The former lives, its moral debts, its affections, its merits and demerits, the role it is fitted to play - all these elements intervene in the fixing of the life in preparation. They help to decide the race, the place, the family. The earthly souls we have loved attract us; the ties of the past are renewed in other alliances and friendships. The same places even exercise upon us their mysterious attraction, and it is rare when destiny does not lead us several times to the country where we have lived, loved, and suffered. Hate, too, is a force which causes us to approach our foes of the past in order to efface old enmities; so we find upon our route the greater part of those who made our joy or torment. It is the same in the adoption of a social class, of conditions of education, and privileges of fortune, health, misery, or poverty. All the causes so varied, so complex, come to combine themselves, to assure to the new incarnation the satisfaction, advantages, merits, and the debts it has contracted. One can comprehend after all this how difficult is the choice. If we do not possess the discernment to adopt with wisdom and foresight the most efficacious means for our evolution and the paying of our past, intelligent directors inspire us, or themselves make the choice to our profit. At the same time, the soul is free to accept or delay the hour of reparation.

At the moment of attaching itself to the human germ, while the soul still possesses all its lucidity, its guide spreads before it the panorama of the existence which awaits it; it shows the obstacles and the difficulties with which the path is strewn, and makes it comprehend their utility in developing its virtues and destroying its vices. If the trial seems too great, if it does not feel sufficiently armed to confront it, the soul can retreat before the experience and find a transitory life which will enable it to gain new moral force and will. In the hour of supreme resolution, before descending into flesh, the spirit perceives the general trend of the life it is about to begin. It sees in large lines the culminative facts, always modifiable, nevertheless, by its personal actions and the use of its free will, for the soul is the mistress of its acts. But as soon as the cords are knotted to the body, and the incorporation takes place, all is effaced, all vanishes. Existence begins to unroll with its consequences, already foreseen, accepted, and willed, but without one intuition of the future existing in the normal consciousness of the being incarnated. Forgetfulness is necessary during material life. Anticipated knowledge of coming misfortune, the prevision of catastrophes which await us, would paralyze our efforts and suspend our onward march.

As to the choice of sex, it is again the soul which decides it in advance. It can be changed from one incarnation to another by a modifying act of the creative will. Certain teachers declare that alternative sex is necessary to the acquirement of special virtues. For instance, will, firmness, and courage for men; tenderness, patience, and purity for women. Nevertheless, we believe according to the teachings of our guides that this change of sex is needless and dangerous, even while possible. The higher spirits, we are told, disapprove of it. It is easy to recognize about us the persons who have adopted a different sex in the previous life, they are always in some manner abnormal. The viragoes with masculine tastes who show the attributes of the other sex in various ways, are evidently reincarnated men. They have nothing aesthetic or alluring about them. It is the same with effeminate men, who have all the characteristics of the daughters of Eve, and seem lost creatures on earth.

When the spirit has taken habitation in sex, it is bad for it to attempt a change; many souls, created in couples, are destined to evolve together, united always in their joys and their sorrows. They are twin souls, and their number is greater than is generally believed. They realize the most perfect form of life and sentiment, and give to other souls and example of faithful, unalterable, and profound love. What would become of their love and attachment if the change of sex were necessary law? We believe rather that noble characters and high virtues multiply in the two sexes at one time in the general ascension. There is but one point, and one alone, which could make the change of sex seem an act of justice, that is where unkind treatment or grave injustice has been inflicted by one sex upon another, and retribution could only come by suffering in the same manner in another life and another sex. But the penalty of retaliation does not reign in an absolute manner in the worlds of souls, as we shall see further on. There exist a thousand forms under which reparation can accomplish the end and efface the causes of evil.

The all-powerful chain of cause and effect unwinds in a thousand diverse links. The objection may be made that it would be unrighteous to constrain half of the spirits to evolve in a weaker sex, often oppressed and humiliated sacrifices of a barbarous social organization. We reply that this state of things is disappearing day by day, to give place to a more equitable order. It is by the moral uplifting education of women that humanity itself will be uplifted. As to the sorrows of the past, they are not lost; the spirit which has suffered from social iniquities obtains by the law of equilibrium compensating results of the trials endured. Our guides tell us that feminine spirits mount with rapid flights toward perfection. The feminine role is immense in the life of people. Sister, wife, or mother, she is the great consoler and the sweet counselor. She prepares man's future. It is the respected, honoured, enlightened woman who makes the family strong and unites a grand moral society.

Formidable are the attractions for some of the souls seeking rebirth: for example, the families of the alcoholics, the debauched, and the demented. How can we conciliate the idea of justice with beings in such environment! We have seen that the law of affinity brings similar beings together: an entire culpable past leads a delayed soul toward a group which presents analogies with its mental and etheric state - a state created by its thoughts and actions. There is no place in these problems for despotism or chance. It is the soul's own prolonged evil use of its liberty, the constant pursuit of selfish and unworthy aims, which leads it to progenitors like itself. They furnish the materials in harmony with its etheric organism impregnate it with the same gross tendencies appropriate to the manifestation of the same appetites and desires. A new existence opens a new path toward vice and crime. It is the descent toward the abyss.

Master of its own destiny, the soul must submit to the state of things which it has willed and prepared. Each time, after having made for its conscience a dark cave, the soul, to repair the evil, should transform it into a temple of light. For faults accumulate will but increase the suffering later: a circle of iron will bind the soul, and whirled on the wheel of causes and effects created by itself, it will comprehend the necessity to react against its tendencies, and to conquer its evil passions.

As soon as the first emotion of repentance touches the soul, it feels born in it new forces and impulsions which carry it toward a purer center. It attracts forms and elements more appropriate to its work of renovation. Step by step, progress is accomplished, and into a repentant soul rays of unknown aspirations penetrate - of desires for useful action - of awakening devotion.

The law of attraction which pushed it toward the underworld now returns, and becomes the instrument of its regeneration. However, the upliftment will not come without pain, the ascension will not be made without difficulty. The faults and errors of the past will send on their obstructions to future lives. The effort must be the more energetic and prolonged, for the responsibilities will become heavier and the resistance more extended with each life. Along the rude ascent the past dominates; the present and its burdens will be heavy on the shoulders of the traveler. But from on high helping hands will be stretched forth to aid him to cross the more difficult passages of his journey; for there is indeed joy in Heaven over the sinner who repents. Our future is in our hands, and our facilities for good increase in the same ratio with our efforts to realize it. Every noble and pure life, every superior mission is the result of an immense past of strife and self-conquest - the crown of long, patient labors, the accumulation of fruits of science and charity, gathered one by one through the ages. The fields of intelligence, painfully cultivated, gave at first but meager harvests; then, little by little, came the more abundant and rich reaping. With each return to space is established the balance of losses and benefits. Progress is measured and established: the soul examines and judges itself. It scrutinises minutely its recent history, written by itself; it passes in review the fruits of wisdom and experience that its last life has procured to more profoundly assimilate the substance. The life in space for the evolved soul is the period of examination and interrogation of the conscience - of a rigorous inventory of what is within itself of ugliness or beauty. The life in space is the life of equilibrium, where the forces are reconstructed, the energies fortified, and the enthusiasm is animated for future tasks. It is repose after effort, calm after torment, peaceful and serene concentration after active expansion and ardent conflict.

According to some theosophists the return of the soul to flesh is effected usually each fifteen hundred years. But our own testimony, gained from great spirits, does not confirm this. Interrogated in great number, and from various centers, they reply that reincarnation is much more rapid than that. The soul eager for progress dwells a brief time in space; they demand a return to this world to acquire new merits. We possess information regarding past lives of certain persons, gathered from the lips of mediums who knew nothing of this people, yet which was in perfect accordance with facts and intuitions of the interested parties. These statements indicated that ten, twenty, thirty years only separated the terrestrial lives of some individuals, but there was no precise rule. The incarnations were separated widely or followed closely, according to the state of the souls, their desire for work and advancement, and the favorable occasions offered them. In the case of premature death reincarnation was often immediate.

We know that the etheric body often materializes or refines, following the nature of the thought and actions of the soul. The vicious by their tendency attract to themselves impure fluids, which thicken their envelope and reduce their radiations. At death they cannot lift themselves above our regions, and remain confined in our atmosphere and near human beings. If they persist in evil thoughts, planetary attraction becomes so powerful that it precipitates their reincarnation. The more gross and material a soul the more the law of gravitation influences him. The inverse phenomenon takes place with pure spirits, and they vibrate with all the sensations of the Infinite, and find in the ethereal regions centers appropriate to their nature and their state of progression. Arrived at a high degree, these spirits prolong more and more their sojourn in space, and planetary lives become for them the exception, soul freedom the rule, until they attain to the perfection which frees them for ever from the servitude of rebirth.

2
RENOVATION OF THE MEMORY

In the preceding pages we have given the logical reasons which militate in favor of the doctrines of successive lives. We consecrate this chapter and the following to a refutation of the objections of those who contradict the idea. We begin with a collection of scientific proofs which every day increase. The most common objection is this: If a man has already lived, why does he not remember his past existences? We have already given a summary of the cause of forgetfulness. It is the rebirth itself - the act of re-clothing a new organism, a material envelope, which in its turn plays the part of an extinguisher. By the divination of its vibratory state the spirit, each time it takes possession of a new body, of a virgin brain devoid of all images, finds itself incapable of expressing the memories accumulated in anterior lives. Its antecedents, it is true, reveal themselves in its tasks, its virtues, and its faults.

But all the detail of facts, the events which constituted its past, remain during earth life in the profound depths of the consciousness. The spirit in its waking state can only express the impressions registered by the material brain; memory is a chain, an association of ideas, facts, and knowledge. As soon as this association disappears, soon as the thread of memories is broken, the past seems to be effaced for us. But that is only an appearance. Professor Charles Richet said in an address, on 6th February 1905, at the Academy of Medicine: 'Memory is an implacable faculty of our intelligence, for no one of our perceptions is ever forgotten. As soon as a fact has struck our sense, then in a manner irremediable it is fixed in the memory. Little matters it that we may guard the consciousness from this souvenir. It exists, it is indelible.' Let us add that it can be reborn. The awakening of memory is but the effect of vibration produced by the action of the will upon the brain cells. To revive the memories anterior to rebirth, we must put ourselves in harmony with the vibrations of the state which was ours at the epoch when those perceptions were established. The brain which registered those perceptions no longer exists, and we must seek them in the depth of consciousness. They remain mute as long as the spirit is prisoned in the flesh. It must go out of the body to recover the plenitude of its vibrations and again seize the hidden memories; then it perceives its past and can reconstruct its smallest wants. That is what is done in the phenomenon of somnambulism and trance.

There are in us profound mysteries which have been slowly placed there through the ages, the sediments of lives of strife, study, and travel. There are engraved all the incidents and the vicissitudes of the obscure past. It is like an ocean of sleeping things, where rock the waves of destiny; a powerful call of the will revives them. The light of the spirit descends into them at moments of clairvoyance, as at times the radiation of a glittering star penetrates the somber depths of the sea.

Let us here recall the essential points of the theory of the ME, to which are attached all the problems of memory and consciousness. The identity of the personality of ME is only maintained by memory and consciousness. There exists in the intelligence a continuity, a succession of causes and effects which we must reconstruct in their ensemble to possess the integral acquaintance of the ME. That is impossible in material life, since the incorporation leads to a temporary effacement of the states of consciousness which formed their continuous ensemble. As the physical life is submitted to alternatives of night and day, so a phenomenon analogous is produced in the life of the spirit. Our memory traverses alternately periods of eclipse or brilliancy, shadow or light, in the state celestial or terrestrial, and even on this last plane during waking hours or different states of sleep.

As there are degrees of eclipse, there are also degrees of light. Many dreams leave no trance on waking, any more than do somnambulic impressions. All the magnetizers know this. But as soon as the subject is again placed in sleep, and finds the dynamic conditions permitting the renewal of memories, they awake. The subject recalls what he has said, done, seen, and experienced in all epochs of his existence. We can then easily comprehend the momentary forgetfulness of past lives. The vibratory movement of the etheric envelopes effected by the material matter in actual life is much too weak for the degree of intensity and duration necessary to the renovation of memories. In reality, the memory is but a mood of consciousness. A recollection is often hidden in the subconsciousness: we do not conserve the memories of our first years, which are nevertheless engraved in us, like all the states traversed in the course of our history. But a mental effort is necessary to awaken the memories of normal life - those most familiar to us - a thousand things studied, learned, forgotten, because they descend into the profound recesses of memory. To recall these things requires first of all an effort of will. Many spirits even in the life in space, because of dogmatic prejudice, neglect all research, and remain ignorant of the past which sleeps in them.

With them, as with us, suggestion is necessary. We see the law of suggestion manifested everywhere under all forms. We submit to it every moment of the day. For instance, near us a song sounds, and a word, a name, an image strikes us, a whole chain of recollections, thanks to the association of ideas. Memories confused, almost forgotten, from the depths of consciousness, arise and unfold. Dr. Pitre Doyen, of the Faculty of Medicine at Bordeaux, in his book on Hypnotism, cites a case where he demonstrates that all the facts registered in us from infancy can be reborn. His subject, a young girl of seventeen, had forgotten the Gascon dialect, and from her fifth year spoke only French. Put into hypnotic sleep and given the suggestion of five years of age, she forgot her French and spoke the Gascon dialect. She related all the minute details of her infantile life, but she was unable to reply to any question asked in French. She forgot utterly her life from five to seventeen. Dr. Durat made similar experiments with identical results. Jeanne, his subject, related experiences at various periods of her life with precision, forgetting all other periods. The facts which these subjects related regarding their past lives were investigated and found to be true in every particular. Numberless cases of this nature are on record, proving how all things are registered in the depths of the mind.

All studies of earthly man furnish us with proof that there exist distinct states of consciousness and personality. We have seen in the early part of this book the co-existence in us of a mental double, of which the two parts join and fuse at death. This is attested by experimental hypnotism and by all psychic evolution. The fact alone of this dual intellectuality considered in its bearings to reincarnation explains to us how part of the ME, with its immense cortège of impressions and old memories, can remain plunged in obscurity during actual life. Telepathy, clairvoyance, and foreseeing the future are powers belonging to this profound and hidden ME. Suggestion, which is an appeal to the will, releases them from their prison temporarily, and enables the soul to enter into possession of its riches for the time being. Frederick Myers in his Human Personality speaks of the 'subliminal faculty,' which evokes the past. This fact, he says, is frequently encountered in artists of highly emotional temperaments.

There are many instances on record of people who in the moment of sudden accident recall every incident of their past lives. Thomas Ribot mentions a number of these cases in his book Maladies of Memory. Admiral Beaufort, in the Journal of Medicine, relates how in two moments of time, having fallen into the sea, his transcendental consciousness recalled all his earth life with prodigious clearness. In these cases the subconscious unites with the normal consciousness and reconstructs the entire memory. For an instant the association of ideas and facts is reformed, the chain of memories united. The same result can be obtained by experimentation with a hypnotic subject. When there is a superior will in control to stimulate its efforts, the two wills combined acquire an intensity of vibration which put in motion the hidden layers of the subconscious.

Another essential point should receive our attention: it is the fact established by all psychological science, that there exists a close correlation between the mental and physical man. Every physical action corresponds to a psychic act, and vice versa. All is registered at once in the subconscious memory in such a manner that one cannot be evoked without the other awakening also. This concordance applies to the least facts of our entire existence, and the present, and the far removed past.

The understanding of all these phases of phenomena, scarcely intelligible to materialists, is made easy for those who know of the etheric envelope of the soul. It is in that and not in the physical organism in which are engraved all these impressions. The etheric body is the instrument which with precision and fidelity notes the least variations of the personality. All our thoughts and acts have there their reproductions; their movements, their vibratory states leave there their successive traces. Certain experimenters have compared this mode of registration to a living cinematograph, upon which is fixed successively our acquisitions and our memories. It un-rolls, either by the suggestion of another will, by autosuggestion, or by a sudden accident, as we have related. The influence of thought on the body is revealed to us by occurrences observable about us every moment. Fear paralyses the movements; astonishment, shame, and terror provoke pallor of color; anguish affects the heart action; grief causes tears to flow, and long continued produces lowering of vital forces. These are all proofs of the powerful action of the mind on the material envelope.

Hypnotism demonstrates in a still more decisive manner this reflex action of the thoughts. The suggestion of a burn can produce on a subject the effect of a real burn. (Authentic instances of this nature are given in chap. XX of my book In the Invisible). If the thoughts and will can exercise such an effect on the material body, we can understand how the action increases and produces more intense effects when applied to the imponderable, etheric form. Less dense, less compact than the material body, it obeys with much more suppleness each volition of the thought. It is by virtue of this law that spirits can appear in their old forms clothed, as in the past, with all their vanished attributes of personality. It is only necessary for them to think strongly of a phase of their past existence to show themselves to clairvoyants as they were at that epoch. The ability to materialise in this manner is furnished by people of mediumistic power. Colonel de Rochas, in his work L'Éthérisation de Sensibilité, relates how he succeeded in separating the etheric body of a subject long enough to demonstrate that it was the seat of feeling and memory. Psychology and hypnotism combined permit us to study the action of the soul released from its material form and united to its etheric body. It furnishes us the means to elucidate the most delicate problems of life.

Psychical research contains the key to all the phenomena of life. It has come to renovate entirely modern science, and cast a clear light on a great number of questions which have been obscure until now. The following authentic statement made by Pierre Jenet, psychologists of Sorbonne, is of vast importance to students of the problems of being. It illustrates how the impressions registered in the etheric body are indelible, and form a close connection with the body.

Rose, the hypnotic subject of Dr. Jenet, was put into sleep (or trance) and told that she was living in the year 1886, in the month of April. Then suddenly Rose began to sigh and complain of fatigue, and said she could not walk; asked what was the matter, she said, 'Oh, it is my condition.' 'What condition?' was asked. She responded with a gesture, and then the doctor observed that her form had suddenly swollen and was twitching with the movements of a woman advanced in pregnancy. Without any knowledge of the fact, Dr. Jenet had put Rose into a period of time when she had been expecting to become a mother. Another subject, Marie, blind in one eye since her seventh year, and with no normal memory of ever having seen with that eye, when put into trance sleep, and told she was six years old, seemed to see perfectly with both eyes and related the entire circumstances of her accident. Memory restored automatically a state of health which in her normal condition was absolutely forgotten. The possibility of awakening in the consciousness of a subject lost memories of childhood bring us logically to memories of anterior lives. This order of facts was first touched upon in the Spiritualistic Congress at Paris, 1900, by Spanish experimenters. Fernandez Colavida announced that he had received from a medium in profound trance a complete detailed account of his life back to birth. Then the medium went still further back to his life in space, and to four former incarnations, the furthest one wholly savage. At each recital the features of the medium changed expression.

In the same congress, Esteve Marata, President of the Union of Catalogne, declared he had, through his wife who was a medium, received the history of his past lives. These experiences have multiplied day by day since then, and experimentation grows. But it is necessary to use great prudence and caution, and to be on guard against fraud and error, and against auto-suggestion. One should not accept from mediums any recitals which cannot be verified by an ensemble of proofs, positive and scientific. It would be wise to imitate on this point the example given by the London Society of Psychical Research, and to adopt its precise and rigorous methods. Even where such methods have been neglected, we find some cases of very striking phenomena, such as that of Helen Smith, a medium studied by Professor Flournoy of the University of Geneva.

Entranced, this medium reproduced scenes of former lives in India, in the twelfth century. She used Sanscrit words of which she knew nothing in her normal state; she gave facts concerning historic personages of that epoch which the Professor after much research found confirmed in a book by Marles, a little known historian, and absolutely beyond the knowledge of the medium. Other better-known historians had not mentioned these facts. In trance, Helen Smith, without education and with no knowledge of the Orient, spoke and sang with an Oriental charm and languorous abandon which the most finished actress after long study could hardly attain. Colonel Rochas, former Administrator of the Polytechnic School, made a careful study of such cases. One of these subjects was put in trance, and sent back to the time of her infancy. Then suddenly a new voice and personality appeared, and the subject gave a history of her former life, even to the name she bore and the country in which she lived. Colonel de Rochas, while dissatisfied with many of his investigations, ended his description as follows: 'It is certain that by magnetic operations one can bring a hypnotic subject progressively back to periods anterior to normal life, with the intellectual and physiological characteristics of those epochs. It is not memories which are awakened but successive states of personality which are evoked. It is certain that in continuing these magnetic operations beyond birth, the subject can be put into analogous states corresponding to former incarnations.'

In the Annals of Physical Science, July 1905, other remarkable experiments with a trance medium are related fully. Mlle. Marie Mayo was the daughter of a French engineer: she had been reared at Bayreuth, where she learned to read and write in the Arabic language. Then she came to France to live with and aunt. The enumeration of her statements during trance fill fifty pages of the Annals, and were testified to by eminent doctors and other men of note.

Mlle. Mayo went back of her earth life, and reviewed three incarnations. She had been twice a man, and had died by drowning in one incarnation: she went through all the agony of this death while in trance, until Colonel de Rochas wakened her. Then again, in trance, she proceeded to more distant incarnations, and said her name was Madeline de Saint Marc; that she had married an attaché to the Court of Louis XIV, that she knew Mlle. De la Vallière. M. Scarron, Molière, and Racine, and that she had died at the age of forty-five. During her waking hours this medium had no knowledge of Mlle. de la Vallière. During one of her incarnations her name was 'Line', and she declared herself about to become a mother, and, greatly to the amazement of Colonel de Rochas, her physical body became enlarged, and she went through all the spasms of childbirth. Later, she wept, saying her husband had died. Mlle. Mayo was on various occasions put into trance state and asked to return to former incarnations, and on each occasion the same conditions and states were repeated without change. With each existence which she described, her attitudes, language, gestures, and appearance changed. When she described masculine incarnations, she spoke in a masculine voice. Mlle. Mayo was a simple young girl in her normal state and incapable of dissimulation. She possessed no knowledge of psychology or pathology, as was attested by the physician of the family, one of the witnesses of these extraordinary séances. It would require a vast talent and art to simulate the dramatic scenes which took place in the presence of these experimenters who were watching for every evidence of error or fraud; such a role could not have been carried out by a young person possessing no experience in life, and with only a limited education. In our estimation, these experiences, joined to many others of a similar nature, are sufficient to establish at the base of the ME a sort of crypt where is accumulated an immense reservoir of memories.

The long past of the soul has left its ineffaceable traces, which alone can tell us the secret of the origin of evolution, the profound mystery of human nature. In a group of researchers at Havre, June 1907, a psychic was asked to obtain from invisible spirits an explanation of how these past incarnations were revealed. The reply was: 'When the mediumistic subject is not sufficiently freed from his body to read for himself the history of his past, we proceed to show him by successive pictures the reproduction of his former lives. From on high we communicate the instructions furnished to experimenters, asking them to make allowance for the circumstances under which they are received. You must not forget that here, free from earth conventions, there is for us neither time nor space; living outside of these limits we easily commit errors in anything connected with them. We consider time and space small things, and prefer to talk of acts good and bad and their consequences. If some dates and names are not found in our archives, you must not conclude that all is false. Difficulties are great for us to give you the precise information you demand; but do not relax your search, for this is the most beautiful of all studies. Light is spreading, but it will be a long time before the masses comprehend toward what dawn they should look.'

There are numerous facts which can be added almost indefinitely in these researches. Prince Adam Wisznieski, 7 Rue du Defarcalese, Paris, related to us the following: Prince Galetzin, the Marquis de B-, and Count de R- were together at Hamburg in the summer of 1862. One evening during a stroll they found a poor woman lying on a bench. Finding she was hungry and penniless, they took her to the hotel and fed her. After she had satisfied a ravenous appetite, the Prince, who possessed magnetic powers, desired to experiment with her. The woman, who spoke a poor ungrammatical German dialect, when in trance condition began to speak correctly in French, and related how her present life was the result of crime committed in a former incarnation in the eighteenth century. She lived in a château in Brittany on the border of the sea. Having a lover, she desired to be rid of her husband, and pushed him over a precipice into the sea. She described the crime and place minutely; and thanks to this description, Prince Galetzin and the Marquis de B- later went to Brittany separately, and each made inquiries and investigation with identically the same results. After careful questioning of many people, they found some old peasants who had been told by their parents the history of a young beautiful woman who had thrown her husband into the sea. All the poor beggar woman had related was exactly verified. The Prince went to Hamburg and made inquiries of the Chief of Police regarding the beggar, and was told that she was uneducated, spoke only a dialect, and lived the life of a common mendicant.

We have said that forgetfulness of past existences is one of the consequences of incarnation. However, this forgetfulness is not always absolute. With many people the past returns under the form of impressions without precise memories. These impressions often influence our actions, and they do not come from education, environment, or heredity. Among the number, we can class our own sudden antipathies and sympathies, our rapid intimacies and our innate ideas. We have only to look inward to study ourselves with attention to find in our tastes, tendencies, and traits of character numerous vestiges of the past, but unfortunately few of us give this personal examination with method and attention.

There are always in every epoch of history a certain number of men who, thanks to exceptional dispositions and psychic organizations, conserve memories of their past lives. For them the plurality of existence is not a theory, it is a fact divinely perceived. The testimony of these men assumes considerable importance, because they usually occupy in the history of their time a high station, and almost all such men have superior minds, and exercise a great influence on their epochs. The rare faculty they enjoy is the result of an immense evolution. The value of a testimony being in exact rapport with the intelligence and integrity of the witness, we cannot pass in silence the affirmation of these men, some of whom have worn the crown of genius.

Pythagoras recalled at least three of his existences and the names he bore in them. Empedocles declared that he recalled having been successively a boy and a girl. Lamartine in his Voyage in the Orient speaks of his distinct reminiscences of a far past. He says, 'I had in Judea, no bible or chart at hand. There was none to give me the antique name of the valleys and mountains. Nevertheless, I at once recognized the Valley and the Battlefield of Saul! When we reached the convent, the Fathers confirmed with exactitude my previsions. My companions could not believe it, and it was the same at Sephora. I had designed with the finger and named a hill whereon the ruin of a château stood, as the probable birthplace of the Virgin. The next day, at the foot of an arid mountain, I recognised the tomb of the Maccabees. With the exception of the Valley of Lebanon, I saw scarcely any spot which was not for me like a memory. Have we then lived two lives, or a thousand? Is nor our memory but a tarnished image that the breath of God revives?'

In the Literary Journal of November 1864, a writer on Joseph Mèry said: 'He had singular theories which to him were convictions. He firmly believed he had lived several times and recalled the small incidents of anterior existences. He said Virgil and Horace had been friends of his, and he had known Augustus and Germanicus, and had fought in Gaul and Germany. He was a general, and commanded

German troops. When they crossed the Rhine, he recognized places in the mountains where his name was then Minius, and he gives an incident to substantiate his idea. One day Mèry was visiting the Library of the Vatican in Rome; he was met by two young men in long brown robes, who spoke to him in pure Latin. Mèry was a Latin scholar, but he had never attempted to converse in the language of Juvenal. But as he listened to these young men, and admired their magnificent idiom, a veil seemed to fall from his eyes, and it seemed to him that it was thus he had conversed of old with his friends. Irreproachable phrases fell from his lips! Immediately he found elegant and correct expressions. He spoke in Latin as he spoke in French. This he could not have done without apprenticeship. He must have journeyed through a century of splendor to have acquired such language, which could not have been attained in an hour. Victor Hugo believed in a succession of lives; he believed he had been Juvenal in one incarnation. Amiel said, "It seems to me I have lived dozens or hundreds of lives. I have been a mathematician, a musician, a monk, a mother; I have been an animal, and a plant."'

To these reminiscences of illustrious men we must add that of a number of children. Here the phenomenon is easily explained. The adaptation of the psychic sense to the material organs at birth takes place slowly and gradually. It is complete at the seventh year usually: later sometimes. Up to this period the spirit of the child floats out of its envelope, and to a certain extent, sees its life in space. In this way we often gather from the lips of children allusions to anterior lives and descriptions of scenes and personages having no rapport with their actual young lives. These visions generally vanish at adult age, when the soul of the child enters into full possession of earthly organs. All the astral vibrations cease, the inner consciousness becomes mute. All the attention which these childish revelations merit is rarely accorded. On the contrary, parents are inclined to regard these childish utterances with inquietude, and to silence them. Science in this way loses valuable material. If the child, trying to translate in its confused language the fugitive vibrations of its psychic brain, were encouraged and questioned, one could obtain interesting indications of past lives. In the Orient this is done frequently. In the Daily Mail London, copied into the Matin, 8th July 1903, a case is related of a child at Simla who remembered that he was assassinated in 1814. His name was Mr.

Tucker, and he was Superintendent of the Council. The child recalled even small incidents of that life and, taken to the place where the assassination occurred, was terror-stricken. In 1880 at Vera Cruz, a seven-year-old child possessed the power to heal. Several people were healed by vegetable remedies prescribed by the child. When asked how he knew theses things, he said he was once a great doctor, and his name was Jules Alpherese. This surprising faculty developed in him at the age of four. When alone with his parents he said: 'Father, you must not think I will stay long with you. I am only here for a little while, then I must go away.' When asked where he would go, he replied, "Far away where it is much better.' He died a few years later.

These cases of children who recall past lives could be enumerated indefinitely. The magazine Filosofia della Scienze, published in Palermo, January 1911, an interesting case, and the Annals of Psychical Science of July 1913 have another.

Meantime, memory of the past lives does not seem desirable for the majority of men: on the contrary, it seems indispensable to their advancement that former existences should be effaced from their memory momentarily. The persistence of such memories would lead to the persistence of erroneous ideas and prejudices of caste, of former times and environments - in a word, of all mental heritage which would be the more difficult to modify and transform if still living in us.

Forgetfulness permits us to profit by the different conditions we find in a new life, and aids us to construct our personality on a better plan, while our faculties gain in depth and extent by our experiences. Then, too, the recollection of a past soiled and sinful, as must be the case with most of us, would be a heavy burden to carry. The will must be well tempered before we can see without giddiness a long series of faults and follies, and even crimes, unroll before us, with all their consequences. The memories of past lives are only profitable to a spirit sufficiently evolved, sufficiently master of itself, to bear the burden without weakening, and sufficiently detached from earthly things to contemplate with serenity the spectacle of its history: to relieve the pains endured, the injustice suffered, and the anguish of betrayal by those if loved. It is a sorrowful privilege to know a vanished past of tears and blood: it is a cause of moral torture and interior wounds. If our former lives have been happy, the comparison with our often bitter present conditions would be almost insupportable.

How many things would we not now efface from our actual lives which are obstacle to our interior peace and hindrances to our liberty! Why add to these the perspective of centuries? All that is important to carry with us are the fruits of the past - that is, the capacities acquired. They are the instruments of labor; the means of action for the spirit. It is all which constitutes character, this ensemble of virtues and faults - of tastes and aspirations; all this which flows from the subconsciousness to the normal consciousness. The recollection of vanished lives would present formidable inconveniences, not only to individuals but to collective society. It would introduce discord and ferment hate and hinder progress. All the criminals of history, reincarnated for expiation, would be unmasked! The terrors and iniquities of past centuries would be newly spread before our eyes. The accusing past would again cause profound, keen suffering. Man has come back to earth to develop his faculties and to conquer new merits, and he should look ahead, not behind. The future opens before him full of promise, and the great law commands him to advance resolutely; to render the journey easier, and to free him from all restraint, it casts a veil upon his past. Let us thank the infinite powers which, by lifting the crushing load of memories, has made the ascension easier and the reparation less bitter.

Sometimes the objection is made that it is unjust to punish a man for a forgotten error. One said to me, 'The justice which moves in secret, and does not permit us to judge ourselves, should be considered an iniquity'. But is not all life a secret to us? The grass which sprouts, the wind that blows, the life which stirs, the stars that glisten in the night silently, all, all are mysteries. If we can only believe in the things we understand, in what will we believe? If a criminal condemned by human laws falls ill and loses his memory, does it follow that all consequences of his acts and all his responsibility vanish at the same time with his memory? No power could wipe away his past actions. All that we need to know here is the aim of life, and that divine justice governs the world. Each one is in the place he has made for himself, and nothing happens that is not merited.

The mind of man vacillates on every wind of doubt and contradiction; one day it finds all is good, and asks for more life, and the next it curses existence and longs for annihilation. Can eternal justice conform its plans for our changing views? To ask the question is to solve it. Justice is eternal because unchangeable. Perfect harmony exists between our liberty of action and the results of our acts. Our temporary forgetfulness or our faults does not change their effect. Ignorance of the past is necessary in order that all the activities of man go toward the present and the future, and that he submits himself to the law and the conditions of the environment in which he is born.

During sleep the soul thinks and acts. Sometimes it mounts to the world of causes and reflects the impressions of lives flown. As the stars shine only at night, so our present is veiled with shadow, that the light of the past may illumine the horizon of our consciousness.

Life in the flesh is the sleep of the soul. It is the dream, sad or joyous, and while it lasts we forget the preceding dreams; that is to say, past incarnations. Nevertheless, it is always the same individuality which persists under its two forms of existence. In its evolution it traverses alternatively periods of contraction and dilation, shadow and light. The personality is restrained or expanded in its two successive states, as it loses and finds itself in the alternating periods. The soul, arrived at its moral and intellectual apogee, finishes forever with dreams. In each one of us there is a mysterious book wherein all things are inscribed in ineffaceable letters; sealed to our eyes during terrestrial life, it opens in space. The advanced spirit reads these pages, and finds there instructions and impressions which the material man cannot comprehend. This book is what we call the etheric or astral form. The more it is purified and refined, the more precise are our memories. Our lives, one by one, emerge from the shadows and defile before us to accuse or glorify us. Then the spirit contemplates the formidable reality - it measures its degrees of elevation. How sweet to the soul in that hour are good actions accomplished! How bitter the works of selfishness and iniquity.

We must remember that, during incarnation, the astral body is covered by the material like a thick mantle. It compresses and smothers its radiations. That is the cause of its forgetfulness. Delivered from this restriction, the spirit rises and finds the fullness of its memory. The inferior spirit remembers little but its last incarnation, that is all that is essential for him, as it gives the sum of his progress, and by it he can measure his situation. Those souls who were not impregnated in this life with the idea of pre-existence remain long ignorant of their former lives. They have not interrogated the depths of their being: they have not opened the book wherein all is engraved.

They retain the prejudices of earth, and these prejudices, in place of inciting them to search, turn them from it. The superior spirits, by a sentiment of charity, knowing the weakness of those souls, and knowing that the knowledge of their past is not yet necessary to them, spare them the painful picture. But a day comes when through suggestions from on high, their wills awake, and they turn the leaves and read the hidden pages of memory. There their past lives appear like a distant mirage. For the purified soul, memory is constant, and the awakened spirit has the power to revive at will his past, to see the present, with its consequences, and to penetrate into the mysterious future, whose depths are illuminated for a moment, and then are plunged again into the sombreness of the unknown.

3

REINCARNATION AND INFANT PRODIGIES

We can consider certain precocious manifestations of genius as proofs of pre-existence, in the sense that they are revelations of work accomplished by souls in anterior cycles. Phenomena of this kind could not have occurred by hazard without attachments to the past. History gives us accounts of prodigies of tender age with faculties so superior to, and having no correspondence with their ancestors, that the most subtle explanations of materialists fail to find an immediate cause. Michael Angelo, Salvator Rosa, Mozart, Paganini, Pascal, Rembrandt, can all be named in this class. Jacques Crichton, a Scottish lad who was called 'The Admirable Crichton,' was one of the word's greatest wonders in precocity. William Hamilton, at the age of thirteen, knew twelve languages, and at eighteen he was called the greatest mathematician of the age. M. Trombette, born of a poor, uneducated family, learned Arabic by reading one book, Abel-el-Kadar; while in primary school he acquired French and German in two months. In several weeks he acquired Persian, while on shipboard in company with a Persian. At twelve, he learned Latin, Greek and Hebrew simultaneously. His friends say he knew three hundred Oriental dialects. The King of Greece made him Professor of Philosophy at Boulogne.

At the International Congress of Psychology in Paris, 1900, Professor Charles Richet presented a Spanish child three and a half years old, named Pepito Arriola, who improvised upon the piano rich and varied airs. At the age of four and a half years he played six compositions of his own at the Royal Palace of Madrid before the King and Queen. His harmony was remarkable and his expression marvelous. The young artist has since become and incomparable violinist. The law of rebirth alone can explain many of these cases; their gifts are the results of immense labors which have familiarized their spirits with the arts and sciences. These manifestations of previous genius, while appearing abnormal, are nevertheless but the consequence of labor pursued through the centuries. Professor Frederick Myers calls this indestructible capital of the being the subliminal consciousness.

The conceptions of right, justice, and duty are much keener in some people and races than in others: they are not merely the result of education, of the present, but of something deeper. Education only develops the germs already there. There are also strange anomalies of savage characters, which can only be explained by anterior lives. We see children exhibiting ferocious tendencies of cruelty to domestic animals and of theft, wholly inexplicable by their environment of heredity. In an opposite manner, we see children displaying devotion and self-sacrifice extraordinary for their age. Angels of goodness and virtue growing up in the midst of depravity, and thieves and assassins in virtuous families can only be explained by the theory of former lives. Each one brings with him at birth the fruits of evolution and the tastes and tendencies he has acquired in all directions. The spirit is capable of diverse studies, but in the limited course of terrestrial life, and through the effect of material conditions, each soul is usually restricted in its studies.

As soon as the will is directed toward one of the domains of vast knowledge by the fact of its accumulated tendencies, its superiority in that direction is displayed and returns more and more accentuated with each life. It is so the child prodigies come, with the genius and talents which are the results of continuous progressive efforts toward a determined object. Nevertheless, the soul being called to enter into all kinds of knowledge and not restrict itself to any one, successive states of education are necessary to its unlimited development. We have behind us infinite reminiscences and souvenirs; before us, another infinity of promises and hopes. But in all this splendor of life, the greater part of humanity sees only and wishes only to see mean fragments of actual existence - and existence which it believes without a yesterday or a tomorrow. This is the cause of the weakness of philosophical thought and moral action in our epoch. The work already effected by each spirit can be easily calculated when measured by the rapidity with which it assimilates the elements of any kind of science whatever. By this explanation the difference in individuals who have here enjoyed the same advantages can be readily understood which would remain incomprehensible otherwise. Two people equally intelligent, studying the same subject with the same masters, do not assimilate in the same manner. One seizes the ideas at a glance, the other can penetrate them only by slow, sustained labor. One has but to penetrate the reservoir of his past, the other is meeting these problems for the first time. One person accepts a great new truth on principle in politics or religion at once, because he has been prepared in former lives to understand it. Another must be convinced by force of arguments, because it is new to him.

Without this explanation of former lives, the diversity without limit in the matter of intelligence and consciousness would remain an unsolvable problem. Genius is not, we have said, explained by heredity or conditions of environment. If heredity could explain it, it would be more frequent. The majority of celebrated men have sprung from mediocre conditions. Christ, Socrates, Joan of Arc, were born of obscure families. Illustrious scientists and philosophers have risen from the most common antecedents. Bacon, Copernicus, Galvani, Keppler, Hume, Kant, Locke, Malebranche, Spinoza, Laplace, J. J. Rousseau, can all be named in this class. No explanation of heredity can give us the key to the genius of Shakespeare. The facts are no less significant regarding the descendants of men of genius. Their power of intellect departs with them, and it is rarely found in their children. The sons of a great poet or a great mathematician are often incapable of the elementary work in those two realms. There is a long list of illustrious men whose sons were stupid or worthless - Pericles, Aristides, Thucydides, Sophocles, Germanicus, Cicero, Vespasian, Marcus Aurelius, not to mention the sons of Charlemagne, Henry IV., etc.

There are, however, cases where talent seems hereditary. That is when the psychic resemblance exists between parents and children, and can be traced back to sympathies existing in former lives. Mozart came from a musical family, yet its musical capacity was not sufficient to explain how he could have a knowledge of the laws of harmony at the age of four! He alone of his family became celebrated, the other Mozarts remaining obscure.

Evidently when the great intelligences can, in order to manifest their faculties more freely, they reincarnate in an environment where their tastes will be understood and encouraged. That is often the case with musicians, for whom special conditions of sensation and perception are indispensable. But in most cases genius appears in the bosom of a family, without precedent or successor in the chain of generations. The great founders of religion and the great moralists were of these - Lâo-Tsze, Buddha, Zarathustra, Christ, Mohammed, Plato, Dante, Newton, Giordano Bruno. If the brilliant or sad exception created in a family by the apparition of a man of genius or a criminal was a simple case of atavism, we would find in the family genealogy some ancestor who served as a model - a primitive type of the manifestation. But this is rarely the case in either sense. The question may be asked us how we conciliate these dissimilarities with the law of attractions of similars, which seem to preside as the coming together of souls. The penetration into certain families of superior or inferior beings who came to give or receive education, to submit to or exercise a new influence, is easily explained. It results from the chain of common destinies, which at certain points rejoins and enlaces again, as a consequence of affection or hate exchanged in the past: forces equally attractive which reunite souls on successive planes in the vast spiral of evolution.

We have said in an earlier book, In the Invisible, that genius owes much to inspiration, and that inspiration is a sort of mediumship. But we must add that when this faculty is specially and clearly indicated, the man of genius cannot be considered a mere instrument, which is all that mediumship proper would make him. Genius is above all an acquisition of the past, the result of patient studies, of slow and painful initiation; these have developed in the being a profound sensibility, which opens the door to high influences.

There is a pronounced difference between the intellectual manifestations of child prodigies and mediumship in its generally accepted sense. One has a character intermittent, abnormal. Mediumship cannot at all times exercise its faculty, but must have special conditions often difficult to obtain. But infant prodigies are able to use their talents at any moment, in a permanent manner, as we do who have acquired control of our mental faculties. If we analyze these cases with care we will recognize the fact that the genius of young prodigies is personal. Its application is regulated by their will, and their works, astonishing as they appear, represent always something of their age, and not that of a high foreign influence, as in the case of mediumship controls.

There is always in their manner of working a hesitation and wavering which would not occur if they were the passive instruments of an occult, superior will. That is why we say that Pepito, notably, indicates a long past of preparation. We find certain individuals who combine the two causes, personal acquisition and exterior inspiration. That does not lessen the theory of reincarnation. We must always have recourse to that to solve certain problems of inequality; we were not all launched at the same moment in the turmoil of life. We have not all traveled the same paths, but have come through infinite routes. By this fact are explained our respective situations and our different views of life. But the goal is the same for all! Under the whip of trials, under the lancet of pain, all mount, all are eventually elevated.

The soul is not made for us, it makes itself through the ages. It faculties, its virtues, grow from century to century. By incarnation each one comes to take up the task of yesterday, interrupted by death, and to perfect it. From this comes the shining superiority of certain souls who have lived much - accomplished much - labored much. From this those extraordinary beings who appear here and there in history and project vivid rays of light on the route of humanity; their superiority is only the result of accumulated experience.

Regarded in this light, the march of humanity is clothed in grandeur. It slowly frees itself from the obscurity of the ages, emerges from the shadows of ignorance and barbarity, and advances with measured steps in the midst of obstacles and tempests. It climbs the steep path, and at every turn in the route sees grander heights, and beholds the luminous summits whereon are throned wisdom, spirituality, and love. And this collective march is also the individual march of each one of us. For this humanity is ourselves; we are the same beings who, after a time of repose in space, come back century after century until we are ripe for a better society and happier world. We are a part of the generation gone, and we will be among those to come. In fact we compose but one immense human family marching on to the realization of the divine plan - the place of its magnificent destiny.

One who will give attention to it finds a long past within himself. If the facts of history awaken in us profound emotion, if we feel ourselves living the lives of those personages of the past, it is because that history is our own. When we read the annals of certain epochs, and feel drawn toward some of the characters with veritable passion, it is because our own past is animated and brought to life again. Through the woof woven by the centuries we have found that our own anguish, our own aspiration and memories momentarily veiled in us are awakened. If we interrogate our subconscious minds, voices sometimes vague and confused, sometimes clear and ringing, will answer from the depths. These voices speak of great epochs, of migrations of man, of furious hordes who passed, carrying all before them, into night and death. These voices speak to us, too, of humble lives effaced, of silent tears, of forgotten sorrows, of heavy and monotonous hours passed in work, in meditation, and in prayer - of the silence of cloisters, and of the misery of existences poor and desolate. At certain hours an entire confused and mysterious world awakes and vibrates in us - a world whose echoes move and enervate us. It is the voice of the past. It speaks in the somnambulistic trance, and relates the vicissitudes of the poor soul struggling through the world. It tell us that the actual ME is made of numerous personalities, which are combined in us like the tributaries of a river: that our principle of life has animated many forms - forms whose dust reposes in the debris of empires, under the vestiges of dead civilizations.

All these existences have left in the profound depths of us traces, memories, and impressions ineffaceable. The man who studies and observes feels that he has lived, and will live. He is his own heir, harvesting in the present what he has sown in some past, and sowing now for the future. It is thus the beauty and the grandeur of this conception of successive lives asserts itself, coming as it does to complete the law of evolution seen by science. Exercised at one time in all domains, it rewards each one according to his works, and shows us above all, the majestic law of progress which reigns in the universe, and leads life ever toward more beautiful and better states.

4
OBJECTIONS AND CRITICISMS

We have responded to many objections regarding the forgetfulness of the past incarnations, but it remains for us to refute others of a character religious or philosophical, which the churches offer to this doctrine. They tell us, first of all, that the doctrine is insufficient from the moral viewpoint in opening to man such vast perspectives in the future, and in leaving to him the possibility of repairing his errors in the lives to come. It is claimed that vice and indolence are encouraged, and that no stimulant is offered powerful enough to produce good actions. For these reasons the fear of eternal punishment after death is preferred by the Church.

The theory of eternal suffering was born in the Church (as we have proven in a former work, Christianity and Spiritism) in order to frighten the wicked. But the menace of Hell, the fear of eternal pain, efficacious perhaps in the era of blind faith, does not hold the modern mind. It is regarded indeed as an impiety toward God, which it represents as a cruel Being, punishing His creatures needlessly, without hope of relief. In its place the doctrine of reincarnation shows the true love of our destinies, and with it the realization of the progress of justice in the universe. In making known to us the anterior cause of our troubles, it puts an end to the iniquitous conception of original sin: that is to say, the burdening of humanity entire with Adam's weakness. Its moral influence is more profound than that of the childish fables of

Hell and Paradise. It offers a bridle for our passions by showing us the consequence of our present acts on the future in sowing seeds of sorrow or felicity. It stimulates our efforts toward good by showing us that just in the degree we are culpable, so will we be unhappy. It is true that this doctrine is inflexible, but it at least proportions the punishment to the fault, and speaks to us of reparation and hope afterward. The orthodox creed instead imbues us with the idea that confession and absolution efface sin and prevent man from rectifying his conduct here and preparing himself carefully for his future Beyond. Another objection offered is, if we are convinced that our evils are merited, that they are the consequence of a just law, such a belief would have the result of extinguishing all compassion for others: we would feel less inclined to console and sympathize with our sorrowing fellows. But modern spirituality teaches us that men are all united by a common fate. The social imperfections from which we all suffer more or less are the result of collective errors of the past, so each one of us carries his responsibility and his duty to work for the amelioration of the whole social body.

In their turn, all souls occupy diverse situations, and all must submit to the tests of poverty and riches, of trouble and sorrow. Before all the miseries of the world selfishness can stand and say, 'After me the Deluge.' It may imagine it will escape the misfortunes of earth and the convulsions of social orders by death, but reincarnation changes the point of view. It tells us we must come again and submit to these evils which we now contemplate lightly, because they have not yet affected us. This social environment which we have done nothing to ameliorate we shall encounter again, and be caught in its maelstrom.

He who crushes others will be crushed in his turn. He who sows discord and hate will suffer its effects. If you would assure your future work, try now to improve the conditions about you. He who does not seek to better the collective social centers fails in the law of solidarity. As for evil individuals encountered on life's path, it is probable we are placed in their route to enlighten and uplift them. It may be a part of our development as well as theirs. It is a part of wrong calculation when we neglect the least occasion to render a service to any soul on earth. 'Hors la charité, point de salut', Allan Kardec has said, and it holds the precept par excellence of moral spiritism. Wherever suffering exists, it should encounter sympathetic hearts ready to succor and aid.

Charity is the most beautiful of virtues: it alone opens access to happy worlds. Many people to whom life has been rude and difficult are frightened at the prospect of its infinite renewal. This large and painful ascension across time and worlds fills with terror who in their lassitude have counted upon immediate repose and happiness after death.

The orthodox conception is certainly more alluring for timid souls and lazy spirits, as it leaves less work for them to do in order to gain salvation. The vision of destiny through many future lives is, on the contrary, formidable. It requires a vigorous spirit to contemplate it and find the necessary stimulant to replace the comfort found in the habit of the confessional. A happiness which must be gained by so much effort alarms rather than attracts them. Many souls are feeble for the most part, and unconscious of their magnificent future.

But the truth must be accepted before all; we are not here to consult our personal conveniences. The law, whether it pleases or not, is the law! It is for us to adapt ourselves to it, not for the law to bend itself to our wishes. Death cannot transform an inferior spirit into a superior one! We are in the Beyond what we are here, intellectually and morally. All spiritual manifestations demonstrate this. Although we are told that only perfected souls enter the highest celestial realms, on the other hand we are told that we reserve our means of perfecting ourselves here on earth. But could we do so vast a work in one short life? If some have succeeded, how vast is the crown of the ignorant and vicious who still people this planet! Is it reasonable to believe that their evolution stops with this life? Those who live an existence of crime here - where will they find conditions for reparation if not in reincarnation? Without that we must fall back on the idea of Hell, and eternal Hell is as impossible as an eternal Paradise. There is no act so worthy, or so frightful, that it merits an eternal recompense or punishment.

We need only consider the works of nature since the beginning of time to observe everywhere the slow and tranquil evolution of beings and things, which proclaims with all the voices of the universe, the wonders of eternal power. The human soul does not escape from this sovereign rule. It is the crown of this prodigious effort, the last link in the chain which has unrolled since the beginning of life, and which encircles the whole globe. It is not in man that the sacred principle of perfection, the sum of all evolution from inferior states, is to be found? This principle is the very essence of man, in truth, the divine seal placed upon him. And being what he is, how can he be outside the laws emanating from the source of all intelligence? The principle of progress is written everywhere in nature and history. Man cannot escape from this law of progress: our existence is not isolated, the drama of life is not composed of one act. It must be followed by other acts, which explain the incoherence and obscurities of the present. There must be a chain of existences to illustrate the economy which presides over the destinies of human beings. Does it result, then, that we are condemned to powerful and incessant labor? No, at the issue of each terrestrial life the soul harvests the fruit of acquired experiences. It gathers its forces and its faculties for an interior and subjective life, and proceeds to make an inventory of its earthly work, to assimilate the parts, and reject the sterile. That is the first occupation of the soul after death - the work of recapitulation and analysis. This contemplative period between active earth lives is necessary. Each being who lives a normal life will benefit by it in his turn. The spirit in its free state does not know much repose - activity is its nature. Do we not see this in sleep? The material organs only feel fatigue, and in the life of space these obstacles are unknown. There the spirit can consecrate itself, without fatigue or restraint, until the very hour of the next incarnation, to the missions which devolve upon it.

At each rebirth the soul reconstructs a sort of virginity. The forgetfulness of the past comes like a healing lethe, benefiting and repairing and creating a new being who recommences the vital ascension with new ardor. Each life means progress - each progress augments the power of the soul, and brings closer its estate of completion. This law shows us eternal life in all its amplitude. We all have an ideal to realize - supreme beauty and supreme happiness. We climb toward this ideal more or less rapidly, following the intensity of our desires. There is no predestination: our will and our consciences are our arbiters. Each human existence indicates the following one. Their ensemble constitutes the fullness of destiny - the communion with infinity.

We are often asked, how can a soul expiate faults when, unconscious of the causes which oppress him, he is ignorant of the result and the reason of his trials.

We have seen that all suffering is not expiation. All nature suffers: all which lives - the plant, the animal, the man, are submitted to pain. Suffering is a means of evolution, of education. But a distinction must be established between actual unconsciousness and the virtual consciousness of destiny in the reincarnated soul.

When a spirit has comprehended, in the intense light of the Beyond, that a life of earthly trials was absolutely necessary to efface the faults of preceding existences, this same spirit, in a moment of full intelligence and full liberty, spontaneously chose or accepted future reincarnation with all its consequences, comprising forgetfulness of the past, which follows the act of reincarnation. This initial view, clear and total, of its destiny at the precise moment when the spirit accepted rebirth, sufficed to establish the consciousness, the responsibility, and the merit of this new life. In veiled intuitions it guards all these, and the least reminiscence, the least dream suffices to awaken them to life. It is by this invisible tie, yet real and powerful, that the present life attaches itself to the anterior life of the same being, and constitutes the moral verity and implacable logic of his destiny. If we recall nothing of our past, it is usually because we make no effort to awaken the sleeping memories. But the order of things exists all the same - the magnetic chain of destiny is never broken.

The mature man does not recall the details of his first youth; but does that prove that he was never an infant? Does not the great artist who, in the evening of a day of labor, yields to fatigue and sleeps, retain in his slumber the plan and vision of his work, which he will take up and continue on awakening?

It is so with our destiny. It, too, is a constant labor broken many times by seasons of sleep which are in reality activities under different forms, illumined by dreams of light and beauty. The life of man is a logical and harmonious dream, where scenes and decorations change with infinite variety, but never depart for one instant from the verity of aim and the harmony of the ensemble. It is only on our return to the world invisible that we comprehend the value of each scene, and the incomparable harmony of all, in its connection with universal unity. Follow then, with faith and confidence, the line traced by an infallible finger. Let us go to the end, as the rivers to the sea, fertilizing the earth and reflecting the heavens.

Two more obstacles present themselves, viz.: 'If the theory of reincarnation is true,' says Jacques Brieu, 'moral progress ought to have been made from the beginning of time, but it is quite otherwise. Man today are as selfish, cruel, and ferocious as they were two thousand years ago.' This statement is excessive. Even if it were exact it proves nothing against reincarnation. As we know, the best men - those who after a series of existences have attained a certain degree of perfection - pursue their evolution in higher worlds, and return to earth, but exceptionally, in the position of masters and missionaries. But meanwhile, contingents of spirits from planes inferior add each day to the population of the globe. It is not astonishing, under these conditions, that the moral level is not greatly elevated.

A second objection is, that the doctrine of reincarnation leads to inevitable abuses and misstatements, and the objector points to the claims of many theosophists and spiritualists that they have been great personages in the past, etc. But cannot this be said of other people - men who pretend to be descendants of noble families, for instance, without substantiating proof? Personally, I know a dozen people who affirm they were 'Joan of Arc'. There is no limit to persons of this order. Yet possibly, among them, one finds a veritable fact. To distinguish them one must analyze their revelations vigorously. First find if their individuality presents striking traits like those of the personage mentioned, then demand of the psychic revealers proofs of identity touching their personalities and details and facts: such as would make verification impossible. These abuses of the doctrine of reincarnation do not reflect on the Law, but on the inferiority of certain minds. They are fruits of ignorance and faults of judgment, and will disappear in time, thanks to education.

Again we encounter a difficulty. It is that which results from the apparent contradiction of spirits regarding reincarnation. In Anglo-Saxon countries this doctrine was not mentioned in messages of spirits for a long period of time, and other messages have denied its truth. We have replied to this objection partly in Chapter XXII. The negations on this subject emanate almost always from spirits not sufficiently advanced to know and to read in themselves the future which awaits them. We know that these souls submit to reincarnation without foreseeing it, and when the hour comes they are plunged in material life as in a sleep produced by anesthesia.

The prejudices of race and religion which have been exercised for a considerable time upon these spirits in earth life persist still in the other life. While those who are in any degree awakened are easily freed from these prejudices by death; the less advanced remain long submerged. The Protestant education leaves no place in the orthodox mind for the idea of successive lives. According to its teachings, the soul at death is judged and fixed definitely in Paradise or Hell. With the Catholics there exists a middle place - Purgatory, where the soul may expiate and purify itself by definite means. This idea leads toward the rebirth conception. The Catholic makes over the old belief into a new creed, while the orthodox Protestant finds himself under the necessity to make a clean sweep and build up a doctrine absolutely different from those suggested by his religion. So here we have the hostilities against multiple lives in Anglo-Saxon countries, which persist even after death among a certain category of spirits. But a reaction is being produced little by little, and the faith in successive lives gains day by day - more in the Protestant domain, in the measure that the idea of Hell has become foreign to them. England and America have many adherents. The principal spiritualistic periodicals of these countries adopt the belief, or discuss it impartially. Mr. Funk, of the firm of Funk and Wagnalls, publishers of the Standard Dictionary, speaks, in The widow's Mite, an important work published in 1905, of reincarnation. The philosopher, Professor Taggar, says, 'It is the only reasonable view of immortality.' Archdeacon Colley, Rector of Stackton (Warwickshire), gave a conference on reincarnation, of a nature which indicates that its ideals have reached even to the bosom of the Church of England.

5
SUCCESSIVE LIVES - HISTORIC PROOFS

Our studies would be incomplete if we did not cast a glance across the role which a belief in successive lives has played in history. This belief dominates all history, and we find it in the greatest religions of the Orient and in the most elevated philosophies. It has guided civilizations on their march, and has been perpetuated from age to age. In spite of persecutions and temporary eclipses, it reappears and persists across the centuries and in all countries. From India it spread over the world, and long before the great revelations of historic times, it was formulated in the Vedas, and notably in the Bhagavad Gita. Brahmanism and Buddhism are inspired with it, and Egypt and Greece adopted this same doctrine. Under symbols more or less obscure, everywhere it appears. It was known to the Roman world, and was the belief of Pythagoras, of Socrates, of Plato, Apollo, and Empedocles. Ovid, Virgil, and Cicero, in their imperishable works, make frequent allusions to it. Virgil, in the Aeneid, speaks of the soul plunging into Lethe, and losing memory of former lives. The school of Alexandria gave it great éclat, by the works of Philon, Plotinus, Ammonius, Saccas, etc. The sacred books of the Hebrews, the Zahar and the Kabala, affirm pre-existence, and under the name of resurrection, reincarnation. It was the belief of the Pharisees and Essenes. The old and the new Testaments, in the midst of obscure and altered texts, contain numerous traces of it - for example, in certain passages of Jeremiah; and in Jesus' own words concerning John the Baptist, Mathew, chapter XI, 'And if ye will receive it, this is Elias which was for to come.' Also chapter XVII, 'But I say unto you, that Elias is come already, and they knew him not, but have done unto him whatsoever they listed. Likewise shall the Son of man suffer of them. Then the disciples understood that he spoke unto them of John the Baptist.' Primitive Christianity possessed, then, the true idea of destiny. But with the subtlety of Byzantine theology, the hidden sense disappeared little by little, and the virtue of secret rites of initiation vanished like a delicate perfume. Scholasticism smothered the first revelations under the weight of syllogisms, or ruined it by specious arguments.

Nevertheless, the first fathers of the Church, and above all, Origen and Clement of Alexandria, pronounced in favor of the transmigration of souls. Origen, in his work called Principles, speaks of the pre-existence and survivance of souls in other bodies. Saint Gregory of Nyssa said that it was a necessity of nature for the immortal soul to be cured and purified, and if it is not done here and now it must be done in the future lives. But in place of this simple and clear conception of destiny, an ensemble of dogmas was given to the world by scholasticism, revolting to the reason and separating man from God.

The doctrine of successive lives reappears again at different epochs in the Christian world under the forms of great heresies and secret schools. But it was often drowned in blood and smothered under the ashes of funeral pyres. In the Middle Ages it was almost wholly eclipsed, and ceased to influence the Occidental thought, to its great detriment. From this came the errors and confusion of this somber epoch, the cruel persecution, the prison of the human spirit. A sort of intellectual night fell upon Europe. However, from afar came a ray of light, an inspiration from on high, illuminating some intuitive souls, and this doctrine remained for the deep thinkers the only possible explanation of the profound mystery of life.

Not only the troubadours in their poems and chants made allusions to it, but powerful minds like Bonaventura and Dante Alighieri mentioned it in a formal fashion. Ozanam, a Catholic writer, recognized the plan of the Divine Comedy as following closely the great lives of antique initiation based on the plurality of lives. Cardinal Nicholas de Cuza sustained in the Vatican the theory of many lives and inhabited worlds with the consent of Pope Eugene IV. Thomas Moore,

Paracelsus, Jacob Bochme, Giordano Bruno, Campanello, affirmed or taught the grand truth, often to their cost. Van Helmont, in De revolutione Animarum, gave in two hundred problems arguments in favor of the reincarnation of souls. Are not these superior intelligences comparable to the summits of the Alps which are the first to receive the fires of the day, and which conserve them when the rest of the earth is plunged in night? Philosophy in the late centuries is enriched with this doctrine. Cudworth and Hume considered this theory of immortality the most rational. Lessing, Hegel, Herder, Schelling, Fichte the younger, discussed it with elevation. Mezzini, in his work Del Concílio a Dio, said: 'We believe in an indefinite series of reincarnations, each one of which constitutes a progress on the preceding: we can recommence the state where we left off, not meriting to pass to a superior one, but we cannot retrograde or perish.'

Returning to the origin of our race, we will see the idea of successive lives spread over the earth by the Gaul's. It vibrates in the accents of the bards, it rings in the grand voices of the forests, saying, 'I have stirred in a hundred worlds, I have moved in a hundred circles.' It is the national tradition, and it inspired in our fathers disdain of death and heroism in combats. Arbois of Jubainville, Professor of the College of France, said, 'In combats against the Romans, the Druids remained immobile as statues, receiving their wounds without fleeing or defending themselves. They knew themselves immortal, and counted on finding in another world a new and always young body.' The Druids were not only brave men, but they were profoundly learned. Their cult was that of nature, celebrated under somber shades of great trees or temples built on cliffs. In the Triads they proclaimed the evolution of the soul climbing from the abyss, and slowly mounting the long spiral of existences, to attain, after many deaths and rebirths, the circle of felicity. The Triads are the most marvelous monuments which have been left to us concerning the antiquity and the wisdom of the Druids. They open up a perspective without limit to the astonished student.

We recommend to our readers The Triads (19, 21, and 36) published by Ed. Williams from original Gaelic and translated by Edward Darydd. The Gaul's taught reincarnation on earth, as well as on other spheres, as is demonstrated by A. de Jubainville in his course of Celtic literature. Find Mac Cumall, the celebrated Irish hero, is described as being killed at the battle of D'Athbrea in 273 A.D., and being reborn in

603, and later being king of Ireland. The author relates that the belief in reincarnation went back to ancient times of Ireland. Long before our era, Eochaid Airem, supreme king of Ireland, espoused Etain, daughter of Etar. Etain had several centuries before being born in Celtic lands as Ailill, wife of Mider, and she was deified after her death.

The Celtic doctrine, after being lost for centuries, reappears in modern France, and has been reconstructed and sustained by a Pleiades of brilliant writers: Charles Bonnet, Dupont de Nemours, Ballanche, Jean Reynaud, Henri Martin, Pierre Laroux, Victor Hugo, Flammarion, etc.

'To be born, to die, to be reborn, and progress without cessation is the law," as Allan Kardec has said. Thanks to him, and to the spiritual school of which he was the founder, the faith in successive lives of the soul spreads over the Occident, where it counts millions of partisans. The testimony of spirits has given it a definite sanction. With the exception of some undeveloped souls for whom the past is still enveloped in shadows, all the messages receive in our century affirm the plurality of existences and the indefinite progress of being. Earthly life, they say in substance, is but a preparation for life eternal. Limited to one existence in its ephemeral duration, the soul could not respond to so vast an object. Incarnations are the stations on the way of ascension - the mysterious ladder which, from obscure regions, by all forms and worlds, conducts us to the Kingdom of Light.

Our existences unroll across the centuries. They pass, succeed one another, and begin anew: and with each one we leave a little of the evil which was in us. Slowly we advance and penetrate further in the sacred way, until we have acquired the merits which open an access for us to the superior circles from which shine eternally, beauty, wisdom, truth, and love.

The attentive study of the history of people does not show us merely the universal character of this doctrine. It permits us also to follow the glorious chain of causes and effects in the social order.

We see above all, that these effects are reborn of themselves, and return to their own principle; that they enclose individuals and nations in the network of a marvelous law. From this point of view the lessons of the past are compelling. The testimony of the centuries is painted in a majestic character which strikes the most indifferent mind, and demonstrates the irresistible force of right. All the evil accomplished, the blood spilled, the tears shed, fall sooner or later fatally upon their authors, individually or collectively. The same culpable acts, the same errors, lead to the same unfortunate consequences. While men persist in living hostile toward one another, to oppress, to fight, works of blood and mourning follow, and humanity suffers to the very depths of its being. There are expiations collective, as there are reparations individual. Through time an immense justice is exercised. It brings into bloom the elements of decadence and destruction, and the germ of death that the nations sow in their own breasts each time they violate higher laws. If we glance over the history of the world we will see that the youth of humanity, like that of the individual, has its periods of trouble and of sorrowful experiences. Across its pages unwinds a cortège of obligatory miseries. Profound depression alternates with high ecstasies - triumphs with defeat. Precarious civilization marked the first ages. The greatest empires crumpled one after another in the maelstrom of passions. Egypt, Nineveh, Babylon, the empires of Persia, are all fallen. Rome and Byzantine, eaten by corruption, went down under the force of barbarians.

After the Hundred Years' War and the execution of Joan of Arc, England was afflicted by a terrible civil war, the War of the Roses, which led it to the brink of ruin. What happen to Spain - responsible for so much suffering and slaughter - Spain with its Inquisition and its Holy Office? Where today is its vast empire upon which 'the sun never set'?

The empire of Napoleon passed like a meteor. Napoleon and Bismarck, in disgrace, began on earth to expiate their lack of respect for moral laws. As for Germany, one can foresee even now what awaits her in the future.[1] History is our great teacher, and we can read in its pages the action of a powerful law. From the center of the night of centuries we see shining the radiations of an eternal thought.

For the people as for the individual it is justice. We can follow this march of justice for the populace silently: often we see it manifesting itself through a chain of facts. For the individual it is more difficult. It is not always visible, as in the life of Napoleon. We do not know how to follow its march when its action, in place of being immediate, is exercised at long periods. It descends into flesh with the reincarnation of the soul, and we lose the succession of causes and effects. But we have seen in the phenomenon of trance that as soon as we can lift the veil stretched over the past, and read what is written engraved in the depths of the human soul, then in the adversities which strike it in its great sorrows, its dreams, its poignant afflictions, we are constrained to recognize the action of an anterior cause - of a moral cause, and to how before the majesty of the laws which preside over the destiny of souls and the societies of worlds.

The plan of history unrolls in formidable lines. God sends to humanity His messiahs, His revealers, both visible and invisible; His guides, His educators of all kinds. But man, free in his thoughts, listens to them or denies them-man is free! Social incoherencies are his work: and he adds his confused note to the universal concert. But this discordant note does not always succeed in dominating the harmony of the centuries. Geniuses sent from on high shine like torches in the black night. Without returning to remote antiquity, without speaking of Hermes, Zoroaster, Krishna, since the dawn of Christian times we have seen arise the numerous figures of the prophets, giants who still dominate history. It was they who prepared the way for Christianity, the master religion, to be born later, with the evolution of time and universal fraternity. Then we see Christ, the Man of Sorrows, the Man of Love, whose thoughts shine with imperishable beauty, and we see the drama of Golgotha, the ruin of Jerusalem and the dispersion of the Jews. We see the flowering of Greek genius, the cradle of education, the splendor of Rome which taught the world discipline and social life. Then came the somber ages of ignorance, a thousand years of barbarism, and the descent of the intellectual level into the night of thought. Then Gütenberg, Christopher Columbus and Luther appeared. Gothic cathedrals arose: new continents were revealed, religion began to be disciplined, and the art of printing spread its ideas over the world. Following the Reformation came the Renaissance-then the Revolution! And so behold, after so many vicissitudes, after strifes and anguish, in spite of religious persecutions and civic tyrannies and inquisitions, thought emancipated itself! The problem of life, which with the conceptions o the Church had become fanatic and blind, remained impenetrable-this problem began to be clarified anew. Like a star over a foggy sea, the great law reappeared. The world saw the life of the spirit reborn. Human existence was to be no more an obscure byway, but a broad route leading into the open future.

The laws of nations and history unite in an imposing verity. One circular law presides over the evolution of beings and things: it regulates the march of centuries and of humanities. Every destiny gravitates in an immense circle, and every life describes an orbit. All human ascension divides into cycles and spirals which are enlarged in the manner that they take their places in the universal scheme.

As natural renews itself without cessation in its resurrection, from the metamorphosis of insects to the birth and death of worlds, so collectively human beings are born, develop, and die in successive forms. But they die only to be reborn, and grow to perfection in arts, sciences, cults, and doctrines. At the hours of a great crisis or danger, messengers come to reestablish the obscure verities and set humanity on its right path. In spite of the flight of the greatest souls to the higher spheres, earthly civilizations and societies evolve. In spite of all the evil on our planet, humanity in its ensemble is slowly mounting at each rebirth. The individual plunges into the mass-the soul takes a new mask, its old personalities are effaced for a time. Nevertheless, across the centuries great figures of the past can be recognized-Krishna in Christ, Virgil in Lamartine, Caesar in Napoleon. In a beggar with altered features, crouched at some door in Rome, covered with ulcers and begging of passers-by, may not one recognize Messalina through our spiritual vision? Doctor Thomas Pascal in The Law of Destiny says: 'The study of the former lives of certain men particularly afflicted, reveals strange secrets. One who has been guilty of treason causing a massacre, centuries later suffers a life- long malady caused by an injury received when a child during a mutiny. Another who took part in an inquisition, returns with a body suffering from youth to age.' These cases are more numerous than we suppose, and we must recognize in them the application of an inflexible law. All our acts, following their nature, are translated into an increase or diminution of liberty. The problems of the lives of individuals and society are explained only by this law of rebirth. All the mystery of being is there. By it our past is made clear and our future is enlarged-our personality attains an unexpected amplitude. We understand that we did not arrive yesterday in the universe, but that our point of origin dates back to the profound depths of time. We feel ourselves united to humanity by a thousand ties woven by the centuries. Its history is ours, and we have journeyed with it upon the ocean of the ages, confronted the same perils, met the same reverses. Forgetfulness of those things is but temporary, for one day a whole world of memories will awaken in us. The past, the future-all history will assume a new character in our eyes, an interest profound. Divine laws will seem greater, more sublime, and life itself will become beautiful and desirable in spite of its trials and its evils.

---

1. This was written three years before the war.

6
JUSTICE AND RESPONSIBILITY

The Problem of Evil

The law of rebirth regulates life universal. By a little attention we can read in all nature, as in a book, the mystery of death and of the resurrection. The seasons succeed one another with an imposing rhythm, the day alternates with the night, repose follows waking hours. The spirit mounts to higher realms to descend again and take up with more force the interrupted task.

The transformations of the plant and the animal are not less significant. The plant dies, to be reborn with each return of sap - it fades but to reflower. The chrysalis and the butterfly are examples of reproductive more or less faithful to the alternating phases of immortality. Could man alone be placed outside this law? When all things are united by numberless and powerful bonds, can our lives be thrown, without attachments to the universal system, into the maelstrom of time and space - nothing before, nothing after? No! man like all else submits to the eternal law. All that he has experienced under other forms revives to evolve and perfect his spirit. Already have we in this one life used numerous physical envelopes through the continual renewing of our molecules. Is it not logical to suppose we will inhabit others in the future?

After each life, the soul harvests and gathers into its body of ether the fruits of vanished existences. All its progress is reflected in this subtle form from which it is never separated - this body etheric, lucid, triumphant, transparent. The marvelous instrument - the harp which vibrates with every breath of the infinite.

So the psychic being finds in each stage of his ascension that which he has made of himself. No noble aspiration is sterile, no sacrifice is vain. We are all associated in this immense work, from the most obscure being to the most radiant genius. An endless chain unites the cosmos. It is an effusion of love and light, and it binds all souls in a communion universal and eternal.

The soul must conquer one by one all the elements and attributes of grandeur, power, and felicity. It will encounter obstacles - resisting and ever hostile nature, material adversity and rude lessons which will provoke its efforts and ripen its experiences. There must be strife to render triumph possible and to create heroism. Without iniquity, and treason, and oppression, would any man suffer and die for justice? Physical suffering and moral anguish refine the spirit, and only the benefactions acquired by ourselves, slowly and painfully, are appreciated. Were the human soul created perfect, it would be unable to appreciate its own perfection. Without means of comparison, and with no goal for its activities, it would be condemned to inertia. Life for the spirit means to act, to grow, to conquer new merits and to attain ever to a higher place in the luminous and infinite hierarchy. To obtain merit, it must first suffer. To enjoy abundance we must have known privation, and to appreciate light we must walk in shadow.

To construct a ME, an individuality, through thousands of lives, accomplished in hundreds of worlds, and under the direction of our older brothers and our friends in space, to climb the paths to Heaven, to mount ever higher, to become one of the authors of the divine drama, one of the agents of God in the eternal work; to work for the universe as the universe works for us, behold the secret of destiny! So the soul mounts from sphere to sphere, from circle to circle. united to the beings it has loved, it goes on its pilgrimage, seeking divine perfection. Arriving at the supreme region, it is freed from the law of rebirth. Reincarnation is no more an obligation for it, but an act of will, and a work of sacrifice when it has a mission to accomplish. Reaching the supreme height, the spirit says: 'I am free! I have broken for ever the fetters which chained me to the material worlds; I have acquired science, energy, love. But that which I have acquired I want to share with my brothers, and for that purpose I will go and live among them, and I will offer them the best that is in me. I will take a body of flesh, I will descend again among those who suffer in ignorance, to console, enlighten and aid.' And then we have Lâo-Tsze, Buddha, Socrates, Christ. We have all the great souls who have given their lives for humanity.

In the course of this study we have demonstrated the importance of the doctrine of reincarnation. We have seen it as the essential base on which reposes the new spiritualism: its doorway is immense. It explains the inequalities of human conditions, tastes, faculties, and characters. It dissipates the mysteries and contradictions of life. It solves the problems of evil. Through it, order succeeds disorder, light comes from the bosom of chaos - injustice disappears, apparent iniquities of fate vanish, to give way to the majestic law of repercussion, of acts and consequences. And this law of immanent justice which governs the worlds, God has inscribed on the foundation of things and in the human consciousness. The doctrine of reincarnation brings men more closely together than any other belief in teaching them their common origin and end, and in showing them the solidarity which unites them in the past, present, and future. It tells them there are no disinherit ones - no favorites, but each being is the son of his own works, the master of his own destiny.

Our sufferings, hidden or apparent, are the consequences of the past; the austere school where we learn high virtues and great duties. We go through all the stations of an immense route. We experience all the social conditions one by one, to acquire the qualities of each environment. In this way we are bound together in a final harmony, all the infinite variety of beings - varied because of the inequality of their efforts and the necessities of their evolution.

The greatest of us has been small - the smallest will be great, and each one in his turn knows joy and pain. In this lies the fraternity of souls. We feel our unity in our collective ascension. We learn to aid, to sustain, to reach out the helping hand.

Across the cycles of time all will attain to perfection. The criminals of the past will become the sages of the future, and an hour will come when our faults will be effaced - our moral wounds healed. Frivolous souls will become serious, obscure minds will be illumined, all the forces of evil which vibrate in us will be transformed into forces of good. From the feeble, indifferent being whose mentality is shut to all great thoughts, at the end of the ages will come forth a powerful spirit which contains all knowledge, all virtue, and realizes the most sublime truths. This will be the work of accumulated existences. A great many indeed will be required to bring forth such a change, but nothing is powerful and durable which has not taken time to germinate in the shadow and mount toward Heaven. The tree, the forest, nature, the plants say it to us in their profound language. No seed is lost, no effort is wasted. The stem does not give its leaf or fruit until its hour comes, and life did not appear upon earth until after immense geological periods of time. Look at the diamond, whose splendor ornaments the beauty of women, shining with a million fires! How many were the changes to which it was submitted before acquiring this incomparable purity. How long was its incubation in the breast of obscure matter. It is here, in this work of perfecting the soul, that the utility is shown of lives of trial, of modest and humble lives, of the existence of labor and duty to vanquish ferocious passions, pride, and selfishness. From this point of view, the roles of the humble and the menial tasks of life reveal themselves to our eyes in grandeur, and we better comprehend the necessity of returning to earth to ransom and purify the soul.

In resolving the problem of evil, the new spiritualism shows again its superiority over other doctrines. To the materialists, evil and sorrow are constant and universal. Taine, Soury, Haeckel declare, 'We see evil spread and regenerate in humanity. Nevertheless, with progress evil becomes less frequent but more painful, because our physical and moral sensibilities are keener.' So we must always suffer, and work without hope, without consolation: for example, in the case of a catastrophe (to their eyes irreparable) as in the death of a beloved being.

Consequently evil always encroaches on good. Certain religious doctrines are no more consoling, for evil seems to predominate in the universe, and Satan appears more powerful than God. Hell is continually peopled with crowds, while only a select few reach Heaven.

With the new philosophy the question takes another aspect. Evil is only a transitory state of being, on the way of evolution toward good. Evil is the measure of inferiority of worlds and individuals, and every ladder has its degrees. Our earth lives represent the inferior degrees of our eternal ascension, everything around us demonstrating the inferiority of the planet that we inhabit. Very much inclined on its axis, its astronomic situation is the cause of frequent perturbations and brusque changes of temperature, tempests, earthquakes, torrid heats, rigorous colds. Earthly humanity to subsist is condemned to arduous labor; millions of men bowed under their tasks know neither rest nor well being. There exist close connections between the physical order of worlds and the moral state of the societies which people them. Imperfect worlds like the earth are reserved in general for the lesser-evolved souls.

Our sojourn in this environment is but temporary, and subordinate to the exigencies of our psychic education. Other and better worlds await us. Evil, sorrow, suffering, are obligatory roles of earth life. They are the whip - the spur urging us on, and so the evils of life have only a relative and passing character. They pertain to the infant soul in its struggling to live, and they will diminish and vanish in the measure that the soul mounts the ladder leading to power, virtue and wisdom.

So justice reveals itself in the universe. Each soul submits to the consequences of his acts, but all repair their faults, and rise sooner or later to evolve from obscure and material worlds to divine light. All those who love one another are united in their ascension, to co-operate in great works, and to participate in universal communion. So there is no real absolute evil in the universe, but everywhere the realization of law and progression, of a superior ideal, everywhere the action of a force, a power, a cause which, while leaving us free, attracts and leads us toward a better state. About us everywhere are great beings working to develop in us, at the price of immense effort, sensibility, sentiment, will, and love.

Let us insist upon the idea of justice, for that is the main point. It is the main point because it is an imperious necessity for all to know that justice is not a vain word; that there is a reward for all good deeds and a compensation for all sorrows. No system can satisfy our reason if we do not feel this law of justice in its amplitude. The idea is engraved in us - it is the law of the soul and the universe, and it is because so many doctrines have ignored it, that they have grown enfeebled, or become extinguished at the present hour about us.

The doctrine of successive lives is resplendent with the ideas of justice. It stands forth in high relief with incomparable luster. All our lives are rigorously enchained; our acts, and their consequences, constitute a succession of elements which are attached to one another by the close relation of cause and effect. We are constantly experiencing in all the events of our lives these inevitable results of past actions. Our will, acting as a generating cause, is producing effects good or bad which will fall on us and form the woof of our destinies.

Christianity renounces this world, and looks to the next for happiness and justice, but justice is not relegated to an unknown realm. It is here - in us and about us that it exercises its empire. Man out to repair on the physical plane the evil he did here. He redescends into the environment where he was culpable, near to those he wronged, to submit to the consequences of those acts. Thus justice, the moral law, is revealed in all its harmony, and compels man to comprehend that this life is but a link in the chain of existences. All that he sows, he must later reap. It is not possible with this belief to disdain our duties or elude our responsibilities, for tomorrow becomes the product of yesterday. Under the apparent confusion of facts we discover the analogy which connects them. Instead of being crushed by inflexible destiny and dominated by fate, man dominates his destiny and creates his own fate by his acts. Justice is not postponed to a transcendental world, but is found in every human life, in the domain of the things real and tangible.

This great light has revealed itself precisely at the hour when the old beliefs are sinking under the weight of time, when the gods of the past veil themselves, and disappear. For a long time human thought had anxiously groped in the night, searching for a new moral edifice which could shelter it, and so the doctrine of rebirths came to offer it the necessary ideal, and, at the same time, the indispensable corrective for violent appetites, for measureless ambitions, and the thirst for riches, place, and worldly honors, and for the sensualism that menaces humanity. With the new faith man learns to support, without bitterness or revolt, his dolorous existence indispensable to his purification. He learns to submit to the natural and transitory inequalities which are the result of the law of evolution, and to disdain the false divisions springing from prejudices of castes, races, and religions. These prejudices vanish utterly the day when one knows that each spirit in the path of ascension must pass through various ways. Thanks to the idea of successive lives in the same time with individual responsibility, that of the collective appears distinctly to us. There is with our contemporaries a tendency to cast the burdens of the present on generations to come. Believing they will no more come to earth, they leave to their successors the care of solving the problems of life, social and political. With the law of destinies the aspect of the question changes. Not only must we pay our own debts to the last penny, but, unless we endeavor to change the evils of social conditions, we must return again to earth to suffer from the same imperfections. This society of which we have demanded much, while giving little, will become anew our society, a stepmother of selfish and ungrateful sons. In the course of our earthly stations, we feel the weight of injustices fall upon us that we at some time have perpetrated.

When the grand doctrine of successive lives becomes the foundation of human education and is shared by all, when the proofs are shown to all eyes, then the wisest and the most reflective, developing the intuitions of the past, will comprehend that they have lived in all social centers, and they will feel more tolerance and sympathy for their weaker brothers, and will endeavor to bestow upon them light, hope, and consolation. Then the benefit of the individual will become the benefit of all. Each will feel he must co-operate in the amelioration of this society in whose breast he may be reborn, to progress with it and advance toward the future.

7
THE LAW OF DESTINY

In the proof of successive lives - the path of existence cleared - the route surely and firmly traced the soul clearly sees its destiny, which is the ascension toward the highest wisdom, toward the most effulgent light. Equity governs the world - our happiness is in our own hands. The universe cannot fail; its goal is beauty, its means justice and love. All chimerical fear, all terror of the Beyond, vanishes. In place of doubting the future, man tastes the joys of eternal certitudes, with confidence in tomorrow, while his strength is doubled and his efforts toward good are increased a hundred-fold.

Yet one more question arises. By what secret springs is the action of justice exercised in the chain of our lives? Let us first say that the working of human justice offers us nothing comparable to the divine law of destiny. That is accomplished of itself, without exterior intervention for individuals and for societies.

It is a law of equilibrium, and establishes order in the moral world, in the same manner that the law of gravitation and weight assures order and equilibrium, (and establishes order in the moral world, in the same manner that the law of gravitation and weight assures order and equilibrium) in the physical world. Its mechanism is at once simple and grand. All wrongdoing is paid for in sorrow. All that man does in accord with the law of good procures peace and elevation, and each violation provokes suffering. Suffering enters into the depths of the being and eliminates the germs of evil. It prolongs its action, and returns again and again, until all unworthy qualities develop into good and vibrate in unison with divine force. But in the pursuit of this great work, the compensations are reserved for the soul. Joys, affections, periods of repose and happiness, alternate in the chaplet of lives with existences of strife, ransom, and reparation. So all is arranged with an art and a science and a beauty infinite in the work of Providence. During his course, man in his weakness and ignorance often transgresses the law - hence his trials, his infirmities, and materials servitude. But as soon as he is enlightened, as soon as he learns to put his actions in harmony with universal laws, he is less and less exposed to adversity. Our acts and our thoughts translate themselves into vibratory movements, and their center of emission, by the frequent repetition of these acts and thoughts, is transformed little by little into a powerful generator of good and evil. The being thus clarifies itself by the nature of the energies of which it is the center. But while good forces destroy themselves by their own efforts as they return to their center and are transformed into unhappy consequences, the evil being is forced like all others to evolve, and the vibrations of his acts and thoughts return to him, oppressing him, and forcing on him, soon or late, the necessity of reforming himself. This phenomenon explains itself scientifically by the correlation of forces, the vibratory synchronism which leads always from effect to cause.

This fact is demonstrated in times of epidemics and contagious maladies. It is always the persons whose vital condition harmonizes with the morbid causes in action who are affected, while those with strong wills and devoid of fear are generally immune. So it is in the mind order. Thoughts of hate and vengeance, desire to injure, coming from outside cannot act on us or influence us unless they encounter in us similar impulses which vibrate in unison with them. If these are not found, they return to the one projecting the evil thoughts, to strike him in his turn, whether in the present or the future, somewhere in the course of his destiny.

∼

The law of repercussion of acts has then something mechanic and automatic in appearance. Nevertheless, when it becomes a question of great expiations, of sorrowful reparations, great spirits intervene to regulate and accelerate the march of souls in evolution. Their hour is exercised particularly at the hour of reincarnation, in order to guide souls in their choice and to determine the best and most favorable conditions for the healing of their moral maladies, and to aid them to ransom anterior faults. We must not think that every trial of humanity is the result of past sins. All those who suffer are not forced to it as an expiation of evil deeds. Many are simply spirits eager for progress who have chosen painful lives of labor for the moral benefit to be so obtained. It is, however, in general the undeveloped soul ignorant of the law of harmony which encounters the greatest suffering. Gradually he must re-establish the law of equilibrium, and must learn that he reaps exactly what he sows.

By continual actions each being refines or materializes his etheric envelope, the vehicle of the soul, the instrument which is used for all manifestations, and upon which is molded the physical body at each birth. We have already seen that our situation in the next plane of existence results from repeated actions which our thoughts and wills have exercised constantly on the etheric double. Following their nature and object, they transform it little by little into a subtle and radiant organism open to the highest perceptions, to the most delicate sensations of space, capable of vibrating harmoniously with elevated spirits. In an inverse sense, they make it an opaque gross form, chained to the earth by its materiality, or even condemned to lower regions. We can understand how continual action of the thought and the will, exercised for centuries of existence upon the etheric body, creates and develops physical tastes as well as our intellectual and moral qualities.

Our tastes for each kind of work, our ability, our dexterity in all things, these are the result of immeasurable mechanical actions accumulated and registered by the subtle body, and the memory of them is engraved on the subconscious mind. At rebirth, these abilities are transmitted by a new education to the external consciousness and material organs. Thus is explained the remarkable and superior ability of many natural musicians which surprises the world. It is the same with the moral faculties and virtues, and all the riches the soul acquires in long cycles of time. Genius is an immense effort of the intellectual order, and holiness has been conquered by secular strife against the passions and inferior attractions.

Every time that we accomplish a good or generous action, or do a work of charity and devotion, or make a sacrifice, do we not feel a sense of exaltation? Something expands within us, and a flame is kindled which revivifies the depths of our nature. This is not illusionary; the spirit is radiated by every altruistic thought, by every act of unselfish love. If these thoughts and acts multiply and increase and accumulate, the man will find himself transformed at the end of his earthly existence. The soul and its etheric envelope will have acquired an intense power of radiation. If the thoughts are bad, the acts culpable, then these wrong habits produce a contraction of the spiritual being, and charge it with gross and dark fluids.

Violence, cruelty, murder, and suicide produce results which return birth after birth on the material body in the form of nervous maladies, deformity, and madness. Impure lives, drunkenness, debauchery, and self-indulgence in luxury, produce in future lives weakness and lack of vigor, health, and beauty. The human being who today is abusing his vital forces by wrong habits is preparing a miserable existence for himself in a future incarnation. Sometimes the reparation is affected by a long life of suffering, which destroys in him the causes of evil; again it may be effected in a short, troubled life with a tragic death. A mysterious attraction sometimes brings together a crowd of people to a given point, that they may expiate in a collective death past conditions, as in great catastrophes on sea or land. Short lives are often the complement of preceding existences, where the individual, by his excesses or other abuses, abridged his normal time on earth. But other causes enter into the death of infants; that is sometimes given as an educating trial for the parents and for the incarnating spirit. Sometimes it is simply a false entrance on the stage of life from physical causes, or the fault of adaptation to the etheric fluids. In these cases the incarnation is repeated in the same environment under more favorable conditions.

To assure the refining of the moral nature, there is a discipline of the thoughts to establish, and a hygiene of the soul to follow, as there is a physical hygiene to observe for the maintenance of the health of the body. We see that the constant action of the thought and will on the etheric body produces absolutely just results. Each receives the imperishable fruits of his past and present. This fruit is not the effect of outside causes, but of interior ones: a chain which produces in us pain and joy, effort and success, fault and chastisement. It is in the intimate secrecy of our thoughts and in the full lights of our actions that we must seek the efficient cause of our present and future situations.

We are placed according to our merits, in the environment created by our former thoughts and acts. If we are unhappy, it is because we have not become enlightened enough to play a better role. But our condition will ameliorate as soon as we know how to awaken in ourselves a disinterested love of justice and truth.

To perfect the being, to unceasingly embellish the inner nature, to augment its value and construct the edifice of the consciousness - such is the aim of evolution. Each one of us possesses that particular primordial genius spoken of by the Druids, a realization of special forms of divine thought. God has placed in the depths of the soul germs of faculties powerful and varied. The soul is called upon to develop above all others one special form of genius, until it is brought to its highest excellence. These multiple aspects of intelligent wisdom and beauty are eternal. Music, poetry, eloquence, invention, prevision of the future and hidden things, the gifts of education, the power to heal, are some of the innumerable forms. In projecting the human entity, the divine thought impregnates that one of these forces assigned particularly to the soul in the vast universal concert.

The mission of the being, his destiny, his actions in the general evolution, grow more and more precise, and from being latent and confused become accentuated and clearly defined in the measure that he climbs the immense spiral. The inspirations that he receives from on high respond to those in his character. According to his need and his appeals will he hear in his own depths the divine melody. It is so God, by the infinite variety of contrasts, causes the great harmony to vibrate in nature and in the breast of humanity. If the soul abuses these gifts, or applies them to evil purposes, if it entertains vanity or pride, it must in expiation be reborn in an organism powerless to manifest them. It will live an unknown genius, humiliated among men, long enough for sorrow to lift it above the excesses of its own personality, and to permit it to take a sublime flight towards its ideal.

Oh, you who peruse these pages, elevate your thoughts and your resolutions to the high tasks which fall to you. The road to the Infinite opens before you, sown with inextinguishable marvels. Wherever your flight is directed, subjects for study will await you, with inexhaustible sources of joy and beauty. Always are there unsuspected horizons succeeding horizons known. All is beauty in the divine work, and in your ascension it is reserved for you to enjoy innumerable aspects smiling or terrible, from the delicate flower to the flamboyant stars: and to wait at the unfolding of worlds and humanities. At the same time, you will feel your understanding of celestial things grow, and there will awaken in you an ardent desire to perpetuate God - to plunge in Him, in His light, His love. In God our source - our essence - our life!

Human intelligence cannot describe the futures presented, the ascension perceived. Our spirit shut in a perishable organism, cannot therein find the necessary resources to express these splendors. The soul, with its profound intuitions, has the sense of infinite things in which it will participate, and to which it aspires. It seeks in vain to express them in feeble human words; in vain to translate those eternal truths in the poor language of earth. But the evolved consciousness perceives the subtle radiations of the superior life. A day will come when the soul will dominate time and space, and a century will be no more for it than an instant, and with a flash of thought it will crown the summits of Heaven. Its subtle organism, refined by thousands of lives, will vibrate to every breeze, to every voice, to all the appeals of immensity. Its memory will plunge into vanished ages, and it will revive at will all that it has lived, and call to it, or join all the cherished souls who have partaken of its joys and sorrows. For all affections of the past are found in the life of space, and new ties are formed, binding us closer and closer in a more powerful and perfect communion.

Believe, love, hope! Man my brother, and then act. Apply yourself and put into your work the reflections, the thoughts and the aspirations of your heart - the joys and certitudes of your immortal soul. Communicate your faith to the intelligent minds which surround you, that they may be able to second your efforts for the uplifting of the world and the opening of a way for the evolution of the spirits. By and by will come science, virile and renewed, no longer the science of prejudices, routines, and worn-out methods, but a science open to all kinds of research, to all investigations, the science of the Invisible and the

Beyond. It will come to fertilize understanding, to enlighten intelligence and to fortify conscience. Faith in the survival of the soul stands upon the rock of experiences and defies criticism.

An art purer and more idealistic, illumined by the light that never dies, will come to vivify the spirit of earth. It will be the same with religious beliefs and systems. In the flight of thought, to lift truths from their relative order to the order superior, they will approach, join, and mingle, making of the multiple faiths of the past, hostile or dead, a living faith which will unite humanity in adoration and prayer. Work with all the power of your being to prepare this evolution. Human activities must be used with more intensity on this route of the spirit. After physical humanity, mind humanity must be created - after the body, the soul. That which has been conquered by material energy has been lost in deeper knowledge and revelation of inner senses. Man has triumphed over the visible world; now it remains for him to conquer the interior world, and to know the secrets of his splendid future.

Instead of arguing, act! Discussion is vain - criticism sterile, but action is grand when it consists of making yourself and others greater. Do not forget that you work for yourself in working for others. The universe, like your soul, renews itself, and is perpetuated and embellished without cessation by work and exchange. God is perfecting his work, enjoy it as you rejoice in embellishing your own: your most beautiful work is yourself. By constant efforts you can make your intelligence and your consciousness an admirable work which you will enjoy indefinitely. From each fertile crucible of a life you should come forth capable to perform new tasks and higher missions appropriate to your strength, and each one should be recompense and a joy.

So with your hands, day-by-day you fashion your destiny. You will be reborn in such forms as your desires construct, until your desires prepare for you forms and organisms superior to those of earth. You will be reborn in the environment you love, near to the being you have loved, and they will live with and for them.

Then when your earthly evolution is finished, when you have exalted your faculties and forces to a sufficient degree of power, when you have emptied the cup of suffering, bitterness, and felicity that the world has offered you, and communed with all the aspects of human genius, then you will mount with your dear ones toward other more beautiful worlds - worlds of peace and harmony.

Your lost earth envelope returning to dust, your pure essence reaching the spiritual regions, your memory and your work still sustaining men in their strife and trials, you can say with serene joy - 'My life on earth has not been sterile - my efforts have not been in vain!'

THE POWERS OF THE SOUL
THE WILL

1
THE WILL

The study of life to which we have consecrated the first part of this work has permitted us to perceive the powerful reservoir of forces and energies hidden within us. It has shown us that therein all our future, in its limitless development, is contained in permanent form. The causes of happiness are not found in determined localities in space, but are in us - in the profound mysteries of the soul.

It is this which confirms that grand doctrine of Christ - 'The kingdom of heaven is within you.' The same thought is explained in the Vedas in another form: 'You carry in yourself a sublime friend whom you do not know.' A Persian sage said, 'You live among stores filled with riches, and you die with hunger at the door!'

All the great teachers are in accord in this subject. It is in the life interior, in the expanding of our powers and faculties and virtues, that the source of our felicity lays. Look attentively into the depths of your being - shut your mind to things external, and after having habituated your psychic senses to the obscurity in the silence, you see the surging of unsuspected lights, you will hear fortifying and consoling voices. But there are few men who know how to read in themselves, how to explore the retreats where sleep inestimable treasures.

We waste our lives in banal things, on things trifling. We walk the road of existence without knowing ourselves and the psychic wealth whose value would procure for us joys without number. There are in each human soul two spheres of action and expression. One exterior to the other manifests the personality - the ME with its passions, weaknesses, and its insufficiency. As long as that regulates our conduct, it is the inferior life, sown with trials and troubles.

The other sphere interior, profound, immutable, is at the same time the seat of consciousness, the source of spiritual life, and the temple of God in us. It is only when this center of action dominates the other - when it's impulsions direct us, that our hidden powers are revealed, and that the spirit affirms itself in all its brilliant beauty. It is at this moment we hold communion with 'the Father who dwells in us,' following the words of Christ - the Father who is the source of all love, the principle of all great actions.

By one of these centers, we perpetuate ourselves in material worlds, where all is inferiority, incertitude, and sorrow. By the other, we unite ourselves to celestial worlds, where all is peace, serenity, and grandeur. It is only by the growing manifestation of the divine spirit in us that we can vanquish the selfish ME, and associate ourselves freely with universal and everlasting work, and create for ourselves a perfect and happy life.

By what means can we put in movement those interior powers, and direct them toward a high ideal? By the will. The persistent, tenacious use of this master faculty enables us to control our natures, to dominate material things, sickness and death.

It is by the will that we direct our thoughts toward a precise goal. With most people thoughts float incessantly: their constant motion, their infinite variety, allows small chance for the higher influences. One must know how to concentrate, how to become in accord with divine thought. Then, is produced the fertilizing of the human soul by the divine spirit which envelops it, and renders it capable of realizing its true tasks, and prepares it for the life in space, by enabling it to perceive in this world a reflection of its splendors. Superior spirits see and hear our thoughts. Their own thoughts are penetrating harmonies, while our own are often confused discords. Let us then learn to use the will, and by it to unite ourselves to all that is great, and to the universal harmony whose vibrations surround space, wherein worlds are rocked.

Will is the greatest of all powers - in its action it is comparable to a magnet. The will to live, to develop life in oneself, attracts new sources of vitality; it is the secret of the law of evolution. The will acting on the etheric body with intensity accentuates its vibrations and prepares it for a higher degree of existence.

The principle of evolution is not in matter - it is in will, whose action reaches to, and affects the invisible order of things, as it affects the order visible and material. The one is but the consequence of the other. The highest principle, the motor of existence, is the will. Divine will is the motive power of life universal.

What is important above all is to know that we can realize all things in the psychic domain. No force remains sterile when it is exercised constantly with an aim conforming to right and justice. That is the case with the will: it can act equally sleepy or waking, for the valiant soul which has fixed its aim pursues it with tenacity in one as in the other phase of life, and so determines a powerful current with silently undermines obstacles.

The will is preservative as well as creative. Will, confidence, optimist are sufficient in themselves often to turn away evil. While discouragement and fear disarm us and leave us without defense. The fact alone that we look trouble in the face and affront it diminishes its effects. The will, it is power! Its prowess is without limit.

The man conscious of himself feels his forces grow with his efforts. He knows that all he desires that is right and good must be inevitably accomplished in the course of his existence when his thought accords with divine law. And in this is verified the celestial words, 'faith can move mountains. It is most consoling to say, 'I am a free intelligence. I made myself through the ages - I build slowly my individuality and my liberty, and now that I know the force and grandeur in myself, I lean upon them. I do not veil them for one moment without, and by them, with the aid of God and my brothers in space, I will lift myself above all difficulties - I will vanquish the evil in me - I will detach myself from all that chains me to gross things, that I may take my flight to happier worlds. I see clear the route which I am called to tread. It leads on and on, without end. But a sure guide conducts me along this infinite way. I have learned to know myself, and I believe in God, and in this immense road which opens before me I walk firmly and will to grow greater, and to elevate myself with the aid of my intelligence, the daughter of God, and to attract to myself all the moral riches, and to participate in all the marvels of the cosmos. My will calls to me - on - always on! Always more knowledge, more divine life: and by it I will obtain the fullness of existence and construct a better and more radiant personality. I have forever left behind me the inferior and ignorant being unconscious of his value and power. I assert the independence and dignity of my consciousness, and reach my hand to all brothers, saying, 'Awaken from your slumber - tear off the material veil which envelops you - learn to know yourself and the powers in you, and learn to utilize them. All the voices of nature and of space cry, 'awake and march on! Hasten and conquer your destiny!'

To you who believe yourselves spent by suffering and disappointments, beings afflicted, hearts torn by bitter trials and wounded by the sword of adversity, I come and say: 'There is no soul incapable of rebirth, of new gloom. You have but to will, and there will awaken in you unknown forces. Believe in yourself - in your immortal destiny! Believe in God, the sun of the sun - immense source of light, of which you are a ray - a ray that can be illumined into a glorious flame. Every man can be good and happy if he wills it with energy and continuity. Divert your thoughts without cessation toward this truth, that you can become what you will to be, and will to be always better and greater.' It is the idea of eternal progress and the means of realizing it: it is the secret of mental force, from which flow magnetic and psychic forces, and when you have acquired this mastery of yourself, you will no longer suffer from the evils of life, but will have made of your ME inferior an individuality high, stable, and powerful.

2
THE INNER SOUL

Consciousness

Our preceding studies have demonstrated that the soul is an emanation from the absolute. Our lives have for their aim the increasing manifestations of what is divine in us, and the growth of the empire it is called upon to exercise over what is within and without, by the aid of its latent energies. We can obtain this result by divers method - by science or by meditation, by work or by moral force. The best procedure is to utilize all those modes of application, each supplementing the others. But the most efficacious method of all is introspection, self-analysis. Add to this the breaking of material fetters, the union with God in spirit and in truth, and the firm determination of self-improvement, and we will discover that all true religions, all profound philosophies find their source in this same formula. Outside of this, doctrines, cults, forms, and practices are but exterior vestments which hide the soul of religion from the eyes of the masses.

The soul is united to the great universal Soul of which it is a vibration. This origin of the soul, this participation in the divine nature, explains the grasps and centralizes the perceptions and transmits those to the soul, which registers all, and disengages those which are useful. But beneath this sensorium of surface is another hidden one, which discovers and regulates the things of the metaphysical world. It is this profound unknown sense, unused by the majority of men, that certain experimenters designate under the name of the subliminal consciousness.

The greater part of the world's wonderful discoveries in the physical domain were ideas perceived first through intuition. For long Newton had entertained the thought of universal attraction, and then the fall of an apple gave his physical senses the objective demonstration. Just as there exists in us a physical sensorium which puts us en rapport with material beings and things, so certain men possess a spiritual sense, by whose aid they penetrate the domain of invisible life. After death, as soon as the veil of flesh falls, this sense becomes the only center of our perceptions, and it is in the extension and the growth of this spiritual sense that lies the law of our psychic evolution, the renovation of our being, and the secret of its interior illumination.

By this law we detach ourselves from the relative and illusionary, from all material contingencies, to attach ourselves more and more to the immutable and the absolute. So experimental science will always be insufficient, in spite of the advantages it offers and the conquests it realizes, if it does not complete itself by intuition and interior divination which enables us to discover the essential truths. A marvel surpassing all other exterior marvels is this marvel of ourselves. It is this mirror hidden in man which reflects all the universe.

Those who are absorbed in the exclusive study of phenomena, in the pursuit of changing forms and exterior facts, often fail to listen to the inner voices and to consult the faculties which develop in the silence. That is why the things of the invisible, the impalpable and the divine, imperceptible to so many scientific minds, are sometimes perceived by the ignorant. The most wonderful book is ourselves - the infinite is revealed therein. Happy is he who can read it! All this domain remains closed to the positivist who disdains the only key by which it can be opened. He tries to experiment by physical senses and material instruments in that which escapes all objective measures. As a deaf man reasons about the rules of melody - a blind man about optical laws - so this man, with exterior senses, reasons about the worlds and beings metaphysical.

Once let the interior senses awaken in him and shine, then compared to the light which inundates him, earthly science, so great to his eyes before, will shrink into insignificance. After this light came to

Professor William James of Harvard, the eminent psychologist, he said: 'All human experience in its vital reality pushes me irresistible to go outside of the narrow limits wherein science pretends to shut us. The real world is richer and more complex than that of science.'

Many men of science have come to the realization that the initial cause of sensation is not in the body, but in the soul. The physical senses are but gross manifestations of inner hidden senses. Professor Lombroso, of the University of Turin, wrote in The Arena, June 1907: 'Until 1890 I was the most opinionated adversary of spiritualism! Then, as a physician, I came in contact with the most curious phenomenon which had ever been presented to my attention. I was called to attend a young daughter of a high officer in my native town. This girl was suddenly attacked by violent spasms, whose symptoms no science of pathology or physiology could explain. She lost for months all use of her eyes, but instead saw by her ears: with bandaged eyes she read printed lines placed against her ear! When a magnifying glass was placed between her ears and the sun, she complained that they were trying to burn her eyes and blind her! So strange were the conditions surrounding this case, that the idea came to me that perhaps spiritualism would aid me to approach the facts.' Gerard Harry, the biographer of marvelous Helen Keller, said that the intensity of her perceptions conferred upon her ability of reading thoughts. The case of Helen Keller proves that behind her atrophied organs of sight and hearing there exists a consciousness long familiarized with ideas of interior worlds. It is a demonstration of anterior lives of the soul with all its perfect senses, and surviving all corporeal disintegration.

To develop and refine the perception in a general manner, we must first awaken the inner senses - the spiritual. Mediumship demonstrates to us that there are human beings more fully endowed with inner vision and hearing than are certain disembodied entities whose evolution has been limited. The purer and more disinterested are our thoughts and acts, the more our spiritual life predominates over the physical, the greater will be our inner development.

The veil which hides the etheric world grows thinner and more transparent, and behind it the soul perceives a marvelous ensemble of harmonies and beauties. At the same time, it becomes more capable of receiving and transmitting the revelations and the inspirations from superior beings, for development of the interior senses coincides generally with increased powers of the mind, and to a more generous attraction of etheric radiations.

Every plane of the universe, every circle of life, corresponds to a number of vibrations which become more subtle and rapid, in the measure that they approach the perfect life. The beings endowed with but feeble powers of radiation cannot perceive the forms of life superior to them. But each soul is capable of obtaining, by will and educations of the inner senses, a power of vibration which will permit him to act upon higher planes of consciousness. We find proofs of the intensity of mental emanations in certain cases of people dying, or in great danger, who telepathically, at a great distance, impress the fact on several minds at one time. In the Annals of Psychic Science, for October 1906, such a case is recorded. In truth, each one of us could, if we would, communicate at any hour with worlds invisible.

We are spirits, and we command matter and disengage ourselves from its bonds, and live in the freer sphere of super consciousness. For that one thing is necessary, viz. to come into the spiritual life with a perfect concentration of all our inner forces. Then will we find ourselves face to face with an order of things which neither instinct nor experience nor reason can seize. The soul in its expansion can break down the walls of flesh which imprison it, and communicate by its new senses with superior and divine worlds. That is what the saints and the great mystics of all time and all religions have done.

William James says: 'The most important result of research into trance conditions is the breaking down of barriers between the individual and the absolute. By this we establish our identity with the Infinite. It is the eternal and triumphant experience of mysticism that one finds in all climates and all religions. All proclaim with the same accents and imposing unanimity the oneness of man with God. These mystic states of trance reveal depths of truth unsounded by reason. They prove that the physical senses are but one mode of consciousness. These mystic states are like windows opening on a wide extended world!'

Spiritualism in a certain measure demonstrates the justice of these words. Mediumship, under varied forms, is the result of a psychic force which permits the soul senses to enter in for a moment, and substitute themselves in place of the physical senses, and to perceive what is imperceptible to others. The spirit desiring to communicate recognizes at sight the organism which in the medium will serve its purposes as an intermediary, and acts accordingly. Sometimes it is the word, or again penmanship by mechanic action of the hand, or the brain when it is a question of mediumistic intuition. In temporary incorporations it is entire and full possession and adaptation of the spiritual senses of the possessor to the physical senses of the subject.

The most common faculty is clairvoyance, that is to say, perception with closed eyes of what is passing afar, whether in time or space – in the past or future. It is the penetration of the spirit of the clairvoyant into etheric centers where are registered facts accomplished or elaborated, plans of things to be. Often the clairvoyant acts unconsciously, without preparation. In such a case it is the result of a natural evolution, but it can be produced, as spiritual vision can be. Colonel de Rochas in his Successive Lives tells what Mireille, his trance subject, said of the effect of magnetism upon her.

'When I am awake,' she said, 'my soul is chained to my body, and I am like a person who is shut in a tower, and sees the exterior world only through five windows, each with a different colored glass. When you magnetize me, you deliver me from my chains, and my soul, which aspires to elevate itself, mounts a stairway of the tower, a stairway without windows, and I see only you who are guiding me, until the moment when I arrive on the upper platform. There, my sight is extended in all directions, with a most acute sense which puts me en rapport with objects I could not see through the windows of the tower.'

Clairaudience can be acquired: the hearing of interior voices, which makes it possible to communicate with spirits. Another manifestation of the inner senses is the reading of registered events, photographed in a certain manner on some antique or modern object. For instance, a fragment of armor, a corner of a sarcophagus, a stone from a ruin, evokes in the mind of the seer a succession of pictures attached to the time and place to which the object belonged. This is called psychometry.

Many people have, without knowing it, the ability to communicate by the inner senses with their friends in space. Such are found among the very religious, the idealists who have keenly suffered, and by a long series of trials have become more subtly attuned to spiritual vibrations. Often human souls in distress have appealed to me, soliciting counsel and advice from the spirit worlds, which I could not procure for them. To all such I recommend the following method: Lean on yourself, in the solitude of the silence. Elevate your thoughts toward God. Call upon your spirit protector, the tutelary guide that Providence attaches to each of us on the voyage of life. Interrogate this guide regarding the things which preoccupy you: if they are worthy of his attention and free from all low or petty interests, then listen attentively in yourself. Listen and wait, and in a short time you will hear in the depths of your consciousness the faint echo of a distant voice, or rather you will feel the vibrations of a mysterious thought which will dissipate your doubts, drive away your anguish, and console and comfort your heart. This is indeed one form of mediumship, and not the least beautiful. All souls can obtain and participate in this communion with the living and the dead. It will one day be known and used by all humanity.

We can indeed by this process correspond with the divine plan. In difficult circumstances of my life, when I hesitated before the task which had been confided to me to spread abroad the consoling truths of spiritualism, making an appeal to the Supreme Entity, I always heard sounding in me the earnest solemn voice which dictated my duty. Clear and distinct, yet this voice seemed to come from a far distance. Its tender accents touched me even to tears.

Intuition is often but one form employed by the inhabitants of the invisible worlds to transmit their instructions. Sometimes they are the revelations of the subconscious mind to the normal consciousness. In the first case, we should regard them as inspiration. Through mediumship the spirit impresses its ideas on the mind of the transmitter, who furnishes the language, according to the degree of his mental development. Each medium gives the imprint of his own personality to the inspiration received from above. The more intellectual and cultured the medium, the more faithfully are transmitted the high and pure communications. The wide sheet of water cannot flow through a narrow canal - so an inspiring spirit cannot succeed in transmitting through the organs of a medium conceptions for which no suitable channel is prepared. By a great mental effort, under the excitation of an exterior force, the medium might express conceptions above her normal knowledge, but in the language used would be found habitual phrases and favorite terms, elevated and amplified at the same time by the spiritual standard.

We see then what difficulties and obstacles the human organism opposes to faithful transmission of spiritual conceptions, and how long training is necessary to render the mind adaptable to the uses of a disembodied intelligence. (Not only such use, but the same may be said of those who seek to delve within the profound depths of their own reincarnated souls for high conceptions, like men of genius, poets, and composers.) Often the medium is conscious in the beginning of her trance state. But as soon as the action of the spirit is accentuated, she finds herself under the influence of a force which acts independently of her will: a sort of weight oppresses her - her eyes are veiled, and she passes under an invisible dominion. Then the medium is but an instrument of reception and transmission. As a machine obeys an electric current which moves it, the medium obeys the current of thought which envelops her.

In the exercise of intuitive mediumship in a waking state, many are discouraged with the difficulty of distinguishing their own ideas from those which are suggested. It is nevertheless easy, we believe, to recognize the difference. The spiritually inspired ideas emanate suddenly from an interior source and jet forth spontaneously, while our own ideas are always at our disposition, and occupy our intellect in a permanent manner. Not only do the inspired ideas surge up as by enchantment, but they rapidly follow one another, and are often expressed in an almost feverish manner. Almost all authors, poets, and orators are mediums at certain moments. They have the intuition of occult assistance in their work. Thomas Paine said: 'There is no one who, being occupied with the progress of the human mind, has not observed that there are two distinct classes of ideas: those produced in ourselves by reflection, and those which are precipitated into our minds. I make a rule of welcoming the politeness these unexpected visitors, and of determining with all possible care if they are worthy of attention. I declare that it is to these stranger guests I we all the knowledge I possess.' Emerson said: 'Thoughts penetrate themselves into my intellect like a ray of light shining into the darkness. The truth comes to me, not alone by reason, but by intuition.'

Walter Scott explained to his astonished friends the rapidity with which he wrote the Bard of Avon, as follows: 'My fingers worked independently of my thought, and it was the same when I wrote Woodstock. I had not the least idea that the story would develop into a catastrophe in the third volume! Often when I take my pen, it moves so fast, I am tempted to let it go alone, to see if it will not write without my assistance.' Jean Jacques Rousseau recounts experiences of similar sources of inspiration. The most extraordinary case of mediumistic inspiration of modern times is that of Andrew Jackson Davies. At the age of fifteen he became celebrated in American for his ability to diagnose sickness and prescribe remedies. He had at age of fourteen been magnetized by a Mr. Livingstone of Poughkeepsie, who discovered the boy's astonishing powers, and retired from business to associate with him. A poor boy, able only to read, write, and compute in simple numbers, he announced at the age of eighteen that he was going to be the instrument of a new and astonishing spiritual power, and he commenced by a series of conferences, which produced considerable effect upon the scientific and religious world of that day. Eminent men attended his conferences, and his work, Divine Revelations of Nature, was of so marvelous a nature, emanating from a person of no education or experience, that it astounded all classes of society. Other voluminous works followed, and this young man, in the course of years, dictated day by day extraordinary and well-conceived books treating of all the great questions of the day: among them, 'Science, and nature in all its ramifications,' 'Man in his numberless modes of existence,' 'God in his depths of love, wisdom and power.' His MSS. were often submitted to high intelligences, who declared them most profound, and acknowledged the impossibility of his having written them in his normal state. The result of the life of this phenomenal person was the revelation that the mind of man could communicate spiritually with spirits of the higher worlds, and acquired knowledge from those spheres.

We have incidentally spoken of the method to follow to develop the psychic senses. It consists in isolating oneself during certain hours of the day or night, suspending the exterior senses, and putting away the sights and sounds of outside life. This it is possible to do, even in the most humble conditions, and in the heart of the most common occupations. We must, so to say, turn in upon ourselves, and in the calm and tranquillity of our thoughts make a mental effort to see and read the great mysterious book within. At these moments, drive away every thought which is light, trivial, and changing. Material preoccupations create horizontal currents of vibrations which are obstacles to the etheric radiations, and restrict our perceptions. On the contrary, meditation and contemplation and the constant effort toward the good and beautiful form ascensional currents which establish a rapport with the higher planes, and facilitate the penetration in us of divine effluvia. By this exercise, repeated and prolonged, the inner being becomes little by little illuminated, fertilized, and regenerated. This work of development is long and difficult, and necessitates more than one existence. It is never too soon to begin. The good results will not fail to manifest themselves. All that you lose in sensations of a lower order you will gain in super-earthly perceptions, in mental and moral equilibrium, and in the joys of the spirit. Your inner senses will acquire an extraordinary acuteness and delicacy. You will one day attain the power of communicating with the higher spheres. The religions have sought to attain these powers by communion and prayer. But the prayers in use by many churches are an ensemble of formulae learned and repeated mechanically, and powerless to give the soul the lofty flight necessary to establish the rapport with superior realms. There must be an interior appeal, a rigorous concentration and profound impulse, to attain results. That is why we have always advocated the improvised prayer – the cry of the soul which in its love and faith flings all the forces accumulated within it toward the object of its desire.

In place of inviting the spirits celestial by means of invocation to descend us, we learn in this manner to free our souls and mount toward them. Meanwhile certain precautions are necessary. The invisible world is peopled with entities of all kinds, and he who penetrates there ought to possess sufficient perfection, and to be inspired by sentiment high enough, to put him above all the suggestions of evil. Above all, he should conduct his researches under sure and safe guides. It is by moral progress that one obtains the necessary force to dominate the earth-bound spirits that often seek to surround us. The full possession of ourselves, and a tranquil and profound knowledge of the eternal laws, will preserve us from dangers and delusions, and at the same time will procure for us the means of controlling the forces in action on the occult plane.

3
LIBERTY

Liberty is the necessary condition for the human soul, which without it cannot build its destiny. It is in vain that the philosophers and theologians have argued this question from all points of view. They have obscured it by their theories and sophisms, condemning humanity to servitude in place of conducting it to the light, yet the idea is simple and clear. The Druids formulated it in the early dawn of history, and expressed it in these terms in the Triads: 'There are three primitive deities, viz. God, Light and Liberty.' At first sight the liberty of man seems to be restrained in the midst of a circle of fatalities which surround it – physical necessities, social conditions and interests or instincts: but on considering the question more closely, we see that this liberty is always sufficient to permit the soul to break through the circle and escape the opposing forces. Liberty and responsibility are correlative in man's being, and augment with his elevation. It is the responsibility of the man which makes his dignity and his morality: without it, he would be but a blind machine – a plaything of Fate! Responsibility is established by the testimony of the conscience which approves or blames our actions.

The sensation of remorse is a more demonstrative proof than all the arguments of philosophers. For each spirit, however slightly evolved, the law of duty shines like a lighthouse through the fogs of passions and self-interest. Everyday we see men in the most humble situations accepting the hardest trials rather than lower themselves, or commit unworthy actions. So if human liberty is restrained, it is at least on the way to perpetual development, for prayer means nothing but the extension of free will in the individual and in collective society. The strife between matter and spirit is precisely for this end – to liberate the spirit and to yoke the blind forces. Intelligence and will reach the place where they predominate over what we call fatality. Free will is then a flowering of the personality and consciousness. To be free, we must will to be free, and make the effort to become so in freeing ourselves from the servitude of ignorance and base passions, and substituting the empire of reason for that of sensation. That can only be obtained by education, and development of the higher faculties: physical liberation by the limitation of the appetites, intellectual liberation by the conquest of truth, and moral liberation by the search for virtue. It is the work of centuries, but at every degree of ascension in the midst of the good and evil things of life, besides the ensemble of causes and effects, there is always a place for the free will of man to exercise itself.

How shall we conciliate free will with divine prescience? Before this anticipated knowledge that God has off all things, can one affirm human liberty? Seemingly complex in appearance, this question which has caused floods of ink to flow is nevertheless simple in solution, but man does not love simple things; he prefers the obscure and complicated, and will accept truth only after having exhausted all forms of error.

God, whose infinite science embraces all things, knows the nature of each man, and the tendencies and impulses which he will be liable to exhibit. We ourselves, knowing the character of a person, can easily foresee whether under certain circumstances he will decide to act for self-interest or for duty. Resolutions are not born for nothing, but come from a series of anterior causes and effects. God knows each soul in its most hidden recesses, and can with certitude deduct from His knowledge of this soul the determination it will, in its freedom, take. This prevision of our acts does not give them birth. If God did not foresee them, they would nevertheless have their free course. It is herein that human liberty and free will are reconciled and combined, when we consider the problem in the light of reason. The circle in which is exercised the will of man is besides too restrained to interfere with divine action whose effects move in their immensity, without limit. The feeble insect lost in a corner of the garden does not trouble the harmony of the ensemble, or fetter the work of the divine gardener, by displacing a few grains of sand.

∼

The question of free will has a large importance and grave consequences for the social order by its effect on education, morality, justice, and legislation. It has determined two opposing currents of opinion – the negators of free will and those who admit it with restrictions. The argument of the fatalist is, 'Man is under the control of his natural impulses, which dominate him, and oblige him to wish and decide in one direction more than another, therefore he is not free.'

The opposite school brings out the theory of indeterminate causes. Charles Renouvier has been its most brilliant representative, and his ideas have been confirmed by Wundt, Fouillée and Boutroux in philosophical works, yet, in spite of the theologians, until now the question has remained practically insoluble. It could not be otherwise, since each one of the systems argues from the inexact idea that human beings have but one life to live. The subject assumes a holly different aspect if we enlarge the circle and consider the problem in the light of the doctrine of rebirth. We then see how each being gains his free will in the course of the evolutions he must accomplish. Supplied with instinct at first, which gradually gives place to reason, our liberty is very limited in our first stations, and during all the period of our early education. As soon as the mind gains and idea of law our free will expands. Always at each step in our ascension, and in hours of important resolution, it will be assisted, guided, and counseled by the great intelligences, the wiser and more enlightened spirits. Free will, the liberty of the soul, is exercised, above all, at the hour of reincarnation. In choosing the family and the environment, it knows in advance what trials await it, but it comprehends equally the necessity for these trials, to develop its qualities, eliminate its defect, and disintegrate its prejudices and vices. These trials may be the effect of a bad past, which it must repair, and it accepts them with resignation and confidence, for it knows that its great brothers in space will not abandon it in difficult hours. The future appears to it than, not in detail, but with all its salient points, or in the measure that this future is the result of anterior actions. These faults represent the part of 'fatality' or 'predestination' that certain men claim to see in all lives. They are simply the reflection of distant causes. In reality, nothing is fatal, and whatever the troubbles and responsibilities we encounter, we can always modify our fate by works of devotion, of goodness and charity, and sacrifices to duty.

The problem of free will is of great importance from the judicial point of view. It is difficult to be exactly just in all the individual cases which come before a tribunal for preservation of social order. This can only be done by establishing the degree of evolution of the culprits. But human justice, little versed in these matters, rests blind and imperfect in its arrests and decisions. Often the wicked and culpable is in reality but a young ignorant spirit in whom reason has not had time to ripen. Duclos said: 'Crime is often the result of false judgment.' That is why there should be established penalties of a nature to compel the offender to enter into himself for instruction, light, and reform. Society should correct without passion or hate, else it renders itself culpable. Each soul is equivalent to its point of departure. They differ by their infinite degrees of advancement: the one young, the other old – diversely developed according to their age. It would be unjust to demand of an infantile mind merits equal to those one expects from a mature mind which has learned much. A great difference exists in their responsibilities.

A human being is not really ripe for liberty until the universal exterior laws become interior and a part of his consciousness, by the fact of his evolution. The day when he is penetrated with the law, and makes it the rule of his actions, he attains the moral point where man possesses, dominates, and governs himself. From that hour he no longer needs social restraints or authority to direct him. It is the same with collective humanity. People are not truly free and worthy of liberty until they have learned to obey this law, eternal and universal, which emanates neither from the power of a caste or the will of crowds but from a higher power. Without the moral discipline which each individual should impose on himself, public liberty is but a mirage. It gives the appearance, but not the manners of a free people. Society remains exposed by its violence, its passions and its appetites, to all the complications and all the disorders of earth life.

All which lifts us toward the light lifts us toward liberty, that flowers freely and beautifully in the higher life. The delayed and unconscious soul is kept down under the weight of material fatalities, while just in the measure it gains freedom, it lifts itself above these trials and comes closely to the divine.

In general terms it may be said that each man arrives at the state of reason and responsibility according to the degree of his advancement. I leave aside the case of one who under the empire of a physical and moral cause, malady or obsession, has lost the use of his faculties. We know that in the strife between the two, the strongest souls triumph always. Socrates said that he had felt germinate in him, and had overcome, most perverse impulses. In this philosopher were two currents, one flowing toward evil – one toward good. It was the latter which carried him on its breast.

There are, too, secret causes working upon us. Often intuition combats reason, and in an unforeseen manner, sudden profound impulses determine our actions. This is not a negation of free will. It is the action of the soul in its wisdom, intervening in the course of our destiny. Or it may, again, be the influence of our invisible guides, or the intervention of an intelligence who looks from afar, and seeks to snatch us away from inferior contingencies and lift us to higher altitudes. But in each case it is ever our own will which accepts or rejects, and makes the final decision. To sum up – man is the artisan of his own liberation. He attains a state of complete liberty only by interior culture and the use of his hidden powers. Obstacles accumulating on his route are in the end but means of compelling him to put in action all his latent powers, until he conquers every material difficulty. We are all united, and the liberty of each one leads toward the liberty of others, and in freeing himself from ignorance and passion each man helps to free those of his own kind. Everything which contributes toward dissipating night and letting in the light of intelligence renders humanity freer and more conscious of its duties and powers. Then let us elevate ourselves to consciousness of our rôle and aim, and we will be free. In place of being passive creatures, bent under the yoke of matter, a prey to inertia and incertitude, let us free our souls form the chains of fatality and display to the world the superiority of our acquired qualities.

4
THOUGHT

Thought is creative. Just as eternal thought is projected ceaselessly in space, and creates beings and worlds, so the thought of the writer, orator, poet, and artists sends forth continual floods of ideas, works, and conceptions, which will influence and impress for good or bad, immense human crowds.

The mission of the workers in the domain of thought is at once great, formidable, and sacred. It is great and sacred because thought dissipates the shadows on the path, solves the enigmas of life, and traces the route of humanity. It is the flame which warms souls and illumines the deserts of existence: formidable also, because its efforts are powerful for descent as well as for ascension. Sooner or later, every product of the mind returns to its author with all its consequences, bringing in its train either suffering and a diminution of liberty, or inner satisfaction and elevation of the being. The present life is but a mere episode in our long history, a fragment of a long chain winding through immensity. Constantly falling on us, in fogs or sunshine, are the results of our works.

The human soul pursues its way, surrounded with an atmosphere radiant or somber, and peopled with creations of its thoughts. There in the life of space lies its glory or its shame.

To give thought all its force and its amplitude nothing is more efficacious than the study of great problems. To express freely we must first feel powerfully – to enjoy the high and profound sensations, we must go to the source from which flows all life, harmony, and beauty. All that is noble and elevating in the domain of intellect emanates from the one eternal source of living thought. The higher is the flight of the mind toward this great cause, the more radiant will be the light it sees, the more intoxicating the joys it feels, the more powerful the forces it will acquire. After each flight the thought redescends vivified, clarified, to the earthly fields to resume the tasks through which it will find greater growth, for it is labor which makes the beauty and splendor of an accomplished work. Lift up your eyes, O thinker – O poet! Send up your appeal of aspiration and prayer! Before the changing reflections of the sea, at the sight of white mountain summits, or the infinite stars, have you not felt hours of intoxicating ecstasy? When the soul was plunged in a divine dream, and when inspiration came like a messenger from Heaven, have you not heard in the depths of your soul the vibration of murmurs from invisible worlds preparing your thought for supreme intuitions? In each poet, artist, or writer lies the germs of the mediumistic power, unsuspected and undeveloped, waiting to blossom. By them the worker becomes through his thought en rapport with the inexhaustible source from which he receives his part of the revelation. This revelation, appropriate to the order of his talent, he has for his mission – to express to the world through his works radiations of divine truths. It will be in the frequent and conscious communion with the world of spirits that the geniuses of the future will obtain the elements for their work. From now, the penetration into the secrets of this double life is going to offer man assistance and light which the failing religions are no longer able to procure for him. In all domains this spiritual idea is going to fertilize thought and work. Science will owe it the discovery of incalculable forces and the conquest of an occult universe. It will owe to it a complete renovation of its theories and its methods. Philosophy will gain from it a more extended and more exact knowledge of human personality. The religions of the future will find in spiritual research the proofs of the survival of the soul and the rules of life in the Beyond, at the same time with the principle of close union toward the common Father.

Art under all forms will discover in it inexhaustible sources of inspiration and emotion. The man of the people, in his hours of lassitude, will find moral courage in it, and he will comprehend that the soul can grow by humble labor as well as by loftier tasks, and that no duty is negligible – that envy is sister to hate – and that often one is less happy in luxury than in mediocrity. In it the skeptic will find faith, the discouraged hope and virile resolutions; all those who suffer, the profound idea that a law of justice presides over all things: that there is not in any domain effect without a cause, no victory without combat – no triumph without hard efforts, and that above all reigns perfect and majestic law, and that no soul is abandoned by God, of whom it is a part.

Thus will operate slowly the renovation of humanity, still so young, so ignorant of itself, but whose desire will carry it, little by little toward the comprehension of its tasks and its aims at the same time that its field of exploration and its perspective enlarge. With each step gained, seeing and desiring more, feeling the center within itself vivified and enlivened, it will see also the shadows disappearing – the somber enigmas of the world resolving – and the way brightened by powerful rays of light. With the shadows will vanish, little by little, narrow prejudices, vain terrors, and apparent contradictions of the universe. Harmony will reign and man will feel his heart and his thoughts enlarged. He will advance anew toward the end of his work, yet his work has no end – for each time humanity lifts itself toward a new ideal which it believes to be the supreme ideal, it has in truth attained only to the system corresponding to its own degree of evolution. But each time, also, from every effort made toward higher ideals will flow new forces and new pleasures, and it will find in the joy of life and progression, which is the law of being, a more intimate communion with the universe, and a more complete possession of goodness and beauty.

O writers, artists, poets, you whose numbers increase daily, whose productions multiply like a rising tide, often beautiful in form, but weak at the foundation – superficial and material, what talents you expend on mediocre results! What vast efforts are wasted on evil passions, on inferior and unworthy interests! While vast and magnificent horizons surround you, while the marvelous book of the universe and the soul lies open before you, while genius invites you to noble tasks which will fertilize the advancement of humanity, you rest contented with puerile and sterile studies, with work which blunts the conscience, and wherein the spirit swoons and languishes in the exaggerated cult of impure instincts.

Who among you will give the world the epic of the soul striving for the conquest of its destiny in the immense cycle of the ages – its sorrows and its joys, its descent into the abysses of life, its rising on wings of aspiration into the light – its immolations and holocausts which are ransoms for past acts – its redeeming missions and its growing participation in divinity? Which one of you will give to earth the powerful harmonies of the universe – the gigantic harp vibrating under the thought of God – the song of worlds, the eternal rhythm which rocks the cradle of the stars and the humanities! Or the slow elaborating, the powerful gestation of the conscience through inferior stages – the laborious construction of an individuality, a moral being? Who will tell of the conquests of life – life always growing greater, more serene, more illumined by rays from on high? The march from summit to summit, the pursuit of happiness – of power and pure love? Who will sing the work of man – immortal toiler, lifting through his doubts, anguish and tears, the sublime and harmonious edifice of his thinking consciousness and personality – always onward – always upward – always higher? Who will teach us these things? The inner voices, and the voices from Beyond! Learn to open and turn the leaves and read the book hidden in you – the book of being. It will tell you what you have been, and what you will be: it will teach you the greatest of mysteries – the creation of the self, by constant effort and sovereign action, which, in the silence of your thoughts, awakens your genius, and stirs you to paint beautiful pictures, sculpture ideal forms, compose harmonious symphonies, and write glorious poems. All is there in you – around you: all is speaking, all is vibrating – the visible and the invisible: all is chanting the glory of life, the intoxication of thought, of creation, of association with the work universal: splendor of seas and starry heavens, majesty of white mountain peaks, perfume of flowers, luster of rays, mysterious voices of the forests, melodies of earth and space, the voices of the Invisible which speak in the silence of the evening: the voice of conscience, that echo of the voice divine – all are teaching and revealing to him who knows how to listen, comprehend, think, and act. Then above all, the supreme vision, the vision without forms, the incarnated thought, the final harmony of the essence of the law which unites all things, from our inner souls to the farthest star in its resplendent unity.

And the chain of life, winding into infinity – a ladder of spiritual power which carries to God the appeals of man by prayer, and brings to man the response of God by inspiration! And now one more question. Why, in the midst of the immense labor and abundant intellectual production which characterizes our epoch, do we find so few notable works and great conceptions? Because we have ceased to see divine things with the eyes of the soul, because we have ceased to believe and love! Let us then return to the celestial and eternal source; it is the only remedy for our anemic morality. Let us turn our thoughts to things solemn and profound. May science illuminate and complete by the intuitions of consciousness the higher faculties of the mind. Modern spiritualism will lend its aid.

5
DISCIPLINE OF THOUGHT AND REFORM OF CHARACTER

We have said that thought is creative. It not only acts about us, influencing others for good or ill, but above all, it acts in us; It generates our words and our actions, and by them constructs each day the glorious or miserable edifice of our life present and to be. We fashion our soul and its envelope by our thoughts. They produce forms and images which are printed on the subtle material of which our etheric body is composed. So little by little our life is peopled with forms frivolous or austere, gracious or terrible, gross or sublime; and the soul shines with beauty, or grows ugly and repulsive. There is no subject more important than the study of thought, its powers and its action. It is the initial cause of our elevation or our abasement. It prepares all the discoveries of science, all the marvels of art, but also all the misery and shamefulness of humanity.

Following its given impulse, it founds or destroys institutions, empires and characters. Man is only great, save through his thoughts, for by them his works shine and are perpetuated through the centuries. Psychical research, better than all anterior doctrines, permits us to seize and comprehend all the force of the projection of thought. We see it acting in spiritual phenomena, which it facilitates or fetters. Its role in experimental séances is always a considerable one. Telepathy has demonstrated to us that minds can influence one another at a distance. This is the means which is employed by the humanities in space, to communicate among themselves across sidereal immensities. In all fields of social activities, in all the domains of worlds visible or invisible, the action of thought is sovereign. It is no less so in ourselves, and upon ourselves, rebuilding and modifying constantly our inner nature. The vibrations of our thoughts and words, reiterated in a uniform manner, drive from us the elements which cannot vibrate in harmony, and attract the elements which accentuate the tendencies of the being. Often unconsciously a work is elaborated – a thousand mysterious workmen labor in the shadows. In the depths of the soul an entire destiny is outlined, and the hidden diamond is polished or marred. If we meditate upon elevated objects, on duty – sacrifice – wisdom – love – our being is impregnated, little by little, with the quality of our thoughts. That is why ardent, improvised prayer – the uprising of the soul to infinite powers – has so much virtue. In this solemn dialogue with the being and its cause, an influx from on high possesses us, and new senses are awakened. The comprehension and compensations of life augment in us, and we feel better than we can express the gravity and grandeur of the most humble existences. Prayer – the communion by thought with the spiritual universe, is the reaching of the soul toward beauty and the eternal verities: it is, for an instant, entrance into spheres of real life - life superior which has no limit. It, on the contrary, our thoughts are inspired by evil desires, by passion, jealousy, and hate, the images which they create accumulate in our etheric bodies gross and dark fluids. So we can at will make in ourselves light or shadow. All the communications from the Beyond tell us this. We are what we think, if we think with force and persistence and will. But almost always our thoughts pass constantly from on subject to another, rarely do we think for ourselves, but instead reflect the thousand incoherent thoughts of the environment where we dwell.

Few men know how to think: how to drink from profound sources - from the great reservoir of inspiration which each one carries within himself - even the most ignorant. They make for themselves an envelope peopled with ephemeral forms. Their minds are like a building open to every passer-by. Rays of light are mingled with shadows in perpetual chaos. It is the incessant combat between duty and passion, where passion usually wins. Before all other things, to learn how to control our thoughts is most important; how to discipline and turn them in one direction toward a noble and dignified goal.

The control of thought leads to the control of actions; for if one is good the other will be equally so, and harmony will regulate our lives. If our acts are good and our thoughts are bad, and we carry in ourselves a false center, sooner or later the influence of our evil thoughts will fall fatally upon us. Sometimes we see a striking contradiction between the thoughts, writings, and actions of certain men, and we are led to doubt the good faith and sincerity of their utterances. But often the acts of these men are but the blind impulsion of thoughts and forces accumulated in past lives. Their high aspirations presented in their thoughts and words will be realized in future actions. Without the theory of successive lives, such contradictions of character are inexplicable.

It is good to live in contact by thought with writers of genius, the veritably great authors of all times and all countries; to read and meditate on their works, to impregnate the being with the substance of their souls. The radiations of their thoughts will awaken in us similar efforts and lead to modifications of our character through the impressions received. It is well to choose our reading with care, then to let our thoughts ripen it until we can assimilate the quintessence. In general we read too much - too hastily - and meditate not at all! It is better to read less and reflect more on what we read. It is a sure method of fortifying our intelligence to gather the fruits of wisdom and beauty which we find in good books: in that as in all things, the beautiful attracts and generates the beautiful, even as goodness attracts and generates the beautiful, even as goodness attracts happiness, and evil suffering. In silent, reflective study lies development of the thoughts. The greatest works are elaborated in the silence. In meditation the mind is concentrated: it turns toward the grave and serious side of things: the light spiritual world inundates it.

About the thinker, invisible great spirits come, eager to inspire him. It is in the half-light of tranquil hours, or in the discreet shade of his study lamp, that they can best enter into communication with him: everywhere and always an occult life mingles with ours.

Avoid noisy discussions, vain words, frivolous reading: read daily papers sparingly. Passing lightly as they do from one subject to another, they render the mind unstable. We live in a period of anemic intellectuality which is caused by the rarity of serious study and the insufficient educative system: let us attach ourselves to substantial works – to works which can enlighten us on the profound laws of life and facilitate our evolution. Little by little we will find growing in us a greater intelligence and consciousness, and our etheric body will shine with reflections of high and pure thoughts. Because of the thousand exterior objects which occupy it without cessation, the mind rarely probes its own depths. Its surface, like that of the sea, is often agitated, but beneath are regions that the storms do not reach.

There lie those hidden powers which await our call to appear. The appeal is made rarely, and man remains ignorant of the treasures which repose in him. It requires the shock of trouble and sorrow to make him understand the fragility of exterior things and to guide him toward the search of himself – toward the discovery of his spiritual wealth. That is why great souls become more noble and beautiful as their sorrows become keener: with each new blow, they have the consciousness of approaching a little nearer to truth and perfection, and this thought is like a bitter tonic. A new star has arisen in the heaven of their destiny – a star whose trembling rays penetrate to the inner sanctuary of their being, illuminating every hidden corner.

In minds of high intelligence and culture sorrow sows rich seeds, and every grief is a blade from which springs a harvest of virtue and beauty. At certain hour of our lives – the death of a mother – the crushing of an ardent hope – the loss of a loved one – each time that one of the ties which binds us to this world is broken, a mysterious voice cries from the depths of our souls – a solemn voice which speaks to us of a thousand laws more august and venerable than those of earth and an ideal world damns on us. But the voices of earth stifle this voice, and the human mind falls again almost always into its doubts and its hesitations, on the vulgar plane of earth existence.

There is no progress possible without attentive self-analysis. We must watch over our impulsive actions in order to know in what manner to improve ourselves. First we must regulate the physical life and reduce the material needs to the necessities, in order to secure health of the body, that indispensable instrument of our earthly role. Then comes the discipline of the emotions and impulses, their domination and utilization as agents for the perfection of character. We must learn the art of forgetfulness of self – of the sacrifice of the lesser ME, and the elimination of all selfishness. He only is truly happy in this life who has learned self- forgetfulness. It is not enough to believe and know - we must live our faith and knowledge; we must penetrate our daily life with the high principles we have adopted. We must habituate ourselves to communicate by thought, will, and heart with the eminent spirits who have revealed themselves to us- with the elite souls who have served as guides for humanity. We must live with them in a daily intimacy, inspire ourselves by their views, and feel their influence by that perception which develops our rapport with worlds invisible.

Among these great souls it is good to choose one who seems the most worthy of our admiration, and in all difficult circumstances, where we oscillate between two decisions, to ask ourselves what this great soul would have done under similar circumstances. We can construct, little by little, upon this model, an ideal which will be reflected in all our actions. The most humble man can make himself a sublime character in this way. The work is slow and difficult, but centuries are given us for it. We must often concentrate our thoughts, and bring them back to the ideal. We must meditate upon it each day at a chosen hour, preferably the morning, when all is peaceful about us. 'The hour divine,' when nature, rested and refreshed, awakens in the rays of the dawn. In those matinal hours the soul, by prayer and meditation, lifts itself more easily to the great heights from which we can see and comprehend that all life is united to something grand and eternal, and that we inhabit a world where invisible powers live and work with us. In the simplest life, in the most modest task, in the most effaced existence, there is always a profound side - and ideal storeroom containing sources of possible beauty. Each soul can, by its thoughts, create a spiritual atmosphere as beautiful, as resplendent as that of any enchanted realm; and in the meanest dwelling, the most miserable lodging, there are windows opening towards God and infinity.

In our social relations we must constantly recall this: all men are travelers on the march, occupying diverse places on the ladder of evolution, which we are all climbing. Therefore we must demand and expect nothing which does not pertain to their degree of advancement.

To each fellow traveler we owe tolerance, good will and even pardon, for those who seek to injure or wound us are merely delayed souls, insufficiently developed. God asks of no man aught that he has not acquired by slow, painful labor. We have not the right to ask more. Have we not been like these unawakened souls in former lives? If each one of us could read in his past what he had been, and what he had done, we would be more indulgent toward the faults of humanity. Let us be severe for ourselves and tolerant toward others - instruct, enlighten, and guide them gently. That is what the law of solidarity commands.

So we must bear all things with patience and serenity: whatever are the acts of other toward us, we must hold no animosity, no resentment, but use the painful experience for our moral education. No misfortune could come to us if by our anterior lives we had not paved the way to adversity. This is what we must often say to ourselves, and in this way we arrive at the acceptance of all trials without bitterness, considering them a reparation for the past. They prove a means of self-possession, and produce that absolute confidence in the future which gives force, quietude, and inner satisfaction, enabling us to keep serene in the midst of the hardest vicissitudes.

When age comes, illusions and vain hopes fall like dead leaves; but the eternal truths shine with greater brilliancy, like stars in winter skies over the leafless trees in our gardens.

It matters little then if it has enriched our souls with one virtue, and with a little moral beauty. The lives of obscurity and torment are sometimes the most fertile; while those which are brilliant with successes chain us to formidable responsibilities. Happiness is not in exterior things, but in ourselves. The wise man creates in himself an assured refuge, a sacred place, a profound retreat, where the discords of the outer world cannot enter. Each soul carries in itself its lights or its shadows, its Paradise or its Hell, but let us remember that nothing is irreparable: the situation of the most inferior spirit is but one point, almost imperceptible, in the immensity of his destiny.

6
LOVE

Love, as generally understood on earth, is a sentiment of impulsion between two beings who desire a closer union. But in reality, love is clothed in infinite forms, from the most vulgar to the most sublime. Principle of life universal, it procures for the soul in its highest and purest manifestation that intensity of radiation which warms and vivifies all and everything about it; and by its power the soul feels itself closely united to Divinity, the ardent center of all life and love.

God is love: it was through love He created beings to associate them with His joys and His works. Love is a sacrifice. God poured out His own life to give it to souls. At the same time with the vital effusion, they received the effective principle, destined to grow and blossom in them through duty and sacrifice to others. So are they ennobled and glorified as they approach the Supreme Center. Love is an inexhaustible force – it constantly renews itself, and at the same time enriches those who give and those who receive. It is by love, the sun of souls, through which God acts in the world. By it He attracts to Himself all the poor beings delayed by human passions and made captive by matter! And He lifts them, and leads them up the spiral of infinite ascension toward the splendors of light and liberty. It has disciplined and fashioned the human soul, and helped to turn the entire race from sensualism and bestiality.

Christ is not the only example of radiant souls on earth. There others who seem to send forth a regenerating exhalation – an atmosphere of peace and protection, as if endowed by a special Providence. All those who live under their moral influence feel a repose of spirit and a serenity which is a foretaste of celestial quietude. In a circle of seekers after spirituals truths, directed and inspired by spirits from high realms, this sensation becomes keener. We have often felt ourselves in the presence of these great entities in the work of our group in Tours.

These impressions become more and more alive, in the measure that one becomes separated from inferior planes, where selfish impulses reign, and climbs the stairs of the glorious spiritual hierarchy, and begins to approach the Divine Center. Then comes the experience which completes the intuitions that each soul is a system of force, and a generator of love whose power of action grows with its elevation. So is explained and affirmed the universal fraternity. Some day, when the true idea of life disengages itself from the doubts and incertitude which obsess human thought, we will comprehend this grand brotherhood of souls.

We feel that all are enveloped by the divine magnetism, by the breath of love which fills space. Apart from this powerful tie, souls also constitute separate groups of families, which are formed during centuries by the community of joys, sorrows, and trials. The real family is that of space, and the one of earth is but an image – a feeble reflection, as are all the things of earth, compared to those of heaven. The true family is composed of spirits who together have climbed the rude paths of destiny, and who have learned how to understand, and how to love. Who can describe the intimate and tender sentiments which unite these beings – the ineffable joy born of the fusion of their minds and consciousness, the fluidic union of souls under the smile of God? These spiritual groups are the hallowed center where selfishness vanishes, where hearts dilate, and where the souls that have suffered and are delivered by death come to rejoin their beloved ones.

Who can paint the ecstasy of purified souls, arriving at the summits of light, filled with divine love! And the celestial lovers, bound together in the bosom of the families of space, assembled to consecrate by solemn rites the symbolic and indestructible union! That is the veritable hymen of twin souls which God binds together by a golden thread for eternity. They will follow each other henceforth in their pilgrimages through the worlds; they will march hand in hand, smiling at misfortune, and finding in their mutual tenderness the force to endure all the bitterness of fate. Sometimes, separated by rebirths, they still conserve the secret intuition that their isolation is but passing. After the trials of separation, they foresee the intoxication of a reunion at the doorway of the immensities. Among those who walk here sad and solitary, bowed under the burden of life, there are those who keep, deep in their hearts, the vague memory of their spiritual family. Those souls suffer cruelly with homesickness for space and celestial love, and nothing in all the joys of earth can console them. Their thoughts go often in the waking hours, but more frequently in sleep, to join the beloved beings who await them in the Beyond. The profound sentiments of expected compensations give them moral force in their struggle and aspirations toward a better world. Hope sows with austere flowers the desert paths they thread.

All the powers of the soul are confined in three words – to will – to know – and to love. To will, that is to converge all the activity, all the energy toward the aim to be attained, and to develop will power and direct it. To know, because without profound study – without the acquaintance of things and laws, the thought and the will can lose themselves in the midst of forces they seek to conquer, and the elements they aspire to command.

But above all it is important to love, for without love, will and science will be incomplete and often sterile. Love illuminates them – fertilizes them, and increases their resources a hundredfold. It is not here a question of love which contemplates without action, but of that which employs itself in spreading truth and goodness in the world. Life on earth is a conflict between good and evil forces. The duty of every virile soul is to take part in the combat, and with all its powers alert, to aid those who struggle in obscurity. The noblest use one can make of his faculties is to work toward the enlarging and developing of the sense of beauty and being in this human society, which has its ugly features, but which is rich with magnificent promises. These promises will be transformed into living realities the day when humanity learns to communicate, by thought and heart, with the center of love which is the splendor of God. Love, then, with all the power of your heart! Love to the point of sacrifice, as Jeanne d'Arc loved France! As Christ loved humanity! And all those about you will feel your influence, and be born to new life.

O men, look about you, and seek to heal wound – to cure evils – to console affliction. Work to build the high city of peace and harmony which will be the city of Love – the city of God. Enlighten, uplift, and purify, and what matters it if some one laughs at you – if ingratitude and meanness rise in your path! Those who love do not fall back before such things. Even if they gather but thistles and thorns, they pursue their work, because duty is there. They know growth lies in abnegation, and sacrifice has its joys. Accomplished with love it transforms tears into smiles. To him who truly loves, the most banal things possess an interest – everything is illuminated, and a thousand new sensations awake in him.

Knowledge requires long and painful efforts to reach the altitudes of thought. Love and sacrifice gain them at a bound, with one stroke of the wings! Love refines the intelligence and enlarges the heart, and it is by the amount of love accumulated in us that we can measure the distance we have traveled on the road to God.

To all the interrogations of man, to his hesitations, fears, and blasphemies, a voice powerful and mysterious responds: "Learn to love! Love is the aim and end and summit of all!" From this summit unfolds without cessation a network of love, woven of gold and light. To love is the secret of happiness; with one word love solves all problems and dissipates all obscurities. Love will save the world. Its natural warmth will melt the ice of doubt, of selfishness, of hate. It will reach the hardest heart – the hearts of the most refractory. Love is always an effort toward beauty. The sexual love of man and woman loses all vulgar characteristics when it is aureoled with the poetic ideal, and mingles with the material, aesthetic sentiment a higher emotion. This depends largely on the woman. She, who truly loves, feels and sees things unknown to man; she possesses in her heart an inexhaustible reservoir of love, a sort of intuition of love eternal. Woman is ever, on one side, sister of mystery, and the part of her being which touches the infinite seems broader than ours. When man responds with her to the call of the Invisible – when their love is exempt from mere bestial desires, then they become one in spirit and one in body; in the embraces of these two beings a light like a flame passes and penetrates – a reflection of the highest felicities.

Yet the joys of earthly love are fugitive and mingled with bitterness. They are never without disappointments and shocks. God only is love in its fullness. He is the foundation of thought and light, from which emanates, and to which returns eternally, the warm effluvia of the stars, the passionate tenderness of all the hearts of women – of mothers and wives, and the virile affection of the hearts of men. God generates and calls forth love, for it is beauty infinite, and the characteristic of beauty is to create love.

Who, on a summer day, with the sun illuminating the immense blue cupola above, with woods, fields, mountains, and seas offering up mute adoration to the Creator, who has not felt these radiations of love filling the universe? One must have refused to open his heart to these subtle influences if he ignores or denies them. Too many earthly souls, it is true, remain hermetically sealed to divine things. Or if they feel the harmonies and beauties, they hide the secret in themselves. They are ashamed to confess their consciousness of these great influences. Open the windows of your prison, O man, to the glory of life eternal, and that prison will be filled with light and melody! Your soul will be flooded with felicities and ecstasies indescribable. It will understand that it is surrounded by an ocean of love and divine force in whose waves it may bathe and be regenerated at will.

A consciousness will come of the sovereign power of the universe which envelops and sustains us, and that by invoking it, and addressing to it an ardent appeal, the soul will be penetrated by its presence and love. These things are difficult to express; they are only understood by those who have tasted them. Nevertheless, all can arrive at this knowledge, and can possess it by awakening the divine in themselves. There is no man so wicked, who in the hour of suffering does not become dimly conscious of higher things, who does not feel a little of the divine love filtering through him. It is only necessary to feel these impressions once never to forget them, and when the evening of life comes with disenchantments, when the twilight shadows fall about us, then these powerful sensations awaken in us the memory of all the joys we have felt; and the souvenir of hours when we have truly loved, like a delicious dew descends upon our souls, dried by the arid winds of trials and sorrows.

7
SORROW

All living things suffer on earth – animals and men. Nevertheless, love is the law of the universe, and by love God formed beings. A formidable contradiction in appearance, an agonizing problem which has troubled many thinkers and carried them to doubt and pessimism.

The animal is subjected to an ardent battle for life. Among the herbs of the prairie, under the leaves in the woods, in the air, in the bosom of the waters, everywhere unknown dramas are enacted. In our cities, inoffensive beasts are continually sacrificed to human needs, or delivered to laboratories for the torture of vivisection. As for humanity, its history is one long martyrdom. Through time, and over the centuries, rises the sad miserere of human suffering. The plaint of the unhappy mounts with the regularity of an ocean wave, and with a heartbreaking intensity. Sorrow follows in the path of each of us and watches all our detours, and before the sphinx who fixes upon him her strange look, man asks the eternal question, 'Why is sorrow?' Is it a punishment – an expiation? Is it a reparation for the past – a ransom for faults committed? At the foundation, sorrow is only a law of education and equilibrium. Without doubt the faults of the past fall upon us with all their burdens, and determine the conditions of our destiny. Suffering is often only the counterstroke of violations of eternal order: but shared by all, it should be considered as an agent of development –

a condition of progress. All beings must submit to it in their turn; its action is beneficial to those who understand it, but only those can understand it who has felt its powerful effects. It is, above all, to those I address these pages – those who suffer, who have suffered, or are worthy to suffer.

~

Sorrow and pleasure are the two extreme forms of sensation. To suppress one or the other, we must suppress sensibility; they are inseparable in principle, and both are necessary to the education of the being, who in his evolution must drain all the illimitable forms of pleasure and of sorrow.

Physical pain produces sensations: moral suffering, sentiments. But as we have seen in chapter XXI, sensation and sentiment become one in the inner sensorium. Pleasure and sorrow reside, then, less in exterior things than within us. Epictetus said: 'Things are only what we figure them to be.' Genius is not only the result of long labor, it is also the crown of suffering. Homer, Dante, Tass, Milton, and all great men suffered. Sorrow caused vibrations in their souls, and it inspired the nobility of sentiment and the intensity of emotion which they expressed in accents of immortal genius. The soul never sings better than when in sorrow. When pain touches the depths of being, it brings forth eloquent and powerful appeals which move the world.

It is the same with heroes and all great characters. Their elevation is measured by the amount of suffering endured. Before sorrow and death, the soul of the hero and martyr reveals itself in touching beauty, or in tragic grandeur, and is aureoled by an inextinguishable light. Suppress sorrow, and you suppress at the same time that which is most worthy of the admiration of the world, that is to say, the courage which supports it. Is not the memory of those who have died for truth and justice the noblest teaching we can offer to humanity? Is there anything more august than their tombs? The centuries seem to render such souls more and more imposing. They are like sources of force and beauty, where the generations come to refresh themselves. Through time and space their light, like the rays of the stars, reaches to earth. Their death brings forth life, and their memory, like a subtle aroma, reaches into the far future.

These souls have taught us that it is by duty and by suffering borne worthily, that we blaze the trail to heaven. The history of the world is but the story of the coronation of the soul by sorrow. Without it, virtue could not be complete, or glory imperishable.

We must suffer, to grow and to conquer; acts of sacrifice increase spiritual radiations. There is a luminous train which follows spirits of heroes and martyrs in space. Those who have not suffered cannot comprehend these things, for they see only the surface of life; their feelings have not been amplified, and their thoughts embrace only narrow horizons. So, by the will, we can vanquish sorrow, or at least turn it to our profit, and make it an instrument of elevation. The idea that we make for ourselves of joy and pain varies infinitely with the evolution of the individual. The good, wise, and pure soul cannot find happiness in the same manner as the vulgarian. As we mount, the aspect of things changes, and the child, growing, disdains the toys which once captivated him. So the growing soul seeks nobler satisfactions and pleasures more profound. The soul which looks from the heights and sees the glorious aim of life finds more felicity and serene peace in a beautiful thought, a good work, an act of virtue, and even a purifying sorrow, than in all material wealth and earthly glories, with their false intoxications. It is difficult to make man understand that suffering is good. Each one would remake and embellish his life to his own taste, pluck from it all annoyances and troubles, not thinking that there is no good without ill, no ascension without toil and effort.

The general tendency of man is to shut himself in the narrow circle of individualism, of self, and in that way he dwarfs and limits all that is great in himself – all that is meant to dilate and grow and soar: the thought, the consciousness – in a word, the soul. To break this circle and give freedom to the imprisoned virtues, sorrow is necessary. Misfortunes and trials stir in us the sources of an unknown life – a more profound life. Sadness and suffering cause us to see, hear, and feel a thousand delicate and powerful things that the happy or the vulgar man never perceives. The material world begins to seem obscure – another is vaguely designed but grows more and more distinct, in the measure that our attention is detached from inferior things and plunged into the illimitable.

Misfortune and anguish are needed to give the soul its richness, its moral beauty, and to awaken its sleeping senses. The sorrowful life is an alembic from which are distilled souls for better worlds. The form, like the soul, is embellished by suffering. There is a charm, at once tender and serious, in the faces which have been often bathed in tears. They take on an austere beauty – a sort of majesty – impressive, yet seductive.

Michael Angelo adopted, as rule of his life, the following principles: 'Enter into yourself, and do as the sculptor does with the work he seeks to make beautiful. Chisel off that which is superfluous, make clear that which is obscure, let in the light from everywhere, and never cease chiseling your own statue.' A sublime maxim, and which contains the principle of inner perfection. The soul is our work – a work which surpasses in grandeur all the partial manifestations of art.

Often the difficulties of execution are in accord with the splendor of the aim; and before this painful task of interior reform, of incessant combat with the passions and material conditions, how often is the artisan discouraged! How often he drops his chisel in despair! It is then God sends him an aid – sorrow! Sorrow goes into the depths of the consciousness where the toiler himself could not penetrate, and remodels the contours, and eliminates or destroys that which is useless or bad. And from the cold marble without form or beauty, from the ugly or coarse statue that our hands have hardly outlined, sorrow brings forth in time the chef- d'oeuvre incomparable, the harmonic form of the divine Psyche.

Sorrow does not, then, strike only the culpable. In our world, honest men suffer as much as the wicked. The virtuous soul, being more evolved, is more sensitive. Besides this, it loves deeply, and so seeks sorrow, knowing the price. There are souls who come to earth for no other purpose than to give an example of grandeur of suffering. They are missionaries, and their mission is no less grand than that of the great revealers. We meet them in all times, and they occupy all planes of life – on high summits, splendid with the light of history, and they are found among the humble and hidden in the common masses. We admire Christ, Socrates, Antigone, but how many obscure victims of duty and love fall every day, upon whom descend silence and forgetfulness. Yet their example is not lost: it illuminates the life of someone who was a witness to it. To be full and fruitful, it is not indispensable that a life should be sown with acts of great sacrifice, or crowned by a tragic death in the eyes of the world. There are many sad, colorless, effaced lives which are a continual effort, a constant strife against misfortune and suffering. If we knew the hidden wounds in these hearts – the cruel disappointments concealed from the world, they would be as interesting in our sight as the most celebrated martyrs.

By this incessant combat with destiny they become heroic souls. Their triumphs are unknown, but all the treasures of energy, of generous impulses, of patience and love which they have accumulated day by day, constitute a capital of moral force and beauty which makes them equal to the noblest figures of history in the world beyond.

In the heavenly workshop where souls are forged, genius and glory are not sufficient to render them truly beautiful. To give them the last sublime touch, sorrow is always necessary. Certain obscure existences become as holy and sacred as those of the celebrated martyrs, because of their continued sufferings. It was not because by some one great moment, or some circumstance of a tragic death, that they were lifted above themselves, to the admiration of the centuries, but because their whole lives were a constant immolation; and this long defile of sorrowful hours which prepared them for ultimate ascension forced the admiration of the spirits themselves; and these touching spectacles inspire the great spirits with a willingness to be born again, and to suffer and die again for all they love, and by a new sacrifice to reach still greater heights of glory.

Physical suffering is often an effort of nature which seeks to save us from excess. Without it we would abuse our organs to the point of untimely destruction. When a serious malady attacks us, it often becomes a benefit by causing us to realize and to detest the vices which have caused it. Sometimes we must suffer to understand the laws of health. To weak souls, sickness comes to teach patience, wisdom, and self-control. To strong souls if offers ideal compensations, in leaving the mind free for flights of aspiration, to the point of forgetting physical suffering. Suffering is no less efficacious for society collective than for the individual. Through it were formed the first human groups.

Through the menace of wild beasts, of hunger and floods, men were constrained to band themselves together, and through their common lives, their common sufferings, through their intelligence and labor, came forth civilization, the arts, sciences, and industries. Again, we can say that physical suffering results often from the disproportion between our corporeal weakness and the colossal forces which surround us. We can only assimilate for ourselves an infinitesimal portion of these forces, but they act upon us constantly, striving to enlarge the sphere of our activity and the power of our sensations. The action on the physical organs reflects on the etheric form, and renders it more impressionable.

Suffering, by its chemical action, has a useful result, but this result varies infinitely according to the state of individual development. In refining our material body, it gives greater force to the interior, more facility for detaching itself from earthly things. Others, more evolved, are affected morally. Sorrow is like a wing lent by the Over Soul to the flesh, to enable it to soar to the heights.

The first movement of unhappy man is that of revolt under the blows of fate. But later, when the soul has climbed to heights where it contemplates the way it has trod, the moving defile of its existences, it is with tender joy that it recalls the trials and tribulations which enabled it to attain to an understanding of truth.

If, in the hours of trial, we know how to watch the mysterious action of sorrow in ourselves, we would better comprehend its sublime work of education and perfectionment. Sorrow always strikes our most sensitive point – the hand which directs the chisel is that of an incomparable artist. It never wearies until all the angles of our characters are rounded and polished. To that end it returns to its work as often as is necessary. Under the repeated strokes of the hammer, conceit, egotism, apathy, indifference, anger and cruelty, all must fall one by one.

For each one of us sorrow has its different methods, varied as the individual, but for all it acts efficiently, in a manner to develop delicacy, feeling, and sympathy, and to give birth to qualities which slept in the depths of the being, or to some new nobility never before acquired. And the more the soul responds and grows under sorrow, the more spiritualizing become the effects of sorrow.

The wicked require innumerable trials, as a tree must bear many flowers before yielding fruit. But the more the nature is perfected, the more admirable become the fruits. To gross souls come violent physical suffering; to the selfish and mercenary, loss of fortune; to the pessimists, torment of mind; for delicate souls, hidden sorrows and heart wound; and to great thinkers, subtle and profound grieves which send forth sublime cries from the source of genius.

Astonishing, as it may seem at first, sorrow is but a means of infinite power to attract us to it, and at the same time to bring us more rapidly to spiritual happiness, which alone is durable. So it is, then, God's love which sends sorrow to us. He corrects us as a mother corrects her child, to teach it to do better. He works without cessation to purify and embellish our souls, which cannot be completely happy, save as they are perfected. For that purpose is the earthly apprenticeship. God has placed beside rare and fugitive joys, frequent and prolonged sorrows, in order that we may realize that our world is only a passageway, not a goal. Joys and sufferings—pleasures and sorrows – God has spread these things in our existence, as a great artist unites on his canvas the lights and shadows to produce his chef-d'oeuvre.

Suffering is a rudimentary method of animal evolution. Through it they acquire the first dawning of consciousness. It is the same with human beings in successive incarnations. If, from its earthly stations, the soul were exempt from suffering, it would remain inert – passive, and ignorant of profound moral truths. Our aim is onward! Our destiny is to march toward the goal without stopping by the way. The joys of this world immobilize us, they retard us; then sorrow comes and pushes us forward. As soon as there opens for us a source of pleasure, for instance in our youth, love and marriage – and we lose ourselves in the enchantment of these blessings, almost always soon afterward an unforeseen circumstance arises, and the blade of sorrow is felt.

In the measure that we advance in life, joys diminish and sorrows increase. The body becomes heavier – the weight of years more burdensome. With most lives, existence commences in happiness and ends in sadness. With age, the light grows dim, dreams vanish – sympathies and consolations lessen. Graves thicken about us; then come the long hours of inaction and suffering. They oblige us to enter into ourselves, and to review our lives. This is a necessary trial for the soul, in order that before it quits the body it may acquire a clear-seeing judgment of the events of its terrestrial careers. So when we curse the hours of age, which are in appearance desolate and sterile, we ignore one of the greatest benefits which nature has offered us. We forget that sorrowful old age is the crucible wherein the soul completes its purification.

At this moment of existence the forces which during the years of virility we dispense in every direction in our exuberance, concentrate and converge toward the profound depths of being, awakening the consciousness and procuring wisdom for the man of maturity. Little by little harmony is established between our thoughts and the exterior radiations, and the inner melody chords with the melody divine. There is then, in resigned old age, more of grandeur and serene beauty than in the éclat of youth or the power of maturity. Under the action of time, all that is profound and everlasting in us frees itself, and the brows of certain aged men and women are aureoled with light from the Beyond.

To all who ask 'Why is sorrow?' I respond: 'Why do we polish the gem – sculpture the marble – hammer the iron – melt the glass?' It is in order to build and ornament the magnificent temple full of rays, of vibrations, of hymns, of perfumes, where all the arts combine to express the divine; to prepare the apotheosis of conscious thought – to celebrate the liberation of the spirit. And behold the result obtained! All that is elementary in us departs. Material unformed, or ruined and broken, is by sorrow used to construct a splendid altar in the heart of man, of moral beauty and eternal truth. In the gross block of marble is hidden the ideal statue, and when man has not the energy, the knowledge, or the will to bring it forth, then comes sorrow. It takes the hammer and the chisel, and little by little, with strokes violent or persistent, the living statue is designed with supple contours and gleaming beauty. Under the broken quartz the glowing emerald shines!

Yes, in order that the form comes forth in all its pure and delicate lines, that spirit triumphs over the substance, that the thoughts keep to sublime heights, that the poet finds his immortal accents, the musician his perfect chords, our hearts must feel the lancet of fate. We must know mourning and tears, ingratitude and treason, the deception of friends, and the anguish of disillusionment. We must see cherished forms descend into the tomb – youth depart, and old age come, with its bitter sorrows. Man must suffer, as the fruit of the vine is pressed that its exquisite liquid may be extracted.

It is in our own consciousness that lies the reward of good and evil. It registers minutely all our acts, and sooner or later becomes a severe judge of the culpable ones who, by the law of evolution, finally yield to its voice and submit to its control. The spirit in space suffers remorse for its far distant wrong acts, as well as for the more recent ones. That is why it often asks to be reincarnated, that it may make reparation for evils committed, and gain freedom from obsessing memories.

On different planes suffering changes its aspect. With us it becomes at once physical and moral, and constitutes a mode of reparation. The sad pages of our early history, where we were ignorant souls, we have been able to efface in later incarnations. By suffering we have learned humility, at the same time with indulgence and compassion for all those about us who succumb to low instincts, as we once did.

It is not, then, by vengeance that the law strikes us, but because it is good and profitable to suffer, since suffering liberates us, while it executes the verdict of the conscience. We hear much of the law of retaliation, but reparation does not always present itself in the form of the act committed. Social conditions and historic evolution oppose that. With the torments of the Middle Ages many scourges have disappeared. Nevertheless, the sum of human suffering under various forms remains proportionally the same. In vain progress is realized, civilization extended – hygiene and well-being developed; new maladies appear which man is powerless to cure. We must recognize in this that superior law of equilibrium of which we have spoken.

Suffering will be necessary as long as man does not think and act in harmony with eternal law. It will cease s soon as the accord is established. All our evils come from what we do in opposition to the currents of divine life. If we enter into this current, pain will disappear with the causes which gave it birth. For a long time to come, earthly humanity, ignorant of these superior laws, unconscious of duty, will have need of sorrow to stimulate it on its way and to transform its primitive and gross instincts into pure and generous sentiments. For a long time man must pass through the bitter initiative before arriving at knowledge of himself and his goal. At present he thinks only of using his faculties to combat physical suffering – to augment riches and well being on the material plane, and to render earthly conditions of life agreeable. But this is all in vain. Suffering changes its aspect as the conditions of earth change, but it is no less suffering, and while selfishness and personal interests govern earthly society – while the human thoughts turn away from profound subjects, just so long the flowers of the soul will not bloom. All the social and economic doctrines of the world will be powerless to reform it, or to alleviate the woes of humanity, because their foundation is too narrow, and they place on one brief earth life the reason of being, the end and aim of this existence, and of all our efforts.

To extinguish the evil in society we must elevate the human soul to the consciousness of its role, make it understand that its fate depends upon itself, and that its felicity will be always proportional to the extent of its triumphs over itself and its devotion to others. Then will the social question be resolved by the substitution of altruism for narrow and exclusive personalism. Men will feel themselves to be brothers, and equal by divine law, which gives to each the good and bad experiences necessary to his evolution, as the means of hastening his ascension. Only when that day comes will sorrow diminish its empire. Fruit of ignorance and selfishness, and of all the animal passions which still agitate the human soul, it will vanish with the causes which produced it, thanks to a higher education, and the realization in us of moral justice and love.

Moral evil is in the dissonance of the soul with divine harmony. In the degree that it mounts to a clearer view, toward a larger truth, toward a more perfect wisdom, the causes of suffering attenuate, at the same time that vain ambitions and material desires vanish. And step-by-step, from life to life, the soul penetrates into the great light and the great peace, where evil is unknown, and where good only reigns.

Often I have heard people whose lives have been sorrowful, say: 'I do not wish to be reborn on earth'. When one has been shaken by the violent storms of life, it is natural to long for repose. I understand how such a soul shrinks from the thought of recommencing this battle of life, where it has received wounds which are still bleeding! But law is inexorable, and to mount up in the hierarchy of worlds, it is necessary to leave here all the baggage of appetites and passions which attach us to earth. Souls that carry those desires beyond the grave are delayed, and tied to lower regions. Often those who believe themselves worthy of attaining high altitudes find themselves riveted to this planet by their tastes. They have not understood love in its divine essence, nor sacrifice for humanity, wherein one life not for self, but for all. To render themselves ripe for the higher worlds, they must re-descend into the crucible – into the furnace where the hardness of the heart melts like wax. And when the dross of the soul has been rejected, and the divine essence extracted, then God calls them to a higher life and a more beautiful task.

Above all, it is necessary to measure at their just value the cares and the sorrows of this life. For us these things are very cruel; but they dwarf and vanish when the spirit, elevated above the details of existence, embraces in a large outlook the perspective of its destiny. It alone knows how to weigh and measure events, and how to sound the depths of the two oceans of time and space – the immensity of Eternity.

8
REVELATION OF SORROW

It is in the face of suffering that we feel the necessity of a robust faith, which at the same time rests on reason and on facts, and which explains the enigma of life and the problem of sorrow. What consolation can materialism and atheism offer a man attacked by an incurable malady? What can they say to one about to die? What language can they use to the father or mother kneeling by the cradle of a dead child? To all those who see the forms of cherished beings descending into the earth? There and then is shown the poverty and insufficiency of those doctrines of nothing. Sorrow is not only the criterion of life – the judge which weighs the character and measures the true grandeur of the man; it is also the infallible process of recognizing the value of philosophical theories and religious doctrines. The best will evidently be that which comforts us, that which says: 'Why, tears are the human lot!' and at the same time furnishes the means of drying them. By sorrow we must surely discover the place from whence shines the brightest, purest ray of truth, which does not become extinguished.

For those whose lives are limited by narrow horizons of materialism, the problem of sorrow is insoluble. If the universe is but a field open to the capricious, blind forces of nature, then sorrow has no sense – no utility, and can find no consolations. Is it not really strange, how impotent have been so many of the sages and philosophers and thinkers, for thousand years, to explain sorrow, or give us consolation, or aid us to accept it! Sorrow is so inevitable! Yet few have comprehended it – fewer have explained it. About us every day, how poor, banal, and childish are the words of sympathy and the efforts at consolation offered to those who are stricken by sorrow. How cold are the words which fall from human lips! What absence of light and warmth in thoughts and hearts! What weakness – what voids – in the processes employed by those who seek to give comfort!

All this results mainly from the obscurity which rests upon the problem of sorrow, and the false doctrines of certain philosophies. They burden and shadow the soul in difficult hours, in place of giving it the means to face its destiny with a firm resolution.

And the religions? You ask. Yes, certainly, without doubt, the religions have given spiritual sustenance to souls in distress. Nevertheless, the consolations they offer repose upon a conception too narrow for the aim of life and the laws of destiny. The Christian religions comprise the grand role of suffering, but they have exaggerated it, and denatured its sense. Paganism expressed joy, and their gods were crowned with flowers at their fêtes. The Stoics, however, and certain secret schools considered sorrow as an indispensable element in the order of the world. Christianity deified it in the person of Jesus. Before the Cross of Calvary humanity found its own cross less heavy. The memory of the great sacrifice has aided man to suffer and die. But in pushing things to an extreme, Christianity has given life, death, religion, and God lugubrious and often terrifying aspects. It is necessary to readjust the religions, or they will lose their empire. Materialism threatens to take possession of their lost territory, for lack of a doctrine adapted to the necessities of the time and the needs of evolving humanity.

That is why we say to all the preachers of all religions: 'Enlarge the compass of your teachings – give man an idea of a more extended destiny – a clearer view of the life Beyond – a higher ideal of the goal to be attained. Make him comprehend that his work consists in reconstructing himself with the aid of sorrow to a higher consciousness for his moral personality through an infinity of time and space.' If, at the present moment, your influence as a teacher is weakened, it is not because of a lack of morale in those you teach – it is because of the insufficiency of your conception of life, which does not show clearly that justice rules: and consequently does not show God. Your theologies have enclosed thought in a narrow circle which stifles. They have given it too constrained a foundation, and on this foundation the edifice trembles and threatens to fall. Stop discussions of texts; come up out of the crypts where you have shut your soul – go forward and act! A new doctrine is rising – growing – extending – which will aid thought to accomplish its work of transformation. The new Spiritualism contains all the resources necessary to console the afflicted, enrich philosophy, regenerate religion, and to attract at one time the affection of the most humble disciple and the respect of the greatest genius. It satisfies the noblest flights of intellect and the aspirations of the heart. It explains human weakness – the torment of the inferior soul, a prey to passions – and it shows it the means of elevating itself to the fullness of knowledge. It offers the world a remedy against sorrow.

In the explanation which it gives, and the consolations it extends to the unfortunate, are found the most evident and touching proofs of its truthful character and unshaken solidity. Better than all other philosophies and religions, it reveals to us the great role of suffering and teaches us to accept it. In making of it an educative and reparative process, it shows us how divine love and justice enter into our trials and sorrows. In place of the despair which negative doctrines give us, in place of lost reprobates, it shows us in the unfortunate an apprentice and neophyte whom sorrow will initiate – a candidate for perfection and happiness.

In giving life an infinite goal, modern Spiritualism offers us a reason for living and suffering which makes life an object worthy of the soul and of God. In the apparent disaster and confusion of things, it shows us order which slowly outlines the future; and above all, it reveals to us an immense and divine harmony. And behold the consequences of this teaching! Sorrow loses its frightful character, an is no longer an enemy – a formidable monster; it is an aid – an auxiliary, and its role is providential. It purifies the soul in its flame, and it re-clothes it with unbelievable beauty. Man, at first astonished – alarmed at its aspect, learns to know, appreciate, and familiarize himself with sorrow, and ends with almost loving it! Certain heroic souls, in place of fleeing from it, go forward and plunge themselves freely in its regenerating waves. Sorrow is but a corrective for our errors, a stimulant on our march. So the sovereign laws show forth, just and good. They afflict no one with useless or unmerited pain. The study of the moral universe fills us with admiration for the power which, by means of sorrow, transforms little by little the forces of evil into good, and brings forth virtue from vice, and love from selfishness. Then, assured of the result of his efforts, man accepts with courage his inevitable trials. Age may come –life roll under the rapid wheel of the years, but his faith enables him to pass through the troubled periods and the sad hours of existence. In the measure that it declines and is shadowed by evening mists, the great light from Beyond grows clearer, and the sentiment of justice, goodness, and love which presides over the destinies of all beings, becomes for him a mighty force in hours of lassitude, and renders easier the preparation for departure.

For the materialist, and even for many believers in immortality, the death of beloved beings opens between them and us an abyss which nothing fills: an abyss of darkness, lighted by no rays – by no hope. Many are so crushed with despair, they do not even pray for their dead. Others are filled with dread of the Judgment Day, which may separate them forever from their loved ones.

But the new doctrine brings a certitude which nothing can shake. Death, like sorrow, has no terrors for them, for every tomb is a door of deliverance, an issue opening toward free space. Every friend who disappears goes to prepare a future dwelling – to mark out a route for us to follow later. Separation is only an appearance: we know that these souls have not left us forever. An intimate communion can be established between them and us. If their absolute manifestations encounter obstacles, we can correspond by thought: you know the telepathic law. It is not by cries and tears, not even by the call of love, that the messages go and come: the admirable solidarity of the souls for whom we pray, and who pray for us, the exchange of vibrating thoughts, and regenerating appeals which traverse space, penetrating agonized hearts with radiations of hope – these never miss their aim. You think you suffer alone; but no! Near to you, about you, there are beings who vibrate with your sorrow, and participate in your grief. Do not make it too intense – spare them useless suffering. To human grief and pain God has given for company celestial sympathy. This sympathy often comes in the form of a beloved being, who in the days of trial descends, full of solicitude, and gathering all our sorrows, makes them into a crown of light in space.

How many lovers, husbands, parents, separated by death, yet live with their dear ones in close intimacy? In the hour of affliction the spirits of a father, a mother, or other dear souls in space, lean down and caress us in affliction. They envelop our hearts with tender radiations of love. How can we let ourselves fall in despair in the presence of such witnesses, knowing that they read our thoughts – see our cares, and that they are waiting to receive us in the doorway of immensity.

Quitting the earth, we will find them, and with them a vast number of spirits we have forgotten: a crowd of those who shared our past lives and composed our spiritual family. All our companions of the great eternal journey group together to receive us; not as pale shadows – vague phantoms animated with fain life, but in the fullness of their accumulated faculties. Active beings, interested in the things of earth, participating in the universal work, co-operating in our efforts, in our labors, in our progress. The ties of the past are renewed with fresh force. Love, friendship – real relationship in multiple existence now cemented newly, are augmented, and given supreme power, which unites them again to those known and love on earth. The sadness of temporary separations, the apparent disappearance of souls caused by death, all melt in effusions of happiness and in the ineffable joy of reunion. Have no faith, then, in the somber doctrines which speak to you of brazen laws of condemnation, or of hells and heavens which separate you from those you love forever. There is no abyss love cannot bridge. God, who is all love, would not extinguish the most beautiful and noble sentiments in the human heart. Love is immortal, as is the soul. In the hour of suffering and anguish rouse yourself, and with an ardent appeal attract to you those beings who were once human like you, and who are now celestial spirits, and unknown forces will penetrate you, and will aid you to bear your miseries and sorrows. Man – sad voyager who painfully climbs the sorrowful mountain of existence, search everywhere upon your route for invisible beings, powerful and good, who are traveling beside you. In the difficult passage their mighty vibrations will sustain your trembling steps. Open your soul to them – put your thoughts in accord with their thoughts, and soon you will feel the joy of their presence. An atmosphere of peace and benediction will envelop you, and sweet consolation will descend upon you.

∽

In the midst of trials, the truths which we have just related do not enable us always to dispense with emotion or tears. That would be contrary to nature, but these truths teach us at least not to murmur, not to be crushed under the blows of sorrow. They drive away impotent ideas of revolt – of despair – of suicide, which often haunt the brains of materialists. If we continue to weep, it is without bitterness and without blasphemy.

Even when a young soul, carried away by mad passion, leaves earth by the door of suicide, the immense sorrow of a mother can find hope in the new spiritual philosophy. By unremitting prayer, by ardent thoughts, remains the hope of helping the unfortunate soul which floats in space, between earth and heaven, awaiting its natural hour of liberation. There is nothing irreparable – no evil without an end: all evolution takes its course upward, when the culpable one has paid his just debts. In all things this doctrine offers us a point of view from which the soul takes its flight toward a brighter future, and consoles itself in the present by that perspective. The faith in our destiny projects an illuminating light before us, our ideas of duty enlarge our sphere of action, and teach us to work for others. We feel that there is in the universe a force – a power – a wisdom incomparable; but also that we ourselves make part of the force, and this power from which we have issued. We comprehend that the source of all things is in God's love. God wishes good for us, and pursues it for us through ways sometimes clear, sometimes mysterious, but constantly appropriate to our needs. If we are separated from those we love, it is to make us find more vivid joys in the reunion. If He permits us to suffer disappointments, sorrows, sickness, reverses, it is in order to oblige us to detach our regard from earth, and to elevate them to Him – to seek higher joys than those we can find in this world. The universe is justice and love, and in the spiral of infinite ascension the divine alchemist changes our sufferings into waves of light and sheaves of felicity.

Sometimes a soul struck by great sorrow sees a great light shine as from an unknown source, more brilliant than the disaster is great. With one leap sorrow lifts it to heights which would have required twenty years of study and effort for it to attain. I cannot resist from citing two examples among many others known to me. Two men of my acquaintance, fathers of two lovely girls, their sole joy in life were suddenly bereaved by death. One was an officer in the East. His oldest daughter possessed all the gifts of intellect and beauty; of a serious character, she disdained the pleasures of youth, and shared the work of her father, a military writer of talent. In a brief time the young girl was attacked by a fatal malady and died. In her papers was found a notebook with this heading – 'To my father, when I am no longer here.' Although in seeming perfect health when she traced the pages, she had the presentiment of approaching death, and addressed consoling words to her father. Thanks to a book which he found in his daughter's desk, we became friends. Little by little, proceeding with method and persistence, he became a clairvoyant medium, and today he has not only the favor of being initiated into the mysteries of survivance, but also that of often seeing his daughter near him, and receiving testimonials of her love. The young girl's spirit also communicates with her fiancé and with one of her cousins, a subaltern in the regiment commanded by her father. The letters of the General also declare that his daughter's spirit was seen by two domestic animals. (An incident which has been described in detail, with all its attendant proofs, in another book.)

The second case is that of Mr. Debrus of Valence, whose only child, Rose, born after several years of marriage, was tenderly loved. All the hopes of the father and mother were bound up in this child: but at the age of twelve she died of meningitis. The despair of the parents was so extreme that the idea of suicide haunted the father. But having some friends who were spiritually awakened, he made researches, and to his joy he developed mediumistic powers, and today he communicates, without an intermediary, freely and surely with his child. Often she appears in the family circle, producing a luminous light of great intensity. Neither of these men knew anything of the life Beyond, and both lived in culpable indifference toward the problems of life and destiny.

But now all is clear to their eyes. After having suffered, they have been consoled, and they console others in their turn; working to spread the truth about them, inspiring all they approach with the dignity of their view and the firmness of their convictions. Their children appear to them, transfigured and radiant, and they have come to understand why God, separated them, and how He will bring about their common life in peaceful space. This has been the work of sorrow!

For the materialist there is no explanation of the world's enigma or the problem of sorrow. All this magnificent evolution and life, all the forms of beauty, slowly developed through the course of centuries, is in their eyes but the caprice of blind chance and ends in nothing! At the end of time all will be as if humanity had never existed. All man's efforts to elevate himself to a higher state – all his sufferings and all his miseries, will vanish like a shadow; all will have been useless and vain. But in place of this sterile and depressing theory, we who have the certitude of a future life and a spiritual world, see in the universe an immense laboratory where the human soul is cleansed and refined, through alternative celestial and earthly lives. This life has but one aim – the education of the intelligences associated with the bodies. Matter is an instrument of progress; what we call evil or sorrow, is but a means of elevation.

Permit me to make an avowal. Every time that the Angel of Sorrow has touched me with his wing, I have felt new and unknown powers awaken in me. I have heard interior voices chanting the eternal canticle of life and light. And now, after having participated in all the evils of life's route, I bless suffering! It has fashioned my soul! It has procured for me a surer judgment and a more certain appreciation of the high eternal truths. My life has been more than once shaken by misfortune, as an oak tree by the tempest; but there has never been a test which has not taught me to know myself better, and to gain in self-control. And now comes age! The end of my work approaches! After fifty years of work, meditation, and experience, it is sweet to me to affirm to all those who suffer – to all the afflicted ones of earth – that there is in the universe an infallible justice. Nothing is lost, there is no pain without compensation, no labor without profit: we all march through vicissitudes and tears toward a glorious goal fixed by God, and we have at our side a sure guide, an invisible counselor to sustain and console us. Man! Brother! Learn how to suffer! For sorrow is holy. It is the noblest agent of perfection. Penetrating and fertile, it is indispensable to the life of each one who does not wish to remain petrified with egotism and indifference.

It is a veritable philosophy that God sends suffering to the souls He loves. Learn how to suffer. I do not say seek sorrow! But when it comes, and stands inevitable in your path, receive it like a friend. Learn to appreciate its austere beauty, to seize its secret knowledge: study its hidden works, and in place of revolting against it, or resting inert and stunned under its action, associate your will with the aim fixed by sorrow, and seek to draw from it all the profit it can offer to a spirit or a heart. Force yourself to be an example for others, and by your acceptation of it, your courage, and your confidence in the future, render it more acceptable to other eyes. In a word, make sorrow beautiful! Harmony and beauty are universal laws, and in this ensemble sorrow has its aesthetic role. It would be puerile to cry out against this necessary element of beauty in the world.

Elevate yourself by higher views and hopes: see in it the supreme remedy for all the woes of earth. You who bend under the burdens of your trials, you who walk in the silence, no matter what comes, do not despair. Remember that nothing comes in vain, or without cause. Almost all our sorrows come from ourselves in the past, and they open the paths to heaven for us. Suffering is an initiation. It reveals the serious inspiring side of life. Life is not a frivolous comedy, but often a poignant tragedy. It is the struggle for the conquest of spiritual life, and in this struggle we must employ all that is great within us – patience – firmness – heroism – resignation. Those old allegories of Prometheus and the Argonauts, and the sacred mysteries of the Orient, had no other meaning. A profound instinct makes us admire those whose existence is a perpetual combat with sorrow, a constant effort to climb the abrupt heights which lead to virgin summits and unviolated treasures. We do not admire only heroism which brings forth the enthusiasm of crowds but also that which strives in obscurity against privations, maladies, and miseries, all that detaches souls from material ties and transitory things.

They strengthen the character for the combat of life – develop force and resistance – take from the soul all that weakens it – elevate the ideal to the pinnacle of force and grandeur. This is what education should adopt for the essential objective.

Let us open our souls to the breath of space, and lift ourselves to the limitless future. This future belongs to us! Our task is to conquer it. O living soul of France! Evoke the great memories, the high thoughts, the sublime inspirations of your genius! From the social fermentation will come forth another life, purer and more beautiful. Under the influx of new ideas France will find again her faith and her confidence. She will arise greater and stronger to accomplish her work in the world. For her genius is not dead! It sleeps, but tomorrow it will awaken!

PROFESSION OF FAITH

I

The first principle is the idea of being – I AM! This affirmation is indisputable: one cannot doubt his own existence. But this idea alone does not suffice; it must be completed by the idea of action and progress. I am! And I will be! Always more and better. Life in me is conscious. The soul is the only living unity – the only monad, indivisible and indestructible in matter, for it exists but in ourselves. The soul remains invariable in its unity, through thousands and thousands of forms – bodies of flesh, which it constructs and animates for the needs of its eternal evolution. It is always changing; by the qualities acquired, and the progress realized, growing more and more conscious and free in the infinite spiral of its planetary and celestial existence.

II

Nevertheless, the soul belongs only half to itself. The other half belongs to the universe of which it is a part: that is why the soul cannot know itself entirely, save in studying the universe. The pursuit of this double knowledge is the reason and the object of its life – of all its lives, death being but the renewing of the vital forces necessary to a new step forward.

III

The study of the universe demonstrates, in the first place, that the action of a superior Sovereign Intelligence governs the world. The essential character of this action is duration, by the mere fact that it perpetuates itself. It knows no limits, and is absolute – Hence – Eternity.

IV

Eternity, living and acting, implies life eternal and infinite – God the first cause – the generating principle – source of all life. We say eternal and infinite, for 'unlimited in duration' leads mathematically to unlimited in extent of time.

V

Infinite action is linked to the necessity of duration. When there is a link of union, a relation, there is a law – the law of the conservation order and harmony. From order flows good, from harmony beauty. The most lofty goal of the universe is beauty in all its aspects – material, intellectual, and moral. Justice and love are its means. Beauty in its essence is inseparable from good; and the two, by their close union, constitute absolute truth – supreme intelligence – perfection!

VI

The aim of the soul, in its evolution, is to attain and realize in itself and about itself, through time and the ascending stations of the universe, by the blossoming of the powers whose germs it contains, this eternal conception of beauty and goodness expressed by the idea of God – of Perfection.

VII

From this far-reaching law of ascension flow the explanations of all the problems of life. The evolution of the soul, which first receives by atavic transmission all the ancestral qualities: then develops them, by its own action, to add new qualities; the relative liberty of relative life in Absolute Life: the slow formation of human consciousness through the centuries, and its growth through the infinity of the future: the unity of the essence, and the eternal solidarity of souls in their march toward the conquest of high summits.

The End

Copyright © 2022 by FV Éditions
Cover design and layout: Canva.com, FV Ed.
Ebook ISBN 979-10-299-1432-4
Paperback ISBN 979-10-299-1433-1
All rights reserved.

www.ingramcontent.com/pod-product-compliance
Lightning Source LLC
LaVergne TN
LVHW031606060526
838201LV00063B/4745